ROUTLEDGE LIBRARY EDITIONS:
ALCOHOL AND ALCOHOLISM

Volume 19

HELPING THE
PROBLEM DRINKER

HELPING THE PROBLEM DRINKER

New Initiatives in Community Care

Edited by
TIM STOCKWELL
AND
SUE CLEMENT

LONDON AND NEW YORK

First published in 1987 by Croom Helm

This edition first published in 2024
by Routledge
4 Park Square, Milton Park, Abingdon, Oxon OX14 4RN

and by Routledge
605 Third Avenue, New York, NY 10158

Routledge is an imprint of the Taylor & Francis Group, an informa business

British Library Cataloguing in Publication Data
A catalogue record for this book is available from the British Library

ISBN: 978-1-032-59082-0 (Set)
ISBN: 978-1-032-60044-4 (Volume 19) (hbk)
ISBN: 978-1-032-60052-9 (Volume 19) (pbk)
ISBN: 978-1-003-45732-9 (Volume 19) (ebk)

DOI: 10.4324/9781003457329

Publisher's Note
The publisher has gone to great lengths to ensure the quality of this reprint but points out that some imperfections in the original copies may be apparent.

Disclaimer
The publisher has made every effort to trace copyright holders and would welcome correspondence from those they have been unable to trace.

HELPING THE PROBLEM DRINKER

New Initiatives in Community Care

Edited by
Tim Stockwell
Sue Clement

CROOM HELM
London • New York • Sydney

© 1987 Tim Stockwell and Sue Clement
Croom Helm Ltd, Provident House, Burrell Row,
Beckenham, Kent, BR3 1AT
Croom Helm Australia, 44-50 Waterloo Road,
North Ryde, 2113, New South Wales

Published in the USA by
Croom Helm
in association with Methuen, Inc.
29 West 35th Street,
New York, NY 10001

British Library Cataloguing in Publication Data

Helping the problem drinker : new
    initiatives in community care.
    1. Alcoholism — Treatment — Great Britain
    2. Alcoholics — Care — Great Britain
    3. Community health services — Great Britain
    I. Stockwell, Tim II. Clement, Sue
    362.2′928′58′0941   HV5283.G7

    ISBN 0-7099-4813-1

Library of Congress Cataloging-in-Publication Data

Helping the problem drinker.

    1. Alcoholism — Treatment — Great Britain.
2. Alcoholics — Rehabilitation — Great Britain.
3. Community health services — Great Britain.
I. Stockwell, Tim. II. Clement, Sue.
HV5283.G6H44 1988   362.2′928′0941   87-21413
ISBN 0-7099-4813-1

Printed and bound in Great Britain
by Billing & Sons Limited, Worcester.

CONTENTS

PART THREE: Specialist Community Alcohol Services

PART FOUR: Prevention of Alcohol Problems

LIST OF CONTRIBUTORS

Peter Anderson, General Practitioner and Senior Registrar in Community Medicine, District Department of Community Medicine, Manor House, Headley Way, Headington, Oxford, OX3 9D2.

Brian Arbery, Director of Turning Point, 9/12 Long Lane, London, EC1A 9HA.

Stephen Baldwin, Research Fellow, Addictive Behaviours Research Group, Department of Psychiatry, Ninewells Medical School, Dundee, Scotland, DD1 9SY.

Alan Cartwright, Principal Psychotherapist, Mount Zeehan Unit, St Martins Hospital, Littlebourne Road, Canterbury, Kent. Also, Chairman, Alcohol Intervention Training Unit, School of Continuing Education, University of Kent at Canterbury, Rutherford College, Canterbury, Kent, CT2 7NX.

Jonathan Chick, Consultant Psychiatrist, University Department of Psychiatry, Royal Edinburgh Hospital, Morningside Park, Edinburgh, Scotland, EH10 5HF.

Sue Clement, Senior Clinical Psychologist, Psychology Department, Dykebar Hospital, Grahamston Road, Paisley, Renfrewshire, Scotland, PA2 7DE.

Nick Heather, Senior Research Fellow, Department of Psychiatry, Ninewells Medical School, University of Dundee, Scotland, DD1 9SY.

Jim Orford, Senior Lecturer, Department of Psychology, Washington Singer Laboratory, Exeter University, Exeter, Devon.

Yiannis Papadatos, Scientific Director, Centre for Mental Health, 58 Notara Street, GR-106 83, Athens, Greece.

Gregory Potamianos, Clinical Psychologist, Centre for Mental Health, 58 Notara Street, GR-106 83, Athens, Greece.

Joe Ruzek, Community Psychologist, ACCEPT, Seagrave Hospital, Seagrave Road, London, SW6 1RQ. Also of Stoneybrook University, New York, USA.

Terence Spratley, Consultant Psychiatrist, Mount Zeehan Unit, St Martins Hospital, Littlebourne Road, Canterbury, Kent.

LIST OF CONTRIBUTORS

Tim Stockwell, Principal Clinical Psychologist, Exeter Community Alcohol Team, 59 Centre, 59 Magdalen Street, Exeter, Devon, EX2 4HY.

Philip Tether, Senior Research Fellow, Addiction Research Centre, Institute for Health Studies, University of Hull, Hull, Yorkshire.

Fred Yates, Research Psychologist, Centre for Alcohol and Drug Studies, Parkwood House, St Nicholas' Hospital, Gosforth, Newcastle-upon-Tyne, NE3 3XT.

EDITORS' ACKNOWLEDGEMENTS

Our thanks go first and foremost to Christine Bird and Juliet Dymoke-Marr for the many hours they spent keyboard tapping and VDU gazing to produce the text for this book. Many people have helped and supported us in various ways while working on this book including both the Exeter and Salford Community Alcohol Teams, Jim Orford, Griffith Edwards, Ralph Barker, Val Taylor, Joan Munroe, Anne Kauder and Ron Wawman. Finally, we warmly thank our fellow contributors who helped us by achieving their writing deadlines despite other commitments and such problems as early drafts being stolen!

INTRODUCTION

Tim Stockwell and Sue Clement

Over the past 15 years a revolution has taken place in the way many scientists, educationalists and clinicians understand the nature of alcohol-related problems. The main shift in thinking has been to progress beyond the idea of there being but two populations of drinkers: a large group of harm-free social drinkers and a tragic minority of pathologically uncontrolled drinkers or "alcoholics". As Jim Orford explains in the opening chapter of this book, it is now clear that there exists a great variation both in types and severities of alcohol-related harm. These may affect not only individuals but also couples, families, work forces and whole communities.

Much has been written already that attempts to chart the extent and severity of alcohol problems in our society. For example, one study of patients registered with a general practice in London found that 11% of men and 5% of women admitted to drinking above "safe" levels (Wallace and Haines, 1985). Economists have conservatively estimated the total annual cost of alcohol abuse to be £1,600 million per annum (McDonnell and Maynard, 1985). Recently, it has been estimated that up to 40,000 people die prematurely each year, as a consequence of alcohol misuse (Report of the Royal College of General Practitioners, 1986).

There are also several excellent theoretical reviews which explore new models for understanding the diverse social, learning and psychobiological processes which result in alcohol-related problems (e.g. Heather and Robertson, 1986).

Alongside this new knowledge and these new understandings there has taken place an upsurge of interest in developing "community-based" responses. We believe this volume collects together for the first time a selection of some of the best and most promising of such initiatives. The varied styles used by the contributors - from the clinical and descriptive through literature review to research report - reflect the diverse approaches and people becoming involved in this important area.

1

Jim Orford's chapter explores the need for a community response to alcohol problems and also places this need with the context of the overall movement towards community mental health. The next four chapters explore the opportunities for identifying and responding to drinking problems at an earlier stage than has been possible with some traditional specialist forms of treatment. The enormous potential for such work both in general practice and in the general hospital setting is discussed by Peter Anderson, Nick Heather and Jonathan Chick. In addition, Joe Ruzek has contributed a detailed account of Drinkwatchers, the first self-help network for controlled drinkers.

In the second part, methods of better equipping primary care workers to deal with problem drinkers are introduced. The opening chapter is an account of the work of the Salford Community Alcohol Team (CAT), a service specifically set up to enable primary care workers to tackle drinking problems themselves by providing training and support for them. Doctor Spratley was a member of the first ever CAT and his chapter is a distillation of his wide experience of working as a consultant to other workers. Steve Baldwin, however, presents a critique of this way of working and describes CAT's as "old wine in old bottles".

One consequence of moving beyond a disease conception of alcohol problems is the realisation that many commonalities exist between all forms of substance misuse. Brian Arbery draws on his wide experience of different forms of service for different types of substance misuse to forcefully argue the case for a combined approach to alcohol and other drug problems.

The third section is concerned with specialist approaches relevant to even severely dependent problem drinkers but which are, nonetheless, community-based initiatives. The first is an account of the Exeter Home Detoxification Project which has attempted to improve the safety and effectiveness of the time-honoured practice of withdrawing from alcohol at home. Greg Potamianos presents an overview of his painstaking study comparing a community day centre approach (ACCEPT) with that of a general hospital psychiatric out-patient clinic. Fred Yates provides a lively discussion of the problems and pitfalls of residential treatment for problem drinkers, and suggests a radical new approach for utilising such a setting. Alan Cartwright's chapter is a thought-provoking and detailed account of the Mount Zeehan therapeutic day unit - a specialised and intensive treatment unit that offers both excellence and accessibility to the community it serves.

The final chapter stands alone and is concerned with prevention. The position and space devoted to this subject we believe to be inversely related to its importance. Prevention of alcohol problems is a much neglected and ill understood area and one to which Philip Tether, the author of this chapter, has made a very unique and valuable contribution.

In short, we believe that anyone concerned with alcohol problems from a community perspective, be they service planners, educators, clinicians or researchers, will find something of value in this book. Most of the contributions include an evaluative element so that even where evidence for effectiveness is tentative, it has been possible to highlight new directions and areas for improvement. It would appear that the overall case for community approaches in this field is unanswerable. We now urgently need the finance and organisational structures within which to provide these new services.

REFERENCES

Heather, N. and Robertson, I. (1986) Problem Drinking: A New Approach. Penguin Books, London and New York

McDonnell, R. and Maynard, A. (1985) The costs of alcohol misuse, British Journal of Addictions, 80, 27-35.

Royal College of General Practitioners (1986) Alcohol - A Balanced View. RCGP, London

Wallace, P. and Haines, A. (1985) Use of a questionnaire in general practice to increase the recognition of patients with excessive alcohol consumption. British Journal of Addiction, 290, 949-53

Chapter 1

THE NEED FOR A COMMUNITY RESPONSE TO ALCOHOL-RELATED PROBLEMS

Jim Orford

THE COMMUNITY SERVICES MOVEMENT

Alcohol-related problems are not alone in demanding a community response, and the movement towards such a response in the alcohol field should be seen as part of a number of overlapping and more general movements in this direction. These include the general move towards "community care", the rather more specific "community mental health" movement, and certain specific professional sub-disciplines such as community nursing, community occupational therapy, community psychiatry, and community psychology. It is important to begin by outlining, however briefly, some of the principles of this general community movement, and to place community responses to alcohol-related problems within this general context. Although the principles underlying community responses to alcohol problems are much the same, understanding and responding to alcohol problems have all too often been treated as a specialism divorced from the wider field of community mental health and community care. In this writer's view this has been to the detriment both of the general services and the alcohol services.

Some of the underlying principles of the community mental health movement are shown in Table 1.1. These include the need to establish the approximate numbers of people in a community who are impaired or who are disabled, and to obtain a picture of how impairment and disability are distributed across areas within the community and across demographically defined sub-groups. Examples from Britain include Bebbington et al's (1981) survey of mental ill health in South London, Goldberg and Huxley's (1980) work on the prevalence of mental health problems amongst general practitioners' patients in Manchester, Morgan et al's (1975) study of the distribution of incidents of deliberate self-harm in different areas and sub-groups in Bristol, and Dean and James' (1980) work on the spatial distribution of admissions to psychiatric hospital in

Table 1.1: Dimensions of Community Mental Health Vs Traditional Clinical Services (Rappaport, 1977)

	Community Mental Health	Traditional Clinical Services
Strategies of service	Strategies aimed at reaching large numbers of people, including brief psychotherapy and crisis intervention	Emphasis on extended psychotherapy
Level of intervention	Emphasis on a total or defined	Emphasis on individual clients
Location of intervention	Practice in the community	Practice in institutional mental health settings
Source of manpower	Mental health professionals together with new, including non-professional, sources of manpower, such as college students and persons indigenous to the target group	Traditional mental health (psychiatrists, psychologists, social workers)
How service is delivered	Emphasis on indirect services through consultation and education	Emphasis on direct clinical services to clients
Kind of planning	Rational planning aimed at specification of unmet needs, high-risk populations, and coordinated services	Unplanned, individual services with no overall community coordination; a 'free enterprise' system
Type of services	Emphasis on preventive services	Emphasis on therapeutic service
Locus of decision making	Shared responsibility for control and decision making with regard to mental health programmes between community and professionals	Professional control of all mental health services
Etiological assumptions	Environmental causes of mental disorder	Intrapsychic causes of mental disorder

Plymouth. Almost all such studies discover a high rate of previously undetected impairment and a very uneven distribution of incidence and prevalence within the study community.

A further principle of community response movements generally is that services should be provided as near as possible to peoples' homes so that regular routines and social ties are as little disturbed as possible and so that institutionalisation is prevented as often as possible. One successful and very carefully evaluated experiment in minimising rates of hospitalisation for schizophrenia has been reported from Australia, for example (Hoult et al, 1984). Where residential provision is required, the principle is that this should be provided not in large institutions, but in small therapeutic hostels or halfway houses which allow for as much residential participation and autonomy as possible and which are located as near as possible to normal community facilities such as shops and entertainment (Apte, 1968; Otto and Orford, 1978).

Other principles are: that amongst the range of services on offer there should be some which deliver relatively "brief" treatments, or 'minimal interventions', to relatively large numbers of people; that services should make as much use as possible of non-professional personnel in the delivery of services (Durlak, 1979); that statutory and non-statutory agencies should collaborate in the delivery of care (Wolfenden, 1978); and that service provision should include indirect or consultancy work with a broad range of health, social service, and other statutory and non-statutory agencies (Brown, 1984; Ketterer, 1981). Finally, to some, the chief hallmark of a thorough-going community response is that prevention should be high on the agenda (Cowen, 1980). In general the community approach can be summarised by saying that those who practise with these principles in mind are "proactive" (rather than reactive) in reaching out to locate and respond to problems in the community; that they attempt to deliver services in settings that are as close to and as similar in form to peoples' own homes as possible; and that they make as much use as possible of the natural resources of people and facilities within the community. These ideas have developed in response to perceived inadequacies in traditional services. The latter failed to take into account the scale of the problem and the lack of specialised man and woman power available. They gave insufficient recognition to the positive role of families, non-professionals, volunteers and self-help. They failed to plan systematically for the needs of whole communities, and to pay particular attention to high-risk groupsroups. Perhaps the most serious failure has been the almost complete neglect of prevention.

NEW DIRECTIONS IN UNDERSTANDING ALCOHOL-RELATED PROBLEMS

At the same time as the community services movement generally has been gathering momentum, so our understanding of alcohol problems has taken a radical new direction. New thinking on the subject has led in the general direction of social learning theories (e.g. British Psychological Society, 1984; Heather and Robertson, 1986; Orford, 1985; Royal College of General Practitioners, 1986). Those who have championed this new approach can point to at least three ways in which it represents an improvement over the pre-existing model of "alcoholism" as a "disease". Each suggests the need for a community response. First, a person's current drinking is viewed as being at a point on a continuum, along which are distributed all members of a community. On the same continuum are those at one end who are at little or no risk of alcohol-related harm because they drink little if at all, and those at the other extreme who are at high risk because they are drinking large amounts. Hence the new model has no place for ideas that imply that a minority of the population are qualitatively different from the rest, or that alcohol is used in a totally trouble-free way by the vast majority of the population and that only a small minority experience any alcohol-related problems.

On the contrary, what the new thinking does is to unite the formerly separate worlds of psychiatry and sociology, the clinic and the social survey. It follows from the idea of continuum that no single estimate of the number of people in a community who have drinking problems will suffice in itself: neither the clinician's estimate based on people referred to him nor the social survey researcher's estimate based on the proportion of her sample who tell her that they drink more than a certain number of "units" of alcohol in a week, is more accurate than the other. Both are relevant. Although there are regional differences within the UK, with some evidence of more heavy drinking (by young men at least) in the north of England than in the south (Wilson, 1980; Breeze, 1985), and evidence of greater alcohol-related harm in Scotland, and especially in the Highlands (Plant, 1982), reasonable average expectations for a health district in England are shown in Table 1.2. Approximately 30 adults per thousand will admit to more than the occasional problem related to the use of alcohol if directly asked. The number of people who will admit to regular heavy drinking is considerably greater, however, whilst the number known to agencies as having problems related to alcohol is very much smaller, and the number admitted to psychiatric facilities for the treatment of alcohol problems is smaller still.

A second advantage to the new way of thinking, based on social learning theory, is a broadening of interest in the

7

Table 1.2: Likely Prevalence of Heavy and Problem Drinking in an Average Health District in England and Wales Serving One Million Adults

22,000 Drinking Heavily[a]

7,500 Admit to Problems[b]

1,250 Known to Agencies[c]

*125 Admitted to Psychiatric Hospital[d]

[a]Based on a rate of 90 adults per 1,000 drinking more than 35 units a week (men) or 20 units a week (women), (Wilson, 1980)
[b]30 adults per 1,000 admitting to problems in a household survey (Edwards et al, 1972)
[c]Adults per 1,000 known to at least one agency to have problems associated with drinking (Edwards et al, 1973)
[d]0.5 adults per 1,000 admitted to psychiatric hospitals or units with an alcohol-related diagnosis (figures provided by DHSS, personal communication)

* Not to scale

determinants of drinking behaviour to include the social, cultural and environmental, in addition to the physiological, psychological and familial. There is now far greater recognition that a person's drinking is determined, not only by inheritance, family environment, and individual factors, but also by the country in which she lives, the nature of his occupation, and the drinking norms of his or her peer group. In particular, the importance of level of availability of alcohol in a community is now acknowledged. People have been impressed, for example, by the correlations that are typically found, both across countries or areas, and across years within one country, between total population consumption of alcohol and deaths from liver cirrhosis. For example, the causal

8

pathway linking availability, level of consumption, alcohol-related morbidity, and mortality, has been specified based upon data collected by Rush et al (1986) in their study of 49 counties in Ontario.

The third advantage of this way of understanding alcohol-related problems concerns our view of the way people make changes in their drinking habits. Formerly, it was held that only very specialised treatment, or attendance at Alcoholics Anonymous, either of them involving a total commitment to abstinence from alcohol, would suffice if "alcoholism" was to be overcome. Two lines of evidence, steadily accumulating since the 1960s, have called into question these earlier views. The first consists of the, now numerous, reports that many people with alcohol problems sufficiently severe to seek specialist help, were found at follow up to have given up excessive drinking but not to have become total abstainers (see Davies, 1962, for an early report of this kind; Sobell and Sobell, 1973, for one of the earliest descriptions of treatment designed with moderate or "controlled" drinking as the goal; and Heather and Robertson, 1983, for a comprehensive review of this literature).

Research on this topic has turned to the question of whether individuals can be matched to drinking goals (abstinence or moderation). There appear to be two leading hypotheses which may be termed the "severity" and the "expectation" hypotheses (Orford and Keddie, 1986). A number of studies appear to support the first: amongst such findings are that successful moderation is predicted by relatively fewer symptoms of excessive drinking, fewer alcohol-related problems, lower pre-treatment alcohol consumption and/or a shorter history of drinking problems (e.g. Edwards et al, 1983; Edwards, 1985). More consistent with the alternative, expectation, hypothesis, are the results of the two recent British studies, although each involved follow up for merely 12 months (Orford and Keddie, 1986; Elal-Lawrence et al, 1986). These studies found that the most powerful discriminators of successful abstinence and moderate drinking were history of attendance at Alcoholics Anonymous, length of previous abstinence, and beliefs in the importance and necessity of one or other goal.

Although the prediction of abstinence or moderation remains a lively issue, the evidence for the successful return of some problem drinkers to moderation is overwhelming, and this has caused a radical revision of ideas about the change process. The second line of evidence about the change process concerns what used to be called, inappropriately, "spontaneous remission". This was once thought to be rare for alcohol problems, but research has shown this belief to be erroneous. There have been a number of studies from the USA including Roizen et al's (1978) study in San Fransisco in which men were interviewed twice, with an interval of approximately four

years between. Estimates of the remission rate varied from
12% to over 60% depending upon the strictness or leniency of
che definition of "remission". A Scottish study in which 60
people who had claimed to have overcome drinking problems were
carefully interviewed about their experience was reported by
Saunders and Kershaw (1979). Getting married and changing
jobs were the two factors to which changes were most often
attributed, and even amongst a sub-group of 19 who had had the
most severe problems, only seven mentioned receiving help from
AA or specialist treatment agencies. This new evidence about
the change process has opened up the way for the application
of theories from the behavioural and social sciences which
would not have been thought relevant whilst alcohol problems
were still viewed as disease entities. One such theory, which
has particular appeal and upon which I have drawn heavily in
my own book, Excessive Appetites (1985) is the theory of
decision-making expounded by American social psychologists
Janis and Mann (1977).

Table 1.3: Hypothetical Balance-Sheet for a Severely
Dependent Drinker

Situation: Mr X's working ability has been impaired by his
drinking for some time. He fears losing his job. His doctor
tells him he has suffered liver damage and must stop
drinking.

Alternative Responses	Anticipated Consequence	
	Positive	Negative
Carry on Drinking	Pleasure of drinking	Serious illness, possibly fatal liver disease
	Drinking relaxes him	Have little money to spare
	Relieves withdrawal symptoms	Social and self-disapproval
	Drinking makes him feel more sociable	
Try to Abstain	Improved work	Withdrawal
	Feel healthier	Difficulty socialising
	Have money to spend on other things	Tension
		Craving
		Past failures

10

The idea of a balance between promoting and restraining forces, a notion of conflict, and the view that the change process is best construed as one in which a person resolves a conflict by making a personal choice, are central to this theory (see Table 1.3 for a hypothetical example of such a conflict). In their book, Janis and Mann write in the same vein about all manner of health decisions (stopping or reducing smoking, dieting, etc.), personal life decisions (marrying, separating, taking or leaving a job, etc.) as well as decisions in the worlds of commerce and international diplomacy. Thus the decision to abstain or moderate drinking is seen as being no different in kind from a whole range of other everyday decisions, large and small.

This movement towards recognising the social and environmental determinants of drinking behaviour, conceptualising people as lying on a continuum rather than in discrete categories, plus the recognition that change is a naturally occurring process and that a variety of drinking goals are possible, amounts to a de-medicalising of a problem of social behaviour which had previously been viewed exclusively as being like a physical disease. This latter, traditional, approach, was successful in drawing attention to the problem, removing it from the exclusive province of morality and the law, and laying the foundations for the development of specialist services. The hope is that the new approach will take this process one step further. In particular it promises the removal of the barriers that still exist between drinking problems as a specialist subject and the mainstream of other disciplines and professions concerned with mental health, education, and the social sciences.

SPECIALIST COMMUNITY SERVICES

In parallel with these changes in ways of understanding alcohol use and alcohol-related problems, there have developed a number of new ways of responding. These may conveniently be divided into those that are specialist and those that are non-specialist, or to put it another way, into those that continue to involve the direct provision of treatment by specialists, and those in which the specialists work indirectly via non-specialist "primary level" agents. Amongst the specialist forms of provision may be included: detoxification services that do not involve hospitalisation; small therapeutic hostels or halfway houses; the use of "minimal" treatments; and the training and deployment of volunteer counsellors.

Community Detoxification Services

In the past supervised detoxification was generally carried out in psychiatric hospitals, but in the last 10 to 15 years forms of service provision have diversified, as Table 1.4 shows. Non-hospital forms of alcohol detoxification service include residential detoxification centres (often referred to as "social setting" detoxification centres to distinguish them from similar centres based in hospitals) and home detoxification. Amongst the suggested advantages of residential social setting detoxification are: a greater concern with the total psychosocial functioning of the individual; the avoidance of indiscriminate use of medication, which may reinforce the use of drugs to cope with stress, as well as carry the danger of misuse, overdose, and dependence; the greater use of support and reassurance from staff in order to reduce clients' arousal levels; and better links with rehabilitation agencies. On this last point, there are two studies from North America (social setting detoxification centres have been popular in Canada and the USA) showing higher percentages of clients successfully referred on for further treatment from social setting units than from hospital units (McGovern, 1983; Rabb, 1981). In England, an experimental social setting detoxification centre was set up in Leeds in 1976, and this was one of a number of detoxification services studied by a DHSS-funded research team (Detoxification Evaluation Project, 1985).

Table 1.4: Types of Alcohol Detoxification Service

Specialist	Non-Specialist
In-patient medical: designated	Psychiatric hospital
In-patient medical: non-designated	General hospital
Residential social setting: designated	Elsewhere, some
Residential social setting: non- designated	supervision Unsupervised
Sobering up station or shelter	
Out-patient medical	
Day centre	
Home, supervised	

Although the literature on alcohol detoxification has focused on residential forms of service, in recent years there has been increasing recognition that detoxification frequently occurs outside such settings. Indeed those who had advocated non-residential detoxification have pointed to certain potential advantages. These include the fact that the patient is not removed from job, family and other community support systems; that it may be easier to provide continuity of care with the same treatment personnel involved in detoxification and further treatment; and that this may be considerably more cost-effective. There is agreement, however, that detoxification must still be intensive, thorough, monitored constantly and regularly, and must involve an effective screening process (e.g. Whitfield, 1982). In North America this has generally been arranged on a hospital out-patient basis, with patients attending daily for medication. The alternative, home-based, detoxification is the form of service that is now finding favour in the UK and this is the subject of Chapter 10.

Therapeutic Hostels or Halfway Houses
Small therapeutic hostels or halfway houses for people with drinking problems were a major community service development in the 1960s in Britain, Canada and the USA. By 1975 in the USA there were nearly three times as many halfway houses for people with drinking problems (totalling 597) than there were similar houses for the mentally ill, and by the end of the 1970s in Britain there were more places (a total of 792 places) for people with drinking problems in small hostels than there were in hospital alcohol treatment units (Orford and Velleman, 1982). The scale, and relatively early development, of this particular movement for community services was no doubt due both to the social instability (and hence need for accommodation) which often follows (and sometimes precedes) the development of drinking problems, and also to the way in which alcohol problems have generally been peripheral to, and neglected by, the mainstream of mental health services.

The expected advantages of small houses such as these, in comparison with traditional hospital units, include the opportunities that they are better able to provide for the involvement of residents in normal community activities including work, family and leisure, as well as the achievement of a milieu in which residents have more involvement in decision-making and therefore in roles involving the taking of normal degrees of responsibility in preparation for full reintegration or integration into ordinary life. Their rehabilitative potential should thus be greater. This form of provision continues to play a major part in the range of available services for people with drinking problems. It is considered in greater detail in Chapter 12.

Minimal Treatments
One of the principles of the community services movement is that a wide variety of treatments should be available, some of them brief rather than intensive, and some of them made more easily accessible to larger numbers of people than has traditionally been the case with mental health treatments. This is consistent with a shift towards prevention. The new understanding of alcohol-related problems, outlined above, with its emphasis on an at risk continuum, a stress on prevention, and a recognition of the legitimacy of reduced drinking for some as well as abstinence for others, has laid

the foundation for the development of such relatively brief, or "minimal", treatments.

That assessment and brief advice can often be as effective as more intensive treatment, even for those with drinking problems severe enough to warrant referral to a psychiatric out-patient department, was demonstrated by our study of treatment vs. advice (Orford and Edwards, 1977) and by Heather et al (1986) in a treatment study in Dundee which involved placing national newspaper advertisements offering written, self-help materials for reducing drinking. Other applications, for example in the contexts of general practice and the general hospital, will be dealt with in later chapters.

Training and Deploying Volunteer Counsellors

A specialist development which deserves particular mention, because in some respects it paved the way for the non-specialist developments to be described next, is the voluntary counsellor movement. A number of trends came together in the 1970s which encouraged the training of volunteers to do some of the basic work of counselling people with drinking problems, work which might otherwise be thought to be the exclusive province of the professionals. One such trend was the general movement within community mental health and disciplines such as community psychology towards recruiting and training "para-professionals" and volunteers, such as college students, "housewife psychotherapists", and teacher aides, to carry out treatment with adults or children (Zax and Specter, 1974; Durlak, 1979). In other cases mental health professionals were trained for new tasks: for example "nurse behaviour therapists" carrying out treatments which would previously have been the preserve of psychologists (Ginsberg and Marks, 1977).

A second trend consisted of research on the treatment of alcohol problems which suggested that commitment to working with people with such problems might be more important than specialised treatment techniques. A whole line of research was beginning to suggest that neither type nor intensity of treatment accounted for much variance in outcome (e.g. Orford and Edwards, 1977; Costello, 1980), although it should be said that others have argued that such research fails to take into account such factors as the need to match individuals to treatment type (e.g. Glaser, 1980). Other research, which will be discussed more fully below, showed the wide variation that existed amongst professional treatment personnel in the extent of their therapeutic commitment to working with alcohol problems (Shaw et al, 1978; Cartwright, 1980).

The third relevant trend is of longer standing and consists of the tradition of self-help which exists in the alcohol and drugs field. Alcoholics Anonymous began in the 1930s in the USA and expanded to Britain in the 1940s and to many other countries since. Its large membership continues to grow and it has provided the model for many other self-help groups. A study of AA in Britain in the 1970s showed that the majority of members who remained with the organisation for more than a few months provided direct help to new members by "twelfth stepping" (the last of the Twelve Steps in the AA programme exhorts members to carry the message to other "alcoholics") and/or by sponsoring them (Robinson, 1979). An important part of the philosophy of drug-free therapeutic communities (or Concept Houses as they are sometimes termed) in the drugs field, and also but less obviously in therapeutic hostels or halfway houses for people with drinking problems, is that people who have themselves experienced drug or alcohol problems are in a strong position to help others with similar problems.

Reports of training schemes for para-professional or non-professional alcohol problem counsellors started to appear from the USA in the 1970s (e.g. Wehmer et al, 1974), and in Britain DHSS made funds available for a pilot project known as the Voluntary Alcoholism Counsellors' Training Scheme administered largely through local voluntary Councils on Alcoholism. A number of such schemes for training and deploying volunteer counsellors were set up around the country and have been evaluated by Marshall et al (1985).

A typical training scheme involves 8-10 sessions of alcohol education, selection for training as a counsellor, an 8-10 session course on general principles of counselling, a residential weekend to consolidate learning and to prepare for the next stage, a period of training in applying the principles of counselling to alcohol problems, a period of a year of counselling under supervision, and the award of accreditation if certain criteria about the quantity and quality of counselling have been met. A useful handbook on the organisation and running of such schemes has been written by Marshall et al (1985).

NON-SPECIALIST COMMUNITY SERVICES

However, the most far-reaching change in ideas about service provision which has followed from the new understanding of alcohol problems and from the community services movement generally, has been the broadening of services to include non-specialist and indirect forms of treatment. When the problem was conceived of purely in terms of treating a distinct group of "alcoholics" with very special treatment needs, it was logical to base services upon specialist treatment units. Alcoholics Anonymous had already shown the demand that existed for this kind of specialist approach, and in Britain from the 1950s to the 1970s the Department of Health encouraged the setting up of specialist psychiatric alcoholism in-patient treatment units. The idea of a continuum of risk of alcohol-related harm, and the broadening of the treatment base to include brief treatments and educational approaches, suggested a different logic. As indicated earlier (see Table 1.2) the prevalence of alcohol problems based upon a survey of all relevant agencies in an area, most of whom do not specialise in the treatment of alcohol-related problems, is likely to be many times greater than the number known to specialist agencies. It follows that the latter (the secondary level agencies) need to provide some of their services indirectly via the non-specialist (or primary level) agencies in order to increase effectiveness. This line was taken in the 1970s by the Maudsley Alcohol Pilot Project whose report, Responding to Drinking Problems (Shaw et al, 1978), has had a very considerable influence on the field. They explored some of the reasons for low therapeutic commitment amongst agents such as general practitioners, social workers, and probation officers, and illustrated some of the ways of providing a consultancy service for members of such agencies.

In the same year there appeared an influential DHSS Working Party Report (The Kessel Report) entitled The Pattern and Range of Services for Problem Drinkers (DHSS, 1978). Although the report was criticised at the time for failing to recommend increased financial resources, it was remarkably forward looking, not only in its abandonment of the language of the disease concept of "alcoholism", but also in its advocacy of a form of service based on the new logic. As the following quotation shows, the report saw the continued need for alcohol specialists, but saw it as their main role to educate, support, and be available to be consulted by, the primary level agencies:

> First and foremost the function of those working at the secondary level of care should be to support and advise those working at the primary level. They should be readily accessible and be prepared to provide advice to those who need it regardless of their professional disciplines. The approach here, as at the primary level, should be multi-disciplinary.
>
> The secondary level workers should also advise, stimulate and, where possible, provide professional in-service training for non-specialist colleagues so as to disseminate their knowledge. They will also have a role to play in more general public education. Part of this educative role will be to help initiate, co-ordinate and monitor research projects in the field of problem drinking.
>
> (DHSS, 1978, 4.19, 4.21).

The report also recommended that statutory and voluntary disciplines and organisations should collaborate in this endeavour, and that this team of specialists could best operate from a common base which should be "in a house in the town" rather than in a hospital. Thus the report paved the way for the future development of Community Alcohol Teams, which have become one of the principal models of service delivery in Britain in the 1980s.

The list of non-specialist agencies with which a community alcohol team might expect to have some dealings is a large one, and includes those in Table 1.5. Some of these, including the general hospital, general practice, and the work-place, are dealt with more fully in later chapters. As illustrations of the ways in which alcohol-related problems may present in non-specialist settings, some expansion of three topics will be given here: the connection between excessive drinking and family problems including family violence; the link with learning disabilities in children; and alcohol problems amongst elderly people.

Alcohol, the Family and Social Services

There is ample evidence that, in the words of the title of one self-help book for partners of people with drinking problems, Drinking Problems Equal Family Problems, (Meyer, 1982). Many studies have shown that women married to men with drinking problems describe experiencing hardships which are variable in extent but which are often severe and of long-standing. They include concern over financial security, social embarrassment, social isolation, rows and quarrels, a poor sex life, possessiveness and jealousy directed towards the wife, and sometimes physical violence (Orford, 1985; McCrady and Hay, 1987). There is evidence, too, that wives living with men who are drinking excessively are at risk themselves and experience raised levels of psychological and psychosomatic symptoms (Bailey, 1967) and consult their doctors more often than most people, complaining of such symptoms as anxiety, depression, and fatigue and with higher rates of gastrointestinal disorders and trauma (Leckman et al, 1984; Roberts and Brent, 1982). Families where the wife is drinking excessively have been much less studied, but research from other countries shows that husbands in such families also experience high levels of distress (Orford, 1986). Marital breakdown is often attributed to excessive drinking. In one recent American study, for example, the partner's drinking was mentioned as a cause of marital breakdown by 36% of divorced or separated women and by 17% of men (Burns, 1984). The same has been reported from many other countries including Russia, where in 1978 63% of women petitioning for divorce cited their husbands' heavy drinking or "alcoholism" (the same was true for only 4.5% of men) (Sysenko, 1982).

Until recently the stresses experienced by children living in families with alcohol-related problems have been

Table 1.5: Community Agents in a Position to Detect and Respond to Drinking Problems

General hospital	A range of physical disorders, including gastritis, peptic ulcer and obesity in men and family and social problems including effects on spouses and children, work attendance, accidents etc.
Health visitors, district nurses	The same range of disorders and problems, but these agents may be particularly likely to see problems in family members
General hospital staff	A range of alcohol-related disorders and injuries, in various departments including gastroenterology and accident and emergency
Psychiatric hospital staff and community mental health staff (CMH teams, community psychiatric nurses etc.)	Excessive drinking with a wide range of mental health problems including anxiety, depression and other drug misuse
Social Services	Excessive drinking with a wide range of family and social problems, especially family violence problems experienced by the elderly and some housing problems
Services for children or adolescents and their families (medical, psychiatric, social and voluntary)	Excessive drinking in a parent is a common cause of abuse and neglect of children and adolescents and a common accompaniment of childhood disorders of various kinds
Services for the elderly	Now recognised that the elderly are a high-risk group for excessive drinking associated with bereavement, loneliness and psychological disorder such as anxiety
Clergy and voluntary organisations (including Citizens Advice, Samaritans, Marriage Guidance, Women's Aid	Particularly likely to be approached by family members affected by excessive drinking and by problem drinkers in despair

Table 1.5 (cont'd)

Local authority housing departments	Drinking problems sometimes come to notice by way of rent arrears or disputes with neighbours. Housing departments also have a role in helping tenants who are undergoing treatment or who need accommodation during a period of rehabilitation
Probation services	A high proportion of clients with drinking problems especially those with many petty offences. Also, many younger offenders whose offences are complicated by very heavy drinking
Magistrates courts	Ditto. Plus a large volume of drunkenness offending dealt with largely by fining. Plus drunken driving offences
Prison	Large proportions of remand prisoners and those serving short sentences, some for non-payment of small fines plus a proportion of long-term prisoners
Police	Public drunkenness, including drunken driving, other offences committed by problem drinkers, control of licensed premises including under-age drinking and domestic disputes
Lawyers	Problem drinking is a common reason for legal separation and divorce especially and one of the factors in many cases of violence towards wives and children
Single, homeless people and casual users of night shelter, reception centres and cheap commercial hostel accommodation	High rates of problem drinking in these groups

Table 1.5 (cont'd)

The workplace (including employers, personnel officers, industrial medical officers, company nurses and colleagues	Drinking problems very often come to notice first in the workplace as a result of absenteeism, accidents and poor work performance. Some forms of employment are particularly associated with excessive drinking including the licensed trade, shipping, hotel and catering and the construction industry
Teachers	Drinking problems in young people may affect attendance and school performance. A sizeable minority of school pupils will also be affected by the excessive drinking of a parent
Licensed premises (especially public houses)	Landlords and bar staff observe much heavy drinking at first hand, are often required to discipline excessive drinkers and can take a responsible and helpful attitude towards individuals
Family and friends	Many quite serious problems are fully known only by family and sometimes by friends. The way they react may be influential in helping to resolve the problem

relatively neglected. These include chronic exposure to a poor family atmosphere with much parental marital tension and discord, disruption of joint family activities, and a restriction on meeting friends or reciprocating invitations because of embarrassment (Wilson, 1982). In our own study in the South-west of England, young adults (aged 16-35 years) who had had parents with drinking problems frequently recalled such things as, "arrangements going wrong", "lack of social life for the family", "being forced to participate in rows between parents", and "having to take care of the parent" (Velleman and Orford, 1985).

On the question of a possible link between excessive drinking and family violence, there is strong evidence of an association between heavy or problematic drinking and violence towards wives (e.g. Gayford, 1975; van Hasselt et al, 1985). A specific link with physical child abuse is less certain. One American review has concluded that there is no satisfactory empirical data to support the existence of such a link (Orme and Rimmer, 1981). However, two out of three studies reviewed by Mayer and Black (1977) found excessive drinking amongst 30% or more of parents of abused children and a later study, also from the USA, found a history of alcohol misuse in at least one parent in 35 out of 51 cases of child abuse at a mental hospital (Behling, 1979). Three reports from Czechoslovakia in the late 1960s and 1970s also reported a link between parental excessive drinking and sexual abuse of children (Orford, 1986). There has been little study of a possible connection with child abuse in Britain, although one small survey of open social work cases in Edinburgh found that families where a parent was considered to have a drinking problem were more likely to be those where a child was thought to be at risk of physical abuse (Lothian Regional Social Work Department, 1981). In our study of young adult children of problem drinking parents, and controls, in South-west England (Velleman and Orford, 1985), those young adults with parents with drinking problems recalled substantially more violence, and more violence that was serious, regular, or prolonged, but the difference between their recollections and those of the control group were more marked in the case of parent-to-parent violence than for parent-to-child violence.

This accumulation of evidence about the link between excessive drinking and marital and family disharmony, marital breakdown, family violence, and stress in relatives, suggests the need for a variety of agencies to be alert to the role that drinking problems may be playing in the family. This particularly concerns agencies that deal with disturbances in children and adolescents, those that deal with problems of mental ill health, particularly in women, and those that deal with family problems. Social Service agencies are clearly high on this list.

Despite the strength of the case for the involvement of social workers in work with alcohol-related problems, there is worrying evidence of the relatively low therapeutic commitment of members of this important occupational group. Research by the Salford Community Alcohol Team (Clements, 1984) found that social workers displayed ambivalence about working with problem drinkers. Most felt that management in their organisations afforded it a low priority. Less than half felt they had the right to ask their clients for information about drinking, and less than half felt that it was part of their job to work with alcohol problems. Most of the rest believed in shared responsibility, referring a client with a drinking problem to a specialist whilst retaining responsibility for the family. Compared to other occupational groups such as community psychiatric nurses, general practitioners, probation officers, health visitors and district nurses, social workers had the smallest percentage (37%) answering affirmatively when asked if they could easily find someone who would be able to help formulate the best approach to a problem-drinking client.

In a comparison of social workers and community psychiatric nurses in Exeter (Lightfoot and Orford, 1987), the former were found to have very significantly lower scores on Cartwright's (1980) scale of therapeutic commitment. Social workers had received less training about alcohol-related problems, and as in the Salford study were less likely to feel that they had support available in working with this client group. Both these factors - education and role support - had been considered important by Cartwright (1980) in providing the necessary background for the development of a positive therapeutic attitude. The Exeter study enlarged on this line of research by incorporating a scale of situational constraint which differentiated the two occupational groups and correlated highly with therapeutic commitment. Social workers were significantly more likely than CPNs to agree with statements such as:

> I feel that I receive little or no encouragement from my seniors to get involved in alcohol-related problems.
> Within my department, the general feeling is that we haven't the right to interfere in peoples' drinking choices.

In a book on alcohol-related problems addressed to social workers in particular, Hunt (1982) has also expressed concern.

> Social workers do not often think of psychological and social problems such as intense jealousy, marital discord, debt and evidence of stress in a child, as being direct consequences of alcohol use, nor have they linked alcohol use to medical problems such as gastritis and the social problems that follow (p. 25).

In addition to some of the stereotyped attitudes and occupational constraints to which reference has already been made, Hunt makes an important point when she says that the excessive use of alcohol by clients is often perceived by social workers as merely a **response** to personal problems or prevailing norms rather than as a **cause** of problems.

There is a clear need, then, to modify the attitudes pertaining in social work departments and the ways social workers identify and counsel or refer on people with drinking problems. This cannot be done by those operating within a traditional form of specialist service alone, but requires an active, educative approach involving a commitment to work that includes consultation and organisational change.

Parental Excessive Drinking and Learning Disabilities in Children

Even less well appreciated than the emotional effects upon children of living in a family where one parent has a serious drinking problem are the effects upon intellectual and educational development. There is now a great deal of evidence, almost all from other countries, that children in such families are likely to find it difficult to concentrate at school, are behind in reading attainment, have lower verbal IQ scores, and are sometimes thought to need special remedial help. Much of the research supporting this conclusion comes from the USA (el-Guebaly and Orford, 1977) but important relevant studies have been carried out elsewhere. One of the best, from Czechoslovakia, involved 200 children from intact families in which the father had registered at one of Prague's anti-alcoholic counselling centres (Matejcek, 1981). They were individually matched, for age, number of children in the family, position in the family, and age and education of parents, with children without parents with drinking problems. Teachers and parents were interviewed and the children were tested, the interviewers and examiners being blind to group membership. The children fell into three age groups: 4-6, 9-11, and 13-15 years old. On intelligence testing, a difference of 7 IQ points was found in favour of the comparison group (almost wholly accounted for by a difference of 8 points on verbal intelligence), in the oldest of the three age groups only. Teachers' assessments, paediatricians' ratings of intelligence, and school mates' nominations of the most gifted, intelligent and quickest children, all showed significant differences in favour of the comparison group.

In a less well controlled study from Portugal the mothers of 100 children with problem drinking fathers were interviewed concerning their children's early development and adjustment, and the results compared with 100 control children. In the former group, breast feeding was reported to have been prolonged to one year or more after birth in more cases, developmental delays (first teeth, first steps, first words, and first sentences) were much more common, sphincter control was more often delayed, and progress at school was much more likely to have been poor (76% vs. 14% had to retake at least one year, de Mendonca, 1976).

In a study from Zurich, parental drinking problems were listed as one of nine psychosocial risk factors differentiating 300 11-year olds with learning difficulties (start of school had been postponed, and/or the child had had to repeat a class, and/or the child had been admitted to a special class or educated in a special school or home for the handicapped) from a contrast group of 200 children of the same age who were in the top third of their classes academically (Schmid, 1983). Memory and attention disturbances, low IQ, slow development, and learning problems have also been reported from Eastern European countries (Orford, 1986).

The exact causes of a link between parental excessive drinking and childhood learning disability are unclear. However, maternal drinking during pregnancy might be a cause, if it were not for the fact that most of these studies were confined to children of fathers with alcohol problems.

Whatever the mechanisms linking parental drinking problems and learning disabilities in their children, there exists strong evidence that teachers, educational psychologists, and others who meet children in an educational setting, should be alert to the possibility that parental excessive drinking may be an important contributory factor in many cases of learning disability. Once again there is a need for a community-oriented alcohol service which makes it its business to acquaint these professional groups with the facts and to help them respond appropriately.

Alcohol Problems Amongst Elderly People

Another neglected group with special implications for the development of non-specialist services, consists of elderly people with alcohol-related problems. The neglect of this group provides a good illustration of the inadequacy of the old concepts. Elderly people with drinking problems fit very uneasily into the stereotyped picture of the "alcoholic". Nor do their needs fit well with the former, exclusively specialised, pattern of alcohol services.

A useful review of what is known about elderly people with drinking problems and their needs is provided by Zimberg (1978). He notes, for example, that two studies (Rosin and Glatt, 1971; Simon et al, 1968) have independently drawn a distinction between elderly people with alcohol problems of "early onset" (long-standing drinking problems that have persisted into older age) and those whose problems are of "late onset" (developing alcohol problems only in later life). Both studies found the former outnumbering the latter by 2 to 1 in their samples, although this ratio may be very different in different agency settings, and others have pointed out that some drinking careers do not fit easily into either category (for example those who have intermittently experienced problems with alcohol earlier in life but who have developed a more persistent problem with alcohol in old age).

Both Zimberg (1978) and Hyatt (1985), who has written from the UK specifically about the detection of alcohol problems amongst the elderly, point out that some of the usual signs of drinking problems amongst younger people may be lacking in the older age group. Interference with work performance, and involvement with police and the courts, are both unlikely, for example, in elderly problem drinkers. Similarly, because of the greater sensitivity of older people to the effects of alcohol, and due to interactions with other drugs which elderly people may be using, quantities of alcohol consumed are likely to be smaller and physical damage from alcohol less apparent as a consequence. Signs and symptoms of alcohol problems in the elderly are more likely to be psychological or social, and include unexplained and repeated falls, self-neglect, anxiety, depression or insomnia, or poor personal hygiene (Hyatt, 1985).

Of particular importance to the present line of argument are Zimberg's (1978) observations about the most productive ways of offering treatments to elderly people with alcohol problems. His view is that treatment of this group, whether alcohol problems are of early or late onset, is best provided by those agencies and within those settings that normally serve older people and not within specialist alcohol treatment settings. He is further of the opinion that treatments should be non-specialised: for example that group therapy should be in mixed groups containing elderly people with a variety of problems, not just those related to alcohol, and that it should not be oriented towards gaining insight specifically about use of alcohol. Furthermore, because of the particular needs of older people many of whom would be reluctant to leave their own homes, the treatment services for this group should have a major outreach component including home-based treatment. Treatment should be specifically directed at the problems of depression, bereavement, retirement, loneliness, marital stress and physical illness which are major contributing factors to drinking problems in older people.

Although as yet largely untested, Zimberg's ideas on the treatment of this important group are particularly stimulating and worthy of test. If he is correct, drinking problems amongst the elderly represent a particular challenge to traditional ways of providing services, and a valuable testing ground for the new, non-specialist, approach.

WIDER SOCIAL AND POLITICAL ISSUES

One of the issues raised by a consideration of alcohol problems amongst elderly people is the question of the appropriate place of alcoholic drinks in residential settings (Zimberg, 1978). Should all residential establishments for older people have bars serving alcoholic beverages? In favour is the argument that older people should have the same rights as younger people to have alcoholic drinks available to them and to exercise the right to choose whether to use them or not and to what degree. Against is the argument that providing a bar is to make very accessible a drug which causes some ill effects to which older people may be particularly prone. Care staff may unwittingly encourage excessive drinking because it appears to make older people in their care easier to handle, or in the mistaken idea that people with little to look forward to might as well ease their burdens by drinking

25

heavily. These kinds of arguments are not, of course, confined to discussions about the elderly. They are representative of differing opinions, each widely held within society in general.

Those responsible for delivering a community service cannot avoid addressing these wider social and political issues. This is yet another consequence of the new ways of thinking about alcohol problems. When the problem was conceived of exclusively in terms of the pathological use of alcohol on the part of a small minority of the population, the role played by the production and distribution of alcohol in society, its availability, its price, and prevailing social norms regarding its use, could all be safely ignored. The new thinking, with its emphasis upon a continuum of risk, varying levels of dependence, a variety of types of alcohol-related harm and awareness of ways in which these problems present in a variety of non-specialist settings, forces attention in other directions. It is no longer sufficient to use exclusively "person-blaming" or "person-centred" constructions in the explanation of drinking problems (Mitchell et al 1985). In the 1970s and 1980s "situation-blaming" explanations have emerged much more strongly. Attention has been directed towards the high correlation often to be found between liver cirrhosis mortality and total population alcohol consumption (RCGP, 1986), the apparently upward trends in indices of alcohol-related harm in Britain in the last three decades at a time when the real price of alcoholic beverages has been falling (RCGP, 1986), and the apparent connection within Europe between relatively stringent laws governing the sale of alcohol and relatively low levels of consumption and of cirrhosis mortality (Davies and Walsh, 1983). Notice is being taken of such factors as the pricing of alcoholic drinks and the economics of alcohol and its use generally (Grant et al, 1983). For example, in 1984, 7.4% of total consumers' expenditure in the United Kingdom went on alcoholic drinks - more than on clothing and footwear (6.8%) or on fuel and power (4.9%). In the case of a typical married couple with only the husband working, two hours and twenty-four minutes at work was necessary to pay for a bottle of whisky in 1981 compared with four hours and seventeen minutes in 1971 (Social Trends, 1986). Much of this evidence calls for action on a national level: consideration needs to be given to the possibility of resisting further falls in the real price of alcoholic drinks and resistance to the liberalising of licensing laws, for example. It might be thought that service providers have no role to play in advocating such action or in joining such debate. It could be argued otherwise however (RCGP, 1986). Because of their special knowledge of alcohol-related problems, and because of their influence as experts, those whose main task is to provide a local community service should nevertheless think of ways of using their influence nationally, either through national bodies of which they may be members, such as Alcohol Concern or Action on Alcohol Abuse, or through their Members of Parliament, letters to the national press, or other normal democratic processes.

It is in their own local areas, however, that community service providers will feel best equipped to take action to prevent alcohol-related problems. The numerous opportunities that exist for such local action have very recently been spelt out in a landmark publication written by Tether and Robinson (1986) entitled, Preventing Alcohol Problems - A Guide to Local Action. The possibilities outlined in this book are wide-ranging and are outlined in Chapter 14 of this volume.

One initiative which has been taken in Exeter, Newcastle, and elsewhere is to open an outlet specifically for the sale of non-alcoholic drinks. The purpose is to promote an interest in such drinks, to demonstrate the viability of a social setting which does not supply alcoholic beverages, and to provide a safe, pub-like environment for people who have had alcohol-related problems.

This chapter has outlined the need for a community response to the full range of alcohol-related problems that present within a geographical area. There is growing awareness of the need to recognise, understand, and respond effectively to a wide variety of problems related to the consumption of alcohol which present in any one of a number of different settings and which may call upon the expertise of any one of a diverse set of workers within the statutory and voluntary health and social care services. Family problems involving both partners and children, learning disabilities in young people, and alcohol-related problems amongst the elderly were given as three examples. Others are discussed at greater length in subsequent chapters. Underpinning the development of a new-style alcohol service is a model of alcohol excess or abuse which sees this as analogous to other forms of social behaviour rather than forms of physical disease. This new understanding and the recognition of the need for a community service demand new roles and set new challenges for specialists and non-specialists alike.

REFERENCES

Apte, R. (1968) Halfway Houses: a new dilemma in institutional care. Occasional papers on social administration, No 27, Bell, London

Bailey, M. (1967) Psychophysiological impairment in wives of alcoholics as related to their husbands' drinking and sobriety. In Fox, R. (ed) Alcoholism: behavioural research, therapeutic approaches. Springer, New York, 134-144

Bebbington, P., Hurry, J., Tennant, C., Sturt, E. and Wing, J. (1981) The Epidemiology of mental disorders in Camberwell. Psychological Medicine, 11, 561-580

Behling, D. (1979) Alcohol abuse as encountered in 51 instances of reported child abuse. Clin. Pediat. Phila., 18, 87-91 (abstract in Journal of Studies on Alcohol, 1979, 40, 628)

Breeze, E. (1985) Women and Drinking: an enquiry carried out on behalf of the Department of Health and Social Security. Office of Population Censuses and Surveys, Social Survey Division, HMSO, London

British Psychological Society (1984) Psychology and Problem Drinking. Report of a working party convened by The British Psychological Society, Division of Clinical Psychology. Robertson, I., Hodgson, R., Orford, J. and McKecknie, R. (eds). BPS, Leicester

Brown, A. (1984) Consultation: an aid to successful-social work. Heinemann, London

Burns, A. (1984) Perceived causes of marriage breakdown and conditions of life. Journal of Marriage and Family, 46, 551-562

Cartwright, A. (1980) The attitudes of helping agents towards the alcohol client: the influence of experience, support, training and self-esteem. British Journal of Addiction, 75, 413-431

Clements, C. (1984) Salford Community Alcohol Team Project. Research progress report. Unpublished

Costello, R. (1980) Alcoholism treatment effectiveness: slicing the outcome variance pie. In Edwards, G. and Grant, M. (eds) Alcoholism Treatment in Transition. Croom Helm, London

Cowen, E. (1980) The community context. In Feldman, P. and Orford, J. (Eds) Psychological problems: the social context. Wiley, Chichester

Davies, D. (1962) Normal drinking in recovered alcohol addicts. Journal of Studies in Alcohol, 23, 94-104

Davies, P. and Walsh, D. (1983) Alcohol Problems and Alcohol Control in Europe. Croom Helm, London

Dean, K. and James, H. (1980) The spatial distributions of depressive illness in Plymouth. British Journal of Psychiatry, 136, 167-180

de Mendonca, M. (1976) Etude pedopsychiatrique sur des enfants de pere alcoolique. Revue de Neuropsychiatrie Infantile, 25, 411-428

Department of Health and Social Security (1978) The Pattern and Range of Services for Problem Drinkers. Report of a working party chaired by Professor N. Kessel. DHSS, London

Detoxification Evaluation Project (1985) Problem Drinking: experiments in detoxification. Bedford Square Press, National Council for Voluntary Organisations, London

Durlak, J. (1979) Comparative effectiveness of para-professional and professional helpers. Psychological Bulletin, 86, 80-92

Edwards, G., Chandler, J., Hensman C. and Peto J. (1972) Drinking in a London suburb II: Correlates of trouble with drinking among men. Quarterly Journal of Studies on Alcohol, Suppl. No 6, 94-119

Edwards G., Hawker A., Hensman C., Peto J. and Williamson J. (1973) Alcoholics known or unknown to agencies: Epidemiological studies in a London suburb. British Journal of Psychiatry, 123, 169-183

Edwards, G. (1985) A later follow-up of a classic case series: Davies, D. 1962 report and its significance for the present. Journal of Studies on Alcohol, 46, 181-190

Edwards, G., Duckitt, A., Oppenheimer, E., Sheehan, M. and Taylor, C. (1983) What happens to alcoholics? The Lancet, July 30, 269-271

Elal-Lawrence, G., Slade, P. and Dewey, M. (1986) Predictors of outcome type in treated problem drinkers. Journal of Studies on Alcohol, 47, No 1, 41-47

el-Guebaly, N. and Offord, D. (1977) The offspring of alcoholics: a critical review. American Journal of Psychiatry, 134, 357-365

Gayford, J. (1975) Wife battering: a preliminary study of 100 cases. British Medical Journal (i), 194-197

Ginsberg, G. and Marks, I. (1977) Costs and benefits of behavioural psychotherapy: a pilot study of neurotics treated by nurse-therapists. Psychological Medicine, 7, 685-700

Glaser, F. (1980) Anybody got a match? Treatment research and the matching hypothesis. In Edwards, F. and Grant, M. (eds) Alcoholism Treatment in Transition. Croom Helm, London

Goldberg, D. and Huxley, P. (1980) Mental Illness in the Community: the pathway to psychiatric care. Tavistock, London

Grant, M., Plant, M. and Williams, A. (eds) (1983) Economics and Alcohol. Croom Helm, London

Heather, N. (1986) Change without therapists: the use of self-help manuals by problem drinkers. In Miller, W. and Heather, N. (eds) Treating Addictive Behaviours. Plenum, New York

Heather, N. and Robertson, I. (1983) Controlled Drinking. Methuen, New York

Heather, N. and Robertson, I. (1986) Alcohol Problems: The New Approach. Penguin, Harmondsworth

Hoult, J., Rosen, A. and Reynolds, I. (1984) Community orientated treatment compared to psychiatric hospital orientated treatment. Social Science and Medicine, 18, 1005-1010

Hunt, L. (1982) Alcohol Related Problems. Community Care Practice Handbooks, Heinemann, London

Hyatt, R. (1985) How to spot the elderly alcoholic. Geriatric Medicine, 15, 20-24

Janis, I. and Mann, L. (1977) Decision-making: psychological analysis of conflict, choice and commitment. Free Press, New York

Kendell, R. (1984) The beneficial consequences of the United Kingdom's declining per capita consumption of alcohol in 1979-1982. Alcohol and Alcoholics, 19, 271-276

Ketterer, R. (1981) Consultation and Education in Mental Health. Sage, Beverly Hills

Leckman, A., Umland, B. and Bailey, M. (1984) Alcoholism in the families of family practice out-patients. Journal of Family Practice, 19, 205-207

Lightfoot, P. and Orford, J. (1987) Helping agent's attitudes towards alcohol-related problems: situations vacant? A test and elaboration of a model. British Journal of Addiction, 81, 749-756

Lothian Regional Social Work Department (1981) Alcohol-related problems in current social work cases. Unpublished paper, Social Work Department, Edinburgh

Marshall, S., Velleman, R. and Lanagan, G. (1985) Training Volunteers to Counsel Problem Drinkers and their Families. Addiction Research Centre, Universities of Hull and York, Occasional paper

Matejcek, Z. (1981) Children in families of alcoholics. II Competency in school and peer group (Cz) Pscyhologija i Patopsychologia Dietata, 16, 537-560. (Translated into English for this review)

Mayer, J. and Black, R. (1977) Child abuse and neglect in families with an alcohol or opiate addicted parent. Child Abuse and Neglect, 1, 85-98

McCrady, B. and Hay, W. (1987) Coping with problem drinkers in the family. In Orford, J. (ed) Coping with Disorder in the Family. Croom Helm, London

McGovern, M. (1983) Comparative evaluation of medical vs. social treatment of alcohol withdrawal syndrome. Journal of Clinical Psychology, 39, 791-803

Meyer, M. (1982) Drinking Problems Equal Family Problems: practical guidelines for the problem drinker, the partner and all those involved. Momenta, Lancaster

Mitchell, C., Davidson, W., Chodakowski, J. and McVeigh, J. (1985) Intervention orientation quantification of "person-blame" versus "situation-blame" intervention philosophies. American Journal of Community Psychology, 13, No 5, 542-552

Morgan, H., Pocock, H. and Pottle, S. (1975) The urban distribution of non-fatal deliberate self-harm. British Journal of Psychiatry, 126, 319-328

Orford, J. (1985a) Excessive Appetites: a psychological view of addictions. Wiley, Chichester

Orford, J. (1985b) Alcohol problems and the family. In Lishman, J. (ed) Research Highlights in Social Work, 10. Approaches to Addiction. Kogan Page, London

Orford, J. (1986) Alcohol Problems and the Family: an international review of the literature with implications for intervention and research. Paper prepared for WHO, Division of Mental Health

Orford, J. and Edwards, G. (1977) Alcoholism: a comparison of treatment and advice, with a study of the influence of marriage. Oxford University Press, London (Maudsley Monograph Series)

Orford, J. and Keddie, A. (1986) Abstinence or controlled drinking in clinical practice: a test of the dependence and persuasion hypotheses. British Journal of Addiction, 81, 495-504

Orford, J. and Velleman, R. (1982) Halfway Houses. In Pattison, E. and Kaufman, E. (eds) The American Handbook of Alcoholism. Spungin, New York

Orme, T. and Rimmer, J. (1981) Alcohol and child abuse: a review. Journal for Studies on Alcohol, 42, 273-287

Otto, S. and Orford, J. (1978) Not Quite Like Home: small hostels for alcoholics and others. Wiley, Chichester

Plant, M. (1982) Drinking habits. In Plant, M. (ed) Drinking and Problem Drinking. Junction Books, London

Rabb, M. (1981) A comparison of the effects of social setting detoxification and sub-acute detoxification on further treatment of problem drinkers seen in public: alcohol and drug abuse treatment programs in a Southeastern State. Unpublished PhD thesis, University of South Carolina

Roberts, K. and Brent, E. (1982) Physician utilisation and illness patterns in families of alcoholics. Journal for Studies in Alcohol, 43, 119-128

Robinson, D. (1979) Talking out of Alcoholism: the self-help process of Alcoholics Anonymous. Croom Helm, London

Roizen, R., Cahalan, D. and Shanks, P. (1978) Spontaneous remission among untreated problem drinkers. In Kandall, D. (ed) Longitudinal Research on Drug Use: Empirical findings and methodological issues. Hemisphere, Washington, DC

Rosin, A. and Glatt, M. (1971) Alcohol excess in the elderly. Quarterly Journal of Studies on Alcohol, 32, 53-59

Royal College of General Practitioners (1986) Alcohol - a Balanced View. RCGP, London

Rush, B., Gilksman, L. and Brook, R. (1986) Alcohol availability, alcohol consumption and alcohol-related damage. I. The distribution of consumption model. Journal of Studies on Alcohol, 47, 1, 1-10

Saunders, W. and Kershaw, P. (1979) Spontaneous remission from alcoholism - a community study. British Journal of Addiction, 74, 251-266

Schmid, W. (1983) Genetic, medical and psychosocial factors as a cause of learning difficulties in a cohort of 11-year-old pupils. Acta Paedopsychiatrica, 49, 9-45

Shaw, S., Spratley, T., Cartwright, A. and Harwin, J. (1978) Responding to Drinking Problems. Croom Helm, London

Simon, A., Epstein, L. and Reynolds, L. (1968) Alcoholism in the geriatric mentally ill. Geriatrics, 23, 125-131

Sobell, M. and Sobell, L. (1973) Alcoholics treated by individualised behaviour therapy: one year treatment outcome. Behaviour, Research and Therapy, 11, 599-618

Social Trends (1986) No 16. The Government Statistical Service, HMSO, London

Sysenko, V. (1982) Divorce: dynamics, motives and consequences. Sotsiologicheskie Issledovaniya, 9, 99-104

Tether, P. and Robinson, D. (1986) Preventing Alcohol Problems: a guide to local action. Tavistock, London

van Hasselt, V., Morrison, R. and Bellack, A. (1985) Alcohol use in wife abusers and their spouses. Addictive Behaviours, 10, 127-135

Velleman, R. and Orford J. (1985) Making sense of what adults who had a problem drinking parent say about their childhood experiences. New Directions in the Study of Alcohol, 10, 29-32

Wehmer, G., Cooke, G. and Gruber, J. (1974) Evaluation of the effects of training of para-professionals in the treatment of alcoholism: a pilot study. British Journal of Addiction, 69, 25-32

Whitfield, C. (1982) Out-patient management of the alcoholic patient. Psychiatric Annals, 12, 447-458

Wilson, C. (1982) The impact on children. In Orford, J. and Harwin, J. (eds) Alcohol and the Family. Croom Helm, London

Wilson, P. (1980) Drinking in England and Wales. HMSO, London

Wolfenden Committee Report (1978) The Future of Voluntary Organisations. Croom Helm, London

Zax, M. and Specter, G. (1974) An Introduction to Community Psychology. Wiley, New York.

Zimberg, S. (1978) Psychosocial treatment of elderly alcoholics. In Zimberg, S., Wallace, J. and Blume, S. Practical Approaches to Alcoholism Psychotherapy. Plenum, New York

PART ONE

EXPERIMENTS IN EARLY INTERVENTION

Chapter 2

THE DRINKWATCHERS EXPERIENCE: A DESCRIPTION AND PROGRESS
REPORT ON SERVICES FOR CONTROLLED DRINKERS

Joe Ruzek

In the minds of most members of the general public, there
exist two distinct groups of drinkers. There are normal
social drinkers, and there are the abusers of alcohol, the
"alcoholics". The concept of the problem drinker who
experiences ill effects through the use of alcohol, but who
would not be described as a severely dependent or severely
impaired alcoholic, is not clearly and commonly used. On the
other hand, most alcohol researchers and counsellors would
probably acknowledge the existence of a very large number of
low-dependence, non-alcoholic drinkers who risk much through
excessive or inappropriate use of alcohol. Notwithstanding
this acknowledgement, most alcohol services have been designed
around the needs of the severe problem drinker, and the
concept of the mild problem drinker has not been used to
develop programmes for action (Skinner, 1985).

In most existing services, the tackling of an alcohol
problem is synonymous with acceptance of the goal of
abstinence. The disease model of alcoholism dominates the
thinking and the actions of many alcohol counsellors. It
seems possible, however, that exclusive emphasis on alcoholism
and abstinence may be ill-suited to the needs of the mild
problem drinker, who does not experience withdrawal symptoms
and experiences fewer drawbacks from his or her drinking than
the users of Alcoholics Anonymous and other non-drinking
approaches. For example, people who have been convicted of
drinking and driving may be hard to persuade to stop drinking
alcohol, even though their way of doing so has been manifestly
unsafe. So may those whose drinking levels exceed the
medically recommended limits for consumption but cause few
problems otherwise.

The limitations of an abstinence model become especially
clear in the context of prevention of alcohol problems.
Certainly, young people can be given an awareness of the risks
attendant upon use of alcohol and encouraged to choose a non-
drinking lifestyle. But even with the best possible

35

presentation of the case for abstinence it seems likely that many people will continue to choose to drink alcohol. If this is the case, it would seem appropriate for safe drinking instruction to complement education for alcohol-free life-styles.

Secondary prevention is concerned with early intervention to prevent the development of more severe problems, and controlled drinking programmes for mild problem drinkers are one possible form of secondary prevention. As a general goal in treatment, there are many possible objections to the concept of controlled drinking. In particular, with severe problem drinkers, the effectiveness of the approach remains to be demonstrated. Even the reported successful controlled drinking outcomes in early influential studies have been called into question (Pendery, Maltzman and West, 1982; Edwards, 1985). However, most recent attempts to use controlled drinking techniques with mild problem drinkers have, as opposed to hospital clinical samples, produced more (consistently) positive findings (Heather and Robertson, 1983). There is growing evidence that any criticisms of the concept of controlled drinking are less relevant in the context of such secondary preventive work (Miller, 1983a). Unfortunately, few studies are available to allow a comparison of the relative effectiveness of abstinence and controlled drinking programmes with mild problem drinkers. Recently, however, Sanchez-Craig and her colleagues (Sanchez-Craig, Annis, Bornet and MacDonald, 1984) conducted a comparative evaluation of abstinence-orientated and controlled drinking programmes for early-stage problem drinkers. Importantly, this study examined two similar cognitive-behavioural interventions which differed only in treatment goals. The authors found that the controlled drinking treatment goal was more acceptable to the majority of their clients, and that controlled drinking clients drank less during treatment than those assigned to the abstinence goal. Clients encouraged to choose abstinence, nonetheless, developed moderate drinking on their own, so that both conditions were equally effective in producing reduced consumption levels. Sanchez-Craig and Lei (1986) conducted further analyses of the same data and found that among the heavier drinkers participating in the study (weekly quantity in excess of 48.5 drinks), imposition of the goal of total abstinence was "ineffective in promoting abstinence" and "counter-productive in encouraging moderate drinking, at least in the short term". They also reported that, regardless of the assigned treatment goal, about 70% of their subjects achieved successful limited drinking throughout the two year follow-up period, compared to 5% or less who continued to abstain.

Although information is not available, it is likely that many of the subjects recruited for participation in other early intervention programmes would have refused to seriously consider an abstinence goal.

The growing body of research on controlled drinking interventions aimed at mild rather than severe problem drinkers is beginning to have an impact on the community response to excessive alcohol use. Safe drinking self-help manuals (Miller and Munoz, 1976; Robertson and Heather, 1986; Grant, 1984) are widely available in book stores. Some (e.g. Robertson and Heather, 1985) play an important role in government-sponsored alcohol education campaigns. In England, television programmes have instructed viewers on guidelines for sensible drinking, and work is under way in various countries to teach moderate drinking skills in the primary health care setting (Babor, Ritson and Hodgson, 1986) as an approach to secondary prevention. In the United States, the proliferation of drink-driving educational programmes can be seen as a related development, since work with first offenders often stresses development strategies to avoid re-offending. Where these strategies do not involve a decision to become a non-drinker, they necessarily become safe drinking training programmes. Clearly, many participants do not have severe drinking problems, although they drink, routinely or otherwise, in an inappropriate way.

As a general rule, however, controlled drinking research has had limited impact on the design of community alcohol services. Safe drinking instructional programmes for mild problem drinkers have been offered in the context of research programmes but have not been widely available to the general public. This state of affairs has recently begun to change in Britain, where many agencies now provide individual counselling focusing on the limited drinking goal as an option for clients showing mild rather than severe problems.

This paper describes an attempt to accelerate the development of community-based sensible drinking programmes in Britain, through the creation of a widely available network of Drinkwatchers services designed around the needs of the milder problem drinker.

DRINKWATCHERS SERVICE OVERVIEW

Drinkwatchers aims to attract heavy drinkers or mild problem drinkers. It is not intended for individuals who could be described as "alcoholic". It assumes that some form of reduced or limited drinking will be the preferred goal of most members, but that some will choose to abstain for shorter or longer periods of time. The approach is loosely based on a social learning model of drinking behaviour (e.g. Orford, 1985; Hodgson and Stockwell, 1985) and its methods derive from behaviour therapy self-control techniques. It is designed to be a limited form of help which will need to be supplemented in many cases by other, more intensive, forms of counselling or advice.

It assumes that individuals may change their drinking habits through a range of interventions, varying from simple physician advice, to the reading of a self-help manual, to participation in long-term intensive skills training programmes, to hospital detoxification and aftercare, to membership of Alcoholics Anonymous. A client is envisaged to engage in a sequential process of treatment selection, whereby progressively more costly and intensive forms of help are used as necessary.

The essence of the Drinkwatchers service is a single individual screening session followed by Drinkwatchers group participation. Persons whose drinking problems are sufficiently severe to require an abstinence treatment goal are referred to a more appropriate service following their individual interview. Where those accepted for Drinkwatchers participation require or request additional counselling, other sources of help are recommended. Commonly, referrals are made to agencies offering marriage guidance, anxiety management, sexual therapy and help for depression. Many referrals are made to a branch of our parent organisation, Accept, which offers individual counselling appointments. This offer of additional individual help is a standing one for all members of Drinkwatchers and may be invoked in time of crisis or otherwise. Also, many members were currently seeing a psychiatrist or psychologist at the time of their initial approach to the organisation.

The screening interview also operates as a brief education/advice service. Because many persons decide not to attend group meetings, or drop out quickly, the interview includes discussion of alcohol information and guidelines for reduction of consumption. Each prospective member is given a Drinkwatchers Handbook (Ruzek, 1982) and diary forms, unless they are being referred to a non-drinking programme. If the person indicates that he or she does not intend to go to the group, efforts are made to schedule a follow-up interview in approximately one month.

At the end of the screening interview clients are actively encouraged to schedule a medical examination to assess health factors related to drinking. A liver function test is recommended. In London and elsewhere, local hospital-based physicians have often enabled us to offer the examination as a Drinkwatchers service. Otherwise, clients are encouraged to approach their own doctors.

Weekly group meetings offer continued opportunity to assess drinking patterns and progress in meeting stated drinking objectives. Members are encouraged to attend regularly, for a period of at least three months, and to use the group as needed for booster sessions once a reduction to acceptable levels has been achieved.

The users of Drinkwatchers have requested a variety of levels of support. Many have contacted the organisation in order to obtain the Drinkwatchers Handbook, preferring to tackle their drinking alone. Many have agreed to attend the single interview for advice, declining to join the group and choosing to change their habits with a minimum of outside help, although a follow-up interview is often welcomed. A minority of those who approach Drinkwatchers are prepared to attend evening meetings, believing that regular contact with like-minded others will aid their chances of success. This range of Drinkwatchers limited drinking services is illustrated in Figure 2.1.

Figure 2.1: The Range of Drinkwatchers Helping Services

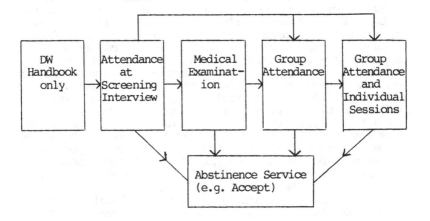

The Initial Interview

There are three reasons for having the screening interview. First, we are able to discuss the relative merits of abstinence and limited drinking with each prospective member. Non-drinking services can be strongly recommended if appropriate. Second, the service can be described, questions answered, and alternative or supplementary avenues of help explored. Third, basic drinking guidelines and information can be clarified.

A "screening" interview seems necessary in such a safe-drinking programme.Drinkwatchers does not wish to establish as an alternative to abstinence services. It does not embrace a general goal of controlled drinking for all comers. It is currently operated within a conservative framework which endorses abstinence as perhaps the "safest" form of drinking behaviour, encourages consideration of non-drinking at all stages of membership and strengthens its recommendations of abstinence as the severity of the problem increases. Moderate drinking goals are welcomed in mild problem drinkers, recommended against for severely dependent individuals, accepted on a trial basis (and sometimes with reluctance) for those in the middle range who refuse abstinence.

While we think this is a responsible approach, there are obvious problems. There are no very clear rules which clarify just who should be encouraged to attempt safe use of alcohol. Even degree of dependence and overall severity of problem, considered by most to be important considerations in choosing a drinking goal, can be questioned on the basis of recent studies (Orford and Keddie, 1986; Elal-Lawrence, Slade and Dewey, 1986). For very mild and very severe cases, a decision seems straightforward. There is, however, a large "grey area" into which the majority of applicants have fallen.

In the absence of clear-cut, well established criteria by which selection for the limited drinking goal can be guided, interviewers form a judgement based on the following considerations: preferences of the client and significant others, health, severity of alcohol-related consequences and severity of alcohol dependence. Clients who wish to abstain but are deemed appropriate for reduction of drinking are not persuaded to change their choice of treatment objective. For those considered obviously inappropriate, attempts at persuasion to abstain and warnings against continued drinking do not necessarily meet with success. If the client steadfastly refuses to consider abstinence, he or she may be given a short-term trial at moderation, which can provide an opportunity for deciding the importance of abstinence. This process of negotiation for drinking goal is similar to that advocated by Heather and Robertson (1983).

In the interview, drinking patterns and levels during the past seven days, a "typical" week during that last three months, and on "typical" heavy drinking occasions are assessed using a questionnaire. Also, the Severity of Alcohol Dependence Questionnaire (SADQ; Stockwell, Hodgson, Edwards, Taylor and Rankin, 1979) is completed by the client. Presence of morning drinking or withdrawal symptoms of shakiness and sweating weigh up strongly against participation in Drinkwatchers. So do apparently serious potential consequences of failure to limit consumption. If a job is clearly at risk, or an important relationship on the line or health is impaired, continued drinking is not encouraged.

If the SADQ and problem discussion lead the interviewer to believe that a non-drinker goal is desirable, the client is asked to describe, at some length, his or her reasons for seeking help. The person is asked, in particular, to describe the "drawbacks" of drinking. The interviewer encourages elaboration of the negative side of the alcohol abuse, so that problems associated with drinking can influence reaction to the abstinence recommendation. Thinking through these drink-related problems often decreases reluctance to discuss abstinence. This process is an adaptation of the "motivational interviewing" technique described by Miller (1983b) and often makes possible constructive feedback without confrontation.

Persons who accept the non-drinking recommendation are referred to Accept, or another service. Most who refuse are asked to use the next 8 or 12 weeks as a limited drinking trial after which they will reconsider their choice of goal. An individual follow-up interview is scheduled, with spouse or partner present, if possible. In this way we hope to encourage an "experimental" decision to abstain, if limited consumption proves unworkable.

Guidelines for "Safe" Drinking

Members ask for guidance about "good" drinking habits, but they often hold strong views with which recommendations need to be integrated. Drinkwatchers has adopted the policy of specifying a general safe, maximum weekly consumption level. Discussion with individuals then makes the target more fitting to the person. The suggested maxima are 30 "standard" drinks or "units" per week for men, and 20 for women. In any discussion of targets these levels are then contrasted with English Health Education Council guidelines, which suggest drinking patterns of 2 or 3 pints of beer, 2 or 3 times per week for men 2 or 3 standard drinks, 2 or 3 times per week for women. This helps emphasise that the former maximum figures are not necesarily desirable. The higher figures are, however, consistent with current British medical recommendations regarding levels of alcohol consumption.

Specification of safe drinking patterns also includes other requirements. The necessity of 2 or more non-drinking days each week is stressed, a daily maxima of 6 drinks or 4 for a woman are strongly recommended. Also important is the concept of "pacing" drinks in order to keep blood alcohol levels low. The idea of a "threshold", after which further drinking leads to trouble, is particularly helpful to members.

Participants will often set their own drinking rules. Common self-imposed guidelines include never drinking alone, avoiding spirits, not drinking during the week (or at lunch times), drinking only on special occasions, never drinking at home and so on. This kind of rule-setting is much discussed in the group and encouraged by leaders.

Conduct of Meetings

Most groups meet one evening each week for about two and half hours per week. An attendance of 6 to 12 people allows for regualar individual weekly reports as well as topical discussions or presentations. Weekly drinking reports are an important part of group operation. Each member describes his or her recent consumption, day by day, and specifies targets for the coming week. Successful weeks are probed by the group leader to identify effective coping methods, and heavy occasions are discussed in order to identify reasons for the break down of coping. These reports sessions help the member, the group and the leader to identify individual "high-risk" situations (e.g. Marlatt and George, 1984) for which more detailed planning is necessary. They enable a group secretary to record progress for each member, which can help evaluation efforts. Individual targets and actual consumption can be compared each week, permitting constructive confrontation when appropriate. It is hoped that the specific goals negotiated in the social context of Drinkwatchers are more likely to be achieved than the privately-generated vague ones characterising many spontaneous self-control attempts (cf. Risley, 1977).

Some aspects of this process of goal setting seem especially important. Goals need to be achievable. Success breeds success in the sense that initial goal attainment may often generate greater effort and persistence in tackling later, more ambitious goals. The leader, therefore, needs to ensure that members set realistic targets and that self-determined goals do not lose their ability, through repeated failure, to influence behaviour. As each member in turn specifies his or her goals for the coming week, this issue can be addressed and discussed by the group.

On some occasions the weekly reports form the structure of the entire meeting, with the leader introducing concepts and prompting discussion of relevant issues as they arise. At other times reports are kept brief, so that other material can be covered. They generally occur each week, however, partly as a means of providing a structured, low-anxiety opportunity for regular active participation on the part of each member. More formal discussion topics vary according to the interest and expertise of leaders and members. They frequently include presentations on medical effects of alcohol, practice in refusing drinks, relaxation training and identification of ways of coping with stress. Workshops on stress allow members to tackle, on a very limited basis, some of the emotional situations related to their drinking.

Reports, discussion and exercises form the basis for the weekly sessions. Some Drinkwatchers branches have chosen a time-related structure, in which new members are recruited and a structured curriculum presented over 6 or 10 sessions. However, we have encouraged the development of "open" rather then "closed" groups. In the "open" format, new members are continuously recruited and begin participation soon after the individual interview. The group runs for an indefinite period, with a gradual turnover in membership. This means that new members have good opportunity to benefit from the experience and encouragement of longer-term members, who have often had considerable success in changing drinking habits. This motivates newcomers and provides experienced members with

an opportunity to share their experience. It is hoped that
the act of helping others may contribute to the maintenance of
the helper's own changed behaviour (cf. Reissman, 1965).

Meetings also include a business segment when small fees
(e.g. £1.00) are collected, books and articles shared, social
activities arranged, or tasks allocated. An effort is made to
involve members in the operation of the group by encouraging
them to act as treasurer, secretary or chairperson. The
treasurer collects weekly fees, out of which room rental,
refreshments and other costs can be met, and if some small
funds begin to accumulate, the group can decide how to use
their money. A group secretary keeps simple records of
members' drinking behaviour and related information which can
be used to construct graphs showing individual consumption
patterns across a period of several months. Acting
chairpersons can conduct meetings in the absence of the
regular leader. Handing over these tasks to members
themselves helps build a commitment to other group members and
to group goals.

After meetings, members often go for a drink together at
a nearby pub. For some, this pub visit allows for exposure to
a high-risk situation within a social climate of moderation
For others, it is a way out of social isolation. Drink
refusal and other exercises can be included during this time,
but the major reason for this after meeting get-together has
been to add a social dimension to participation in
Drinkwatchers.

Roles of the Leaders
Leaders have in most cases been counsellors trained by and
working with local community alcohol services. Also,
probation officers, social workers and other professional
helpers have taken on leadership of a group as part of their
ordinary work role. In London, members have sometimes acted
as leaders, with support from the author. Any prospective
group leader is asked to attend a one-day workshop outlining
Drinkwatchers goals and procedures. This straightforward
training assumes a basic working knowledge of alcohol problems
and counselling skills, and local leaders are encouraged to
work closely with existing alcohol agencies which can provide
back-up services for the group. In London, local leaders meet
regularly to discuss current concerns, and when members act as
leaders on a more than occasional basis, they are given more
intensive support.

Leaders concern themselves with maintaining the structure
of the sessions, encouraging participation, giving information
about alcohol and its effects, resolving conflict and
prompting action as well as talk. They are especially
concerned with managing the "airtime" of group meetings, which
means encouraging certain types of talk and discouraging
others. Content to be encouraged includes concrete

descriptions of high-risk situations, practical anticipation of and planning for risky circumstances, identification of the positive consequences of changed drinking practices, and stated commitment to action. Talk to be discouraged might include repetitive excuse making, rambling and support for excessive drinking. Leaders are not non-directive. Rather, they try to influence the group discussion to make it productive and practical, through using social reinforcement and the opportunites afforded by their role as chairperson.

As needed, leaders also guide the group in structured exercises. In particular, they help members to use a group application of the technique of "problem solving" (D'Zurilla and Goldfried, 1971). A high-risk situation is identified and given concrete description. The group then generates a sizable list of possible ways of coping with it. Finally, the individual member for whom it is a problem selects the new responses he or she is willing to try, and reports on progress at the next meeting. Another common exercise is the structured "role play" rehearsal of drink refusal.

Finally, group leaders are expected to report on their own drinking practices whether or not they have ever experienced problems with alcohol. Likewise, all visitors to the group participate in the drink report section of the meeting. The practice helps to underline the idea that safe drinking is everybody's business, and to include descriptions of very different, very moderate drinking styles contrasts usefully with the "taken for granted" heavier consumption considered "normal" in members' drinking circles.

DISSEMINATION: THE ORGANISATIONAL CONTEXT OF DRINKWATCHERS

Drinkwatchers aims to encourage the development of local groups around Britain so that services which complement existing abstinence ones can become widely available. Currently, local alcohol agencies other than AA have a limited profile among problem drinkers and are often virtually unknown to the general public. It seems possible that the creation of a network of safe drinking groups, sharing the name "Drinkwatchers" and loosely unified by a set of goals and procedures can achieve large public visibility and contribute significantly towards the secondary prevention of alcohol problems. In line with this reasoning, efforts have been under way to disseminate the Drinkwatchers concept, and some influences bearing on the success or failure of our attempts can be described.

First, the goal of moderate drinking for clients with less severe problems is acceptable to most British community alcohol agencies. The work by Heather and Robertson and others has made the concept a mainstream one. Government prevention campaigns centre around the notion of safe levels of alcohol consumption, and a survey conducted as early as

1979 (Robertson and Heather, 1982) indicated that at least 38 agencies in the United Kingdom were offering the goal of moderation to some of their clients. Therefore, for many potential sponsoring agencies, the idea of a Drinkwatchers service merely extends existing practice or planning.

Second, the parent organisation of Drinkwatchers is Accept, a London-based charitable organisation concerned with education, prevention and treatment of alcohol problems (see Chapter 11). Location of the project within an established agency has provided advantages for Drinkwatchers in terms of legitimacy, community contacts, access to media fund raising possibilitites and advice of experienced colleagues. It has proven disadvantageous in other respects. Within Accept itself, Drinkwatchers has been accorded relatively low priority. The parent agency justifiably concerns itself with running more intensive abstinence-orientated day centres which serve large numbers of clients. Drinkwatchers is in some sense an altruistic exercise from the standpoint of a community agency like Accept, in that successful growth means the establishment of new branches by other existing alcohol agencies and professionals, and it is never likely to attract much in the way of funds. Externally, one potential sponsoring organisation has challenged Accept's role in promoting such a national programme, and some have been concerned that Drinkwatchers might be used as a sort of "Trojan horse" to extend Accept's services into new regions, draining funds from the local sponsoring agency. With time these political difficulties have become less of a problem, but they do indicate the importance of considering the point of origin of the Drinkwatchers movement.

Obstacles aside, the overall British organisational context has seemed very favourable for the development of Drinkwatchers. Originally, our hope was that local branches would operate as self-help groups, convened and run by members themselves. This was because self-help groups have demonstrated a capacity to develop and expand to a greater extent than professional services. But because Drinkwatchers was to be aimed at persons with less severe alcohol problems, it seemed imperative to "screen" prospective members. This would provide one means of ensuring that Drinkwatchers would not offer controlled drinking advice to all applicants. The natural providers of these screening interviews were existing community alcohol agencies, and as a result they have been encouraged to establish local Drinkwatchers services. The concept of self-help Drinkwatchers branches has been tried with success in London, but awaits further development elsewhere.

Anticipation of a widespread dissemination of the service has guided the design of Drinkwatchers procedures. Simple, non-aversive self-change techniques were selected to improve the likelihood of use by members. Compatible with individual or group work, with closed or open groups, and with didactic or discussion-based formats, the programme was made flexible to allow local sponsors the freedom to modify it in line with their specific circumstances. The network of local groups operates in a decentralised manner designed to encourage local experimentation with the approach. Flexible, decentralised programmes may be more compatible with the social context of the communities in which they will be implemented and therefore more likely to be effectively disseminated (Fawcett, Matthews and Fletcher, 1980). Since the start of the project, active dissemination efforts have included the following:

1. A self-help manual, The Drinkwatchers Handbook (Ruzek, 1982) has been written not only to provide guidance to individual members, but to advance the Drinkwatchers concept among alcohol professionals and referral agents

2. A leaflet and posters have been produced, and they allow space for local sponsors to promote their own service

3. Leader training has been offered to interested counsellors and agencies at no cost

4. The author has met with potential sponsors, clarifying questions, exploring obstacles and, most importantly, making presentations to executive committee

5. National network meetings have been held, providing for discussion and planning by local sponsors

6. A "Drinkwatch" newsletter has been circulated, reporting on local branch developments, innovative practices, useful responses to obstacles, and so on

7. A "Branch Handbook", in preparation, will give concrete advice on all aspects of establishing a local group. It will include sessional outlines for use by new group leaders.

PROGRESS REPORT

The Drinkwatchers concept is an evolving one. We intend that the design of the service, group procedures and national network interaction will develop according to the influence of research findings, branch experience and member involvement. At this stage, however, it is useful to assess progress and prospects for the continued development of the approach as outlined in this paper. The following paragraphs describe the users of the service, present limited evaluation information, and outline the current results of our efforts at dissemination.

Drinkwatchers Clientele

Given the rationale of the project, it is important to examine the characteristics of users of the service. There follows some simple descriptive information collected from recent samples of clients attending the screening interview.

First, source of referral data is available for 90 individuals, and is presented in Table 2.1. One quarter of all referrals were from Accept, the parent abstinence treatment centre. The large majority of these were persons refusing to accept the non-drinking goal advocated in the Accept intake interview and required by the Accept treatment programme. A few of these individuals presented with problems sufficiently mild for the abstinence-orientated intake interviewers to recommend a limited drinking goal. These Accept referrals illustrate the potential complementary nature of abstinence and limited drinking services. Without the Drinkwatchers referrals option, these refusers of abstinence could have been offered no further help. Referrals from alcohol agencies (Accept and others) were equalled in number by self-referred persons, who responded to posters, written media and radio coverage.

These referrals were recruited by a variety of means, as part of general Drinkwatchers service development. Specific recruitment activities included written media coverage (especially newspaper and magazine stories describing the concept of safe alcohol use and the Drinkwatchers organisation), talks to community referral groups (e.g. doctors, social workers), poster mailings to general practitioners, and listings in various community directories. Many who approached the service had, in fact, seen Drinkwatchers mentioned several times over a considerable period of time. The recruitment of a sample of 100 attenders

Table 2.1: Source of Referral of Attenders of the Drinkwatchers Screening Interview

SOURCE OF REFERRAL	N	%
Accept	22	24
Self-referral	26	29
Physician	18	20
Workplace	7	8
Family and Friends	7	8
Professional Helpers	6	7
Other Alcohol Agencies	4	4
TOTAL	90	100

of the initial interview required about 8 months, a time period which is lessening as the rate of referrals gradually increases. The catchment area was London and surrounds.

The ages of interviewees ranged from 21 to 73, with the majority being under 40. Table 2.2 displays the ages of participants categorised by sex. Roughly two-thirds of those of those interviewed were men.

Table 2.2: Age of Clients Attending the Drinkwatchers Screening Interview

AGE	% MEN (n=64)	% WOMEN (n=33)	% TOTAL (n=97)
20-29	22	21	22
30-39	37	36	37
40-49	27	21	25
50-59	6	15	9
60 +	8	6	7

Attenders of the interview were asked to complete the Severity of Alcohol Dependence Quesitonnaire (SADQ), a twenty item self-rating measure focusing on withdrawal symptoms, withdrawal relief drinking and quantity consumed during a heavy drinking day (Stockwell, Hodgson, Edwards, Taylor and Rankin, 1979). Participants' SADQ scores, catgorised by sex, are presented in Table 2.3. On this measure, three-quarters of those interviewed scored 20 or less, suggesting only mild degrees of alcohol dependence.

Candidates for Drinkwatchers were also asked to indicate their typical weekly alcohol consumption over the 3 months prior to their interview. Figure 2.3 shows this weekly consumption represented as "standard drinks" for men and women. Forty-four of the 57 men sampled (78%) reported a mean daily consumption of a half bottle of spirits or less (8 pints or less of ordinary strength beer). Approximately one-third of the men were drinking less than or equal to 8 or 9 drinks per day. Four-fifths of the women were drinking under the latter amount, and 43% reported consuming under 6 drinks per day (one bottle of wine or less per day). These data indicate high levels of consumption among many of those interviewed, resulting in many being strongly recommended to stop drinking. However, they also suggest that many relatively mild problem drinkers were using the service, consistent with the data on severity of dependence.

Table 2.3: Severity of Alcohol Dependence Questionnaire (SADQ) Scores of Clients Attending the Drinkwatchers Screening Interview

SADQ SCORES	% MEN (n=60)	% WOMEN (n=31)	% TOTAL (n=91)
1-10	31	45	36
11-20	41	39	41
21-30	20	16	19
over 30	6	0	4

As shown in Figures 2.2 and 2.3 some members reported that they had been abstaining prior to their initial interview. However, these data describe a typical drinking week over the last 3 months. Some members had quite frequent weeks with no alcohol at all, but did drink during other weeks. Some had a general pattern of abstinence, punctuated by the occasional heavy session or heavy week, and some had

Figure 2.2: Typical Weekly Drinking Levels for 30 Female Clients Attending the Drinkwatchers Screening Interview

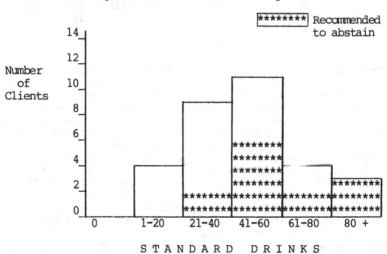

STANDARD DRINKS

been more or less abstinent during the last 3 months, with problems occurring earlier, but had no intention of attempting complete abstinence (and in fact were not doing so).

Ninety-two candidates provided information about previous help for alcohol problems. Forty-eight (52%) reported receiving no prior help. Fifteen (16%) had previously approached AA, although contact in a number of cases amounted to as little as one telephone call or attendance at one

Figure 2.3: Typical Weekly Drinking Levels for 57 Males Attending the Drinkwatchers Screening Interview

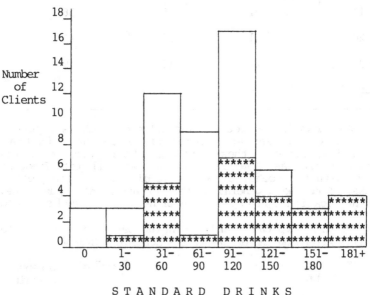

STANDARD DRINKS

meeting. This confirms our clinical experience that many Drinkwatchers members have been along to one AA meeting and have not returned because of difficulty in identifying with those present. Seven interviewees (8%) had attended our parent abstinence service (Accept) in the past, and two (2%) had discussed the issue with their general practitioner,five (5%) had done so with a psychiatrist and ten (11%) had received help in a hospital out-patient or in-patient setting. Eight individuals had received aid from more than one source. Nearly all of the clients who had previously involved themselves in AA or attended a hospital-based programme were recommended to abstain. Five previous AA members indicated acceptance of this advice and were referred to a suitable agency. Four of the ten previous users of hospital-based services were referred for the Drinkwatchers interview by

Accept, where they had earlier voiced their refusal to give up alcohol altogether. Three of the remaining six accepted an abstinence referral.

Generally, it is significant that a large number of applicants for participation in Drinkwatchers were judged better suited to an abstinence programme. Of 100 clients, 39 were recommended to abstain, on the basis of one or more of the following criteria: high SADQ scores, very high levels of consumption, severe alcohol-related consequences, previous participation in abstinence-orientated hospital or community-based services. Of these 39 persons, 15 (38%) agreed to pursue an abstinence goal within an appropriate treatment setting. Eight (21%) failed to decide on a course of action during the interview, and discontinued contact against advice. Seven (18%) refused to accept the non-drinking recommendation and wished to have a try at moderation for a short time within a Drinkwatchers group. Another seven (18%) were also determined to pursue moderation, but refused to attend the support group, preferring to tackle the problem on their own. Of these, six asked for an individual follow-up interview. The remaining two clients were referred to other agencies and their choice of drinking goal was unknown.

On the basis of self-report information gathered during the initial interview, it can be argued that the Drinkwatchers service attracts considerable numbers of heavy drinkers appropriate for the limited drinking goal. Many are dependent only to a mild degree, consume amounts of alcohol below those reported by many clinic alcoholics, are under 40 years of age and have little or no previous contacts with AA - all possible indicators for assignment to a controlled drinking goal (Heather and Robertson, 1983). Also encouraging is the fact that many of those for whom abstinence is advised do indicate a willingness to attend a more suitable treatment service. The initial interview does provide an opportunity to review drinking habits and choice of drinking goal.

While information describing the above sample is restricted to self-report data, limited medical assessments are available for an additional, earlier sample of applicants to the Drinkwatchers programme (Barrison, Ruzek and Murray-Lyon, in press). Following an initial interview with a Drinkwatchers counsellor, 124 heavy drinkers were referred for a medical screening as part of the Drinkwatchers service. The physician examined patients for signs of chronic liver disease and conducted blood tests. Table 2.4 presents the results of his examination.

These data support the indications from the sample already described that Drinkwatchers is attracting many relatively mild problem drinkers who have not yet experienced serious health problems as a result of their drinking patterns. Only 4 of 135 successive referrals had signs of advanced liver disease. Nonetheless, one-half of those examined presented with abnormalities on at least one of the three measures commonly used to screen for heavy alcohol consumption. The physician's recommendation in each of these cases was one of abstinence and was communicated to patients several days after their examination. A follow-up visit at three months was organised for all 63 persons with abnormality on initial testing. Only 30 (47.6%) of these individuals did, in fact, re-attend, and few reported compliance with the non-drinking recommendation. Most did report a reduction in drinking levels, and of the 19 subjects with initial liver enlargement who attended at follow-up, 17 were found to have reduced their liver size to within the normal range. Nine out of 13 patients with a raised level of gamma-glutamyl transpeptidase (GGT) showed reduction back into the normal range at follow-up.

Table 2.4: **Frequencies of Raised Mean Cell Volume (MCV), GGT and Hepatomegaly in a Sample of Attenders of a Drinkwatchers Medical Screening Examination**

	N	MEN (%)	N	WOMEN (%)	N	OVERALL (%)
Raised MCV	17	(27.8)	29	(46.0)	46	(37.1)
Raised GGT	18	(29.5)	5	(7.9)	23	(18.5)
Hepatomegaly	28	(45.9)	17	(27.0)	45	(36.3)

No individual showed a significant fall in MCV during the 3 month period, reflecting the long time lag between changes in drinking behaviour and resulting changes in this measure.

Our experience with medical screening suggests that it should certainly be included as a component of limited drinking interventions with mild problem drinkers, to ensure that appropriate drinking and non-drinking recommendations can be made. It also illustrates some limitations of advice to abstain with milder problem drinkers, even when a clear relationship between drinking and health risk can be demonstrated to the client. Finally, it suggests that some short-term health benefits can be achieved through recruitment of persons who would like to drink less, coupled with medical examination and advice. Interestingly, this sample was different in some respects from the one described earlier in this section. Sources of referrals were very different. The sample for whom medical data are available was contacted largely through the media publicity, with 85% being self-referred. Accept referred clients relatively infrequently, as did physicians. These differences probably reflect the fact that Drinkwatchers received some excellent radio and magazine coverage during the period in which the earlier sample was recruited. Since that time, the service has become better known locally, accounting for an increase in referrals from physicians. And the higher rate of Accept referrals is probably due, in part, to the increasing acceptance of the role of Drinkwatchers (and the controlled drinking goal) in a service committed to abstinence.

Evaluative Information
Short-term data is available for a small sample of 39 subjects who participated in a Drinkwatchers evaluation project. Some joined a Drinkwatchers group while others received brief individual advice. Table 2.5 describes drinking patterns for a "typical" week during the preceding 3 months, before and after a 3 month period of participation. The figures show reductions in total consumption levels and amounts consumed per drinking day, as well as an increase in number of alcohol-free days and days during which limited amounts of alcohol

Table 2.5: **Mean Self-Reported Alcohol Consumption, for a "Typical" Week over the Last Three Months, in a Sample of Thirty-Nine Drinkwatchers**

DRINKING VARIABLES	PRE	POST
No. days drinking sensibly	1.4 (n=38)	2.9 (n=36)
No. days abstinent	0.8 (n=38)	1.8 (n=36)
No. days over over limits (over 6 units-men; over 4 units-women)	4.6 (n=39)	2.3 (n=37)
Total weekly consumption (units)	59.9 (n=38)	31.9 (n=37)
Amount consumed per drinking day (units of alcohol)	9.80 (n=38)	5.91 (n=36)

were taken. Six or fewer standard drinks during a day were
considered a limited amount for male subjects, and four or
less for women. Despite improvements, on average, subjects
continued to drink over these limited amounts more than twice
during a typical week.

Participants were also asked to rate their degree of
progress in changing drinking habits during the intervening 3
months. While only 3 individuals reported no progress and no
individual indicated a worsening problem, 10 out of the 38
persons interviewed reported only slight progress. About two-
thirds of the sample considered themsleves to have made more
substantial improvements, but only 39% were more than
"somewhat satisfied" with their pattern at the end of the 3
month period. Satisfaction ratings were higher among those
who participated in a Drinkwatchers group, comparing
favourably with the ratings of recipients of less intensive
advice.

An attempt was made to follow up 24 participants over a
longer period of time. Seventeen subjects were located and
interviewed between one and three years after the initial
assessment. On the basis of their self-report, 11 of the 17
appeared to be drinking in a relatively harm-free way, and
were much improved in comparison with their status at the
start of the project. These improvements were accomplished in
many different ways. A 53-year old male reported drinking 113
units in a typical week before joining Drinkwatchers,
averaging about 16 units on each drinking day. He dropped out
of the group after only two meetings and reduced his
consumption to 70 units at the 3 month evaluation, clearly
continuing to drink heavily. He then decided to re-join a
group, brought his levels down to around 5 drinks per week at
another 3 months follow-up, and continued to drink under 10
units per week for the three years during which he continued
to maintain contact with Drinkwatchers. A more common pattern
was shown by a 57-year old woman who was drinking 51 units per
week initially, averaging 8.5 units per drinking day with one
alcohol-free day each week. At long-term follow-up she
reported consuming 23 drinks in a typical week, with two non-
drinking days and an average of 4.6 drinks per drinking day.
She was no longer experiencing any black-outs, and had almost
eliminated hangovers. She had far fewer of what she
considered to be "heavy" days, and consumed markedly less on
those days. Difficulties in judging success are illustrated
by the change in pattern demonstrated by a 27-year old man.
At long-term follow-up he was drinking 14 drinks in a typical
week, compared to 36 before receiving the Drinkwatchers
Handbook. However, he achieved this by abstaining on 5 days
each week and consuming 7 drinks on each of the other two. He
experienced fewer hangovers, had fewer self-perceived heavy
drinking days, consumed less on heavy drinking occasions and

pronounced himself completely satisfied with his present pattern.

Few of the successful subjects abided by all our guidelines for safe and sensible drinking. Some continued to drink 6 or 7 times per week, but stayed to very low levels on those occasions. Others continued to exceed our recommended weekly limits, but to a very small degree and apparently with very few negative consequences. Most continued, at times, to drink over the recommended daily maxima of 6 drinks for men and 4 for women, but these occasions became much less frequent. Self-perceived heavy drinking days occurred far less often and involved much lower levels of alcohol. Many of the occasions in excess of the daily limits took place over long periods of time and did not necessarily produce a high blood alcohol level. Clearly, it is necessary to go beyond self-report data in examining outcome. We experienced much difficulty in gathering data from a third party, because many subjects were single and unable or unwilling to nominate anyone to provide the needed information. Also, many of the partners of our subjects reported problems in commenting on changes in alcohol consumption. They were not present during most of our subjects' drinking and unable to observe changes in level.

Obviously, the data summarised above do not permit firm conclusions regarding the effectiveness of Drinkwatchers services. However, they do suggest that participation in the programme is associated with improved patterns of alcohol use in the short term. Very limited longer-term follow-up information is also encouraging. It is hoped that development of Drinkwatchers will permit more rigorous evaluation studies.

Network Development
The growth of the Drinkwatchers network has met with moderate success. There are, at the time of this writing, 14 local Drinkwatchers branches in 11 cities in England, Scotland and Wales, and 4 new branches are currently at the planning stage. Groups are available in many of the localities. All provide individual counselling towards the limited drinking goal and all call themselves by the name of "Drinkwatchers". Organisers of local services include community alcohol agencies, probation services, workplace employee assistance programmes and community psychiatric nursing teams. Leaders are drawn from the ranks of alcohol agency workers, social workers, community psychiatric nurses, clinical psychologists, probation officers and volunteer counsellors. Many of the branches involve a joint effort by, for example, an agency member and a probation officer, or a psychologist and an agency worker. Some degree of interdisciplinary cooperation has been achieved in many of the branches. One has formed a steering committee made up of representatives of the local community alcohol agency, the local hospital-based alcohol

treatment unit, the general practitioner committee, the community health council and other interested groups.

Local efforts have also varied in other ways. Some branches have had a quite short life span, owing to difficulty in recruitment coupled with a high drop-out rate, or to funding crises in the parent agency, or to the departure of the group leaders. Others have continued to operate for several years. Some have developed their own instructional materials, and altered the structure of the service to fit with local circumstances and priorities. This Drinkwatchers development appears to have been permitted by an increasing awareness of the need to prevent rather than treat severe alcohol problems and by the widespread acceptance of the controlled drinking goal in Britain. Small community agencies wanting to expand their services have looked toward the development of a Drinkwatchers programme with a more preventative orientation. Probation officers, psychiatric nurses and social workers, aware of large numbers of heavy drinkers (not alcoholics) on their case-loads, have needed a response more acceptable to their clients than referrals to abstinence treatment. There has been a general growth of programmes focusing on alcohol in moderation in Britain, and the development of Drinkwatchers services has been part of that growth.

DRINKWATCHERS IN PERSPECTIVE: ISSUES AND OBSTACLES

The guiding idea behind the development of a Drinkwatchers service has been the perceived opportunity to provide community-based intervention targeted at the mild problem drinker, focusing on the limited drinking goal and complementing existing abstinence-dominated approaches. The service is designed to offer support and instruction to that population of at risk drinkers who are the intended audience for related secondary prevention attempts, including self-help manuals, televised instruction in safe drinking and interventions in the primary health care setting. With this rationale in mind, the crucial question is whether mild problem drinkers will use a Drinkwatchers service. In our experience, it has proven very difficult to recruit persons who are drinking in excess of recommended limits but remain virtually free of negative health, social and personal consequences. Certainly, the experience of local developers of Drinkwatchers branches has underlined this difficulty. They have consistently found it hard to recruit appropriate clientele for their fledgling service, often being forced to limit their work to an individual rather than a group approach. Unfortunately, we are not unique in this regard and other writers have reported similar recruitment problems (e.g. Vogler, Compton and Weissbach, 1976)

Perhaps one-third of our applicants have been considered by us to be unambiguously representative of that group of drinking men and women for whom the Drinkwatchers approach has been explicitly designed. As has been indicated earlier, many applicants to the programme have been better suited to non-drinking treatments. This is not in our view a major problem, since many of these individuals have been persuaded to abstain and those who have refused to do so would almost certainly have been no better off had Drinkwatchers not been in existence.

As is the case with abstinence programmes, there are likely to be considerable numbers of users of limited drinking services who fail to change their pattern of alcohol abuse. The accusation will be made that these services in effect collude with problem drinkers and delay their entry into non-drinking treatments like AA. This is a real possibility which could be evaluated by, for example, randomly assigning applicants judged inappropriate for limited drinking and refusing to accept the abstinence recommendation either participation in Drinkwatchers or to no further help.

Why are only a small proportion of heavy drinkers coming forward for help before alcohol has become a relatively serious problem in their lives? Perhaps this is only to be expected. Perhaps drinkers will seek help as a late resort, preferring to take action on their own in less worrying circumstances. However, part of the rationale for development of Drinkwatchers-style services has seen the assumption that "early stage" or "mild" problem drinkers balk at asking for help because of the nature of the help being offered (i.e. abstinence only treatment for "alcholics"). If this assumption is correct, the Drinkwatchers experiment would have been expected to generate greater involvement on their part. Clearly, many of our members do approach us because they see a sensible or safe drinking goal as more suitable for their needs and more fitted to the severity of their problems. But the numbers of suitable applicants remain relatively small. Interestingly, some investigators of controlled drinking interventions with less severe problem drinkers have apparently experienced less difficulty in recruiting appropriate subjects, judging from their ability to locate samples reporting quite modest pre-treatment drinking levels. However, Miller (1986) has recently indicated that the recruitment of his samples of around 40 such clients involved a considerable struggle. He noted similar difficulties reported by other research clinics in the United States and elsewhere, although not with some Scandinavian efforts.

It seems, nonetheless, that the target audience will come forward in at least some circumstances. For example, Sanchez-Craig et al (1984) reported mean consumption of 51 drinks per week in their sample, and noted that this figure was higher than that reported in some similar investigations. The mean weekly consumption for non-abstainers in our sample was 60.8 units (men, 73.5; women, 39.5) higher than that of most other studies. These slightly higher drinking levels probably reflect a higher threshold for recommendation of the non-drinking-orientated context in which the Drinkwatchers service is offered. The number of programme applicants who report quite moderate levels (say, between 20 and 50 units) has remained a modest proportion of those coming forward, and a fairly small number in absolute terms.

This difficulty with the recruitment of milder problem drinkers does not necessarily spell disaster for the general enterprise of early intervention. Larger numbers of persons have contacted the Drinkwatchers service for information than have attended an interview. Literature, especially the Drinkwatchers Handbook self-help manual, has been in high demand. It is possible that those with less problematic drinking habits seek less problematic forms of help. Importantly, there is probably quite limited awareness of the existence and aims of limited drinking services among the appropriate potential users of these services. Coupled with the continued stigmatisation and stereo typing associated with problem drinking and the popular confusion between drinking problems and alcoholism, this limits the likelihood that suitable persons will approach a Drinkwatchers-style service. Nor do potential referral agents currently lay a facilitative role in the development of such services. Physicians, social workers, welfare officers and other helpers do not routinely assess alcohol use among their patients and clients, and largely restrict their referrals to relatively severe cases, for whom abstinence is far more advisable.

If such factors account for the difficulty in attracting the mild problem drinker, then there is some reason for optimism. Old-fashioned referral practices can be changed, as physicians and other helping professionals begin to routinely enquire about the drinking behaviour of their patients/clients, and screening procedures are more regularly implemented in hospital consulting rooms, workplace health services and other community settings. The community can become more aware of the risks of heavy, but non-alcoholic, use of alcohol. Awareness of the availability of early intervention, moderation-orientated services can grow.

Safe drinking services for mild problem drinkers seem likely to continue to become more widely available. Preliminary evidence suggests that they can help produce clinically significant reductions in drinking level, and that the goal of moderation is more acceptable, to this population, than that of abstinence. This description of Drinkwatchers has outlined one form that such services might take. Although controversies surrounding controlled drinking for severely dependent drinkers are very much alive, and advocates of disease and non-disease models are frequently in conflict, it

is hoped that the development of safe drinking interventions
for mild problem drinkers can be explored at some distance
from these quarrels. A Drinkwatchers-style service is not
intended for use by severely dependent alcoholics, and
provided that it remains reasonably true to its intentions it
can, in our experience, be accepted or even welcomed by those
for whom abstinence is the only path to recovery from
alcoholism. Certainly, the developers of these programmes
must be concerned to prevent their misuse by drinkers for whom
they are inappropriate, and remain aware of the risks of
collusion. If these conditions are met, perhaps we can get on
with the pragmatic business of taking earlier action in the
lives of excessive drinkers and promoting safe use for all who
choose to drink.

REFERENCES

Babor, T., Ritson, E. and Hodgson, R. (1986) Alcohol-related problems in the primary health-care setting: a review of early intervention strategies. British Journal of Addiction, 81, 23-46

Barrison, I., Ruzek, J. and Murray-Lyon, I. (in press) Drinkwatchers: description of subjects and evaluation of MCV and GGT as markers of heavy drinking. Alcohol and Alcoholism

D'Zurilla, J. and Goldfried, M. (1971) Problem solving and behaviour modification. Journal of Abnormal Psychology, 78, 107-126

Edwards, G. (1985) A later follow-up of a classic case series: D.L. Davies' 1962 Report and its significance for the present. Journal of Studies on Alcohol, 46, 181-190

Elal-Lawrence, G., Slade, P. and Dewey, M. (1986) Predictors of outcome type in treated problem drinkers. Journal of Studies on Alcohol, 47, 41-47

Fawcett, S., Matthews, R. and Fletcher, R. (1980) Some promising dimensions for behavioral community technology. Journal of Applied Behaviour Analysis, 13, 505-518

Grant, M. (1984) Same Again: a guide to safer drinking. Penguin, Harmondsworth

Heather, N. and Robertson, I. (1983) Controlled Drinking. Methuen, London

Hodgson, R. and Stockwell, T. (1985) The theoretical and empirical basis of the alcohol dependence model: a social learning perspective. In Heather, N., Robertson, I. and Davies, P. (eds) The Misuse of Alcohol: crucial issues in dependence, treatment and prevention. Croom Helm, Beckenham, 17-34

Marlatt, G. and George, W. (1984) Relapse prevention: introduction and overview of the model. British Journal of Addiction, 79, 261-273

Miller, W.R. (1983a) Controlled Drinking: a history and critical review. Journal of Studies on Alcohol, 44, 68-83

Miller, W. (1983b) Motivational interviewing with problem drinkers. Behavioural Psychotherapy, 11, 147-172

Miller, W.R. (1986) Haunted by the Zeitgeist: reflections on contrasting treatment goals and concepts of alcoholism in Europe and the United States. Annals of the New York Academy of Sciences, 472, 110-129

Miller, W. and Munoz, R. (1976) How to Control Your Drinking. Prentice-Hall, Englewood Cliffs, New Jersey

Orford, J. (1985) Excessive Appetites - A Psychological View of Addictions. Wiley, London

Orford, J. and Keddie, A. (1986) Abstinence or controlled drinking in clinical practice: a test of the dependence and persuasion hypothesis. British Journal of Addiction, 81, 495-504

Pendery, M., Maltzman, I. and West, L. (1982) Controlled drinking by alcoholics? new findings and a re-evaluation of a major affirmative study. Science, 217, 169-174

Reissman, F. (1965) The helper therapy principle. Social Work, 10, 27-32

Risley, T. (1977) The social context of self control. In Stuart, R. (ed) Behavioural Self-Management. Brunner/ Mazel, New York

Robertson, I. and Heather, N. (1982) A survey of controlled drinking treatment in Britain. British Journal on Alcohol and Alcoholism, 17, 102-105

Robertson, I. and Heather, N. (1985) So You Want To Cut Down Your Drinking?. Scottish Health Education Group, Edinburgh

Robertson, I. and Heather, N. (1986) Let's Drink to Your Health. British Psychological Society, Leicester

Ruzek, J. (1982) Drinkwatchers Handbook. Accept Publications, London

Sanchez-Craig, M. and Lei, H. (1986) Disadvantages of imposing the goal of abstinence on problem drinkers: an empirical study. British Journal of Addiction, 81, 505-512

Sanchez-Craig, M., Annis, H., Bornet, A. and MacDonald, K. (1984) Random assignment to abstinence and controlled drinking: evaluation of a cognitive-behavioural programme for problem drinkers. Journal of Consulting and Clinical Psychology, 52, 390-403

Skinner, H. (1985) Early detection and basic management of alcohol and drug problems. Australian Alcohol/Drug Review, 4, 243-249

Stockwell, T., Hodgson, R., Edwards, G., Taylor, C. and Rankin, H. (1979) The development of a questionnaire to measure severity of alcohol dependence. British Journal of Addiction, 74, 79-87

Vogler, R., Compton, J. and Weissbach, T. (1976) The Referral Problem in the Field of Alcohol Abuse. Journal of Community Psychology, 4, 357-361

Chapter 3

EARLY INTERVENTION IN GENERAL PRACTICE

Peter Anderson

INTRODUCTION

General practice is in a unique position in this country for
promoting health (Gray and Fowler, 1984; Fry and Hasler,
1986). Over 98% of the population is registered with a
general practitioner. There are a million consultations with
general practice in the United Kingdom each day. Two-thirds
of the practice population consult their doctor within a one
year period and nine-tenths within a five year period. This
presents a unique opportunity for preventing illness and for
promoting health.
     This chapter argues for a new approach to alcohol and
alcohol problems in general practice. It is suggested that
alcohol should be viewed as a preventive risk factor and that
the use of this risk factor can be modified following quite
simple advice.
     The chapter begins with a review of alcohol and general
practice and is then followed by discussion of a new framework
of understanding. This is followed by a review of the
effectiveness of minimal intervention for heavy drinking. It
is then argued that the practice population should be screened
for the extent of consumption of the risk factor, alcohol. A
model of responding both within and outside the practice is
then presented. The chapter concludes with a short agenda
for change.

ALCOHOL AND GENERAL PRACTICE

The clients
It is difficult to obtain figures of the contribution of heavy
drinking to general practice workload. The General Household
Survey has demonstrated that, compared to light drinkers,
heavy drinkers experience more health problems and consult
their general practitioners twice as often as light drinkers
(OPCS, 1984). In the second national study of general

practice morbidity, 0.9 per thousand patients consulted for "alcoholism and drug dependence", a rate of 1.1 for the age group 25-44 and 1.7 for those aged 45-64 with a consultation rate per thousand population of 4.5 and 6.5 respectively (OPCS, 1979). Wilkins (1974) estimated a prevalence rate of 11.1 per 1,000 population aged 15-65 for present "alcoholics" in his practice.

Based on national data (Wilson, 1980), a general practitioner will have amongst an average list of 2,000 patients some 55 people who are drinking at levels posing a high risk of harm, and over 200 people who are faced by an intermediate risk. There are a further 1,150 whose drinking presents little risk, unless personal vulnerability or changed circumstances indicate otherwise.

It is clear that patients themselves believe that alcohol is an important part of general practice work. A postal survey of 2,572 patients in a North London practice revealed that four-fifths believed that GPs should be interested in drinking problems, and two-fifths believed that their GP was actually interested (Wallace and Haines, 1984).

The Therapists

A number of studies have demonstrated that general practitioners find helping people with alcohol problems a difficult business (Clement, 1986; Thom and Tellez, 1986; Tether 1984).

Table 3.1: Attitudes of General Practitioners to Working with Drinkers

Attitude	Agree (%)	Neither (%)	Disagree (%)
I feel I have a legitimate role to work with drinkers	93	6	1
I feel capable of working with drinkers	44	44	13
I am motivated to work with drinkers	39	42	19
I am satisfied with the way I work with drinkers	29	51	20
I get work satisfaction from working with drinkers	9	57	34

Table 3.1 summarises the attitudes of a sample of 312 general practitioners in the Oxford region to working with individuals with alcohol problems (Anderson, 1984; Anderson and Clement, 1986). Although most of the respondents believed that they had a legitimate role in dealing with

drinkers, less than one-half felt adequately equipped to perform this role. Only a minority felt motivated to work with drinkers, were satisfied with the way in which they worked with drinkers, and fewer than one in ten received work satisfaction from working with drinkers.

It is suggested that general practitioners find working with drinkers a difficult business because many are restricted to working within a narrow medical model of alcohol problems. Such a model tends to focus on individuals with serious problems, foster negative feelings and a belief in a poor outcome. Such a model is not suitable for working in general practice. A model which puts alcohol in the arena of health promotion is likely to be more valuable and is discussed below.

One important finding of general practice studies is that the doctors' attitudes are related to the number of patients seen with alcohol problems and the amount of education about alcohol. The larger the number of patients seen and the more education received, the more positive the attitude.

We know little of the activities of general practitioners in relation to alcohol, and what information is available tends to be self-reported data, rather than obtained from an audit of medical records. Table 3.2 gives the distribution of the frequency with which the doctors in the Oxford study performed several activities related to alcohol. The more positive the doctors' attitudes to working with drinkers, the more tasks the doctors were likely to perform.

Table 3.2: Distribution of Frequency of Activities for Alcohol-Related Advice (312 General Practitioners)

	Initiate discussion about alcohol (%)	Advice to reduce drinking (%)	Use health education literature (%)	Refer patient outside practice (%)
More than once a week	49	29	2	2
Once or twice a month	31	45	5	6
Less than once a month	20	26	93	92

In an audit of the recording of risk factors in a sample of 2,000 notes in general practice, it was found that alcohol was mentioned in 12% of notes examined (range 8-16%) (Mant and Phillips, 1986).

In the Oxford study, the general practitioners were also asked about their own alcohol consumption. The amount of alcohol consumed was obtained by using a quantity/frequency question. The respondents were divided into light, moderate or heavy drinkers, according to the consumption of units of alcohol per week (where one unit is equivalent to half a pint of beer, a single of spirits or a glass of wine or sherry): women - light = less than seven units; moderate = 7-27 units; heavy = more than 27 units; men - light = less than 14 units; moderate = 14-34 units; heavy = more than 34 units. The distribution of alcohol consumption was as follows: women - light 69%; moderate 28%; heavy 5%; men - light 68%; moderate 19%; heavy 13%. Surprisingly, there was no relationship between the doctors' alcohol consumption, their attitudes towards working with drinkers, or their reported activities.

THE NEED FOR A NEW APPROACH

There is a need for a new framework within which alcohol and alcohol problems can be understood and responded to in general practice. Components of the framework have been described in greater detail elsewhere (Robertson, Hodgson, Orford and McKechnie, 1984; Royal College of General Practitioners, 1986).

There are two elements to the framework: the continuum and the balance sheet.

A main component of the framework sees everyone's drinking as spread along a continuum from harm-free drinking at one end to harmful drinking at the other. There is no group of people within the continuum who are qualitatively different from anyone else. An individual's drinking, or position on the continuum, can be seen as a behaviour learned and modified by experience. At any stage in a person's life, their drinking behaviour is determined by the balance of the advantages and disadvantages, pleasures and harms of drinking.

Everyone, whatever their current level of drinking, has the choice to move forward or backward along this drinking continuum.

An important implication of this framework is that no fundamental difference exists between spontaneous improvement and improvement which occurs in response to therapeutic intervention. There is good evidence that individuals with alcohol problems often treat themselves and that people are able to move out of harmful alcohol use by drinking less. Vaillant (1983), for example, has reported the results of the longitudinal study of 456 Boston 14-year olds followed up for 35 years from 1940. During this 35 years 110 developed symptoms of alcohol abuse. Of that 110, 48 subsequently achieved at least one year of abstinence and 22 were able to return to social drinking. About one-third of the 48 who became abstinent and nine of the 22 men who returned to social drinking did so with the aid of professional treatment and about one-third who became abstinent had also been helped by Alcoholics Anonymous. Most, however, helped themselves. There were a number of factors that enabled the men to become abstinent: of particular relevance is the finding that 48% had developed a medical problem that was instantly made worse by further drinking, hence reminding them constantly of the need to change their drinking habits.

RISK AND LEVEL OF ALCOHOL CONSUMPTION

The concept of the continuum taken together with the epidemiological evidence relating alcohol consumption to harm leads to the view that alcohol should be regarded as a risk factor for physical, psychological and social harm.

Any user of alcohol is at risk of disabilities but, by and large, the more alcohol is consumed, the greater risk of problems. In this way, alcohol is similar to both blood pressure and serum cholesterol which both exist within continua and are risk factors for disease. The higher the level of blood pressure, the greater the risk of cerebrovascular disease and the higher the serum cholesterol level, the greater the risk of coronary heart disease.

Unfortunately, there is a wide variety of opinion about risk and levels of alcohol consumption (Anderson, Cremona and Wallace, 1984; Wallace, Cremona and Anderson, 1985).

A number of authors have studied the relationship between consumption and damage (Turner, Mezey and Kimball, 1977). Whilst it is clear that heavy drinkers have higher rates of morbidity and mortality than light drinkers, heavy consumption in many studies is not defined. It is either implied a priori, for example in studies of alcohol clinic attenders, or defined loosely without reference to any minimum volume of intake.

One exception to this is the study of Pequignot et al (Pequignot, Tuyns and Berta, 1978). This study showed that men who consumed between 28 and 42 units of alcohol a week had a risk of developing cirrhosis six times that of men with a weekly consumption of less than 14 units of alcohol a week, and this risk increased to 14 times for men drinking between 42 and 56 units a week. Another exception is the civil servant study (Marmot et al, 1981) which demonstrated an increased mortality for men consuming more than 30 units of alcohol a week.

Of course the averages of alcohol consumption referred to in most studies simply represent the total volume of alcohol consumed over a given period of time divided by the numbers of days or weeks involved. Clearly such a measure does not take into account differences in patterns of drinking. However, with respect to most alcohol-related organic conditions, the pattern appears to be irrelevant except in so far as it affects the total amount of alcohol consumed. One exception to this may be liver cirrhosis where it seems that the steady daily drinker is more at risk than the spree drinker whose total alcohol intake may be no less (Sherlock, 1982).

On the other hand, it is evident that the pattern of drinking is highly relevant to the acute problems of alcohol use, such as accidents. Nor does the type of beverage seem to make much difference to most alcohol-related problems, though folate-deficiency is associated with wines and spirits, cancer of the oesophagus is possibly associated with spirit drinking, and colo-rectal cancer with the consumption of beer.

Furthermore, many studies do not take into account individual susceptibility to alcohol. A number of studies have suggested that women may be more susceptible to the toxic effects of alcohol than men. Following a standard oral dose of alcohol women achieve significantly higher blood alcohol values than men. Tissue ethanol concentrations are correspondingly higher in women and it is reasonable to suppose that over a period of time this might result in earlier or more severe tissue damage. Drinking in pregnancy is particularly hazardous and alcohol influences women differently at different times of the menstrual cycle. At the extremes of youth and old age alcohol may have disproportionate effects. Finally, ethnic origin may be an important factor in determining susceptibility to the effects of alcohol.

With these caveats borne in mind the figures in Table 3.3 represent a reasonable guide to personal risk at different levels of alcohol consumption (Royal College of General Practitioners, 1986).

Table 3.3: Levels of Risk and Weekly Consumption

	WOMEN	MEN
Low risk	Less than 16 units per week	Less than 21 units per week
Moderate or intermediate risk	16-35 units per week	21-49 units per week
High risk	36 units per week or more	50 units per week or more

EFFECTIVENESS OF MINIMAL INTERVENTION

There is now an increasing amount of evidence that general practitioners' advice is likely to be effective in helping

heavy drinkers cut down on their drinking.   The effectiveness
of minimal intervention in assisting smokers give up smoking
has clearly been demonstrated (Russell, Wilson, Taylor, and
Baker, 1979; Jamrozik et al, 1984).

In the Russell study, one group was given simple but firm
advice to stop smoking during a routine consultation.
Another group was given the same advice, warned that they
would be followed up, and provided with a four-page
information leaflet entitled "How you can give up smoking".
A third group was assigned to a control condition in which
neither advice nor information was given.   Follow-up data
were obtained at one month and one year after the
consultation.   The results showed that motivation and
intention to stop smoking were increased in the advice groups,
as was the proportion of patients who attempted to stop.   At
one year follow-up 5.0% of the smokers in the information
leaflet group had stopped smoking, compared with 0.3% in the
control group and 3.3% in the advice only group.   Light
smokers were more likely to stop successfully than heavy
smokers.   There were also pronounced differences in the
success rates achieved by different doctors.   Although the
effects of the programme were not dramatic, it was concluded
that if all general practitioners in Britain were to adopt
this simple measure, the intervention could produce half a
million ex-smokers in a year.

It is likely that minimal intervention by general
practitioners to heavy drinkers will be equally effective.
Currently there are three on-going projects testing the
effectiveness of general practitioners' advice to heavy
drinkers to reduce their alcohol consumption and one project
testing the effectiveness of the practice nurse in advising
heavy drinkers to reduce their alcohol consumption.   The
study of the DRAMS pack is discussed in Chapter 4.   Relevant
research in clinic and hospital settings is discussed in more
detail in Chapter 5.

FINDING OUT

Screening for Alcohol Consumption

Having accepted that in primary care the main function with
regard to alcohol is the assessment of alcohol as a risk
factor for each individual and that for each individual the
degree of risk from alcohol is a function mainly of the level
of alcohol consumed, it becomes essential to ascertain from
all individuals registered with the practice how much alcohol
is consumed and to record this information in suitable and
accessible form.

Instruments

To ascertain the alcohol consumption of all patients requires
a brief and easy to use instrument.   The quantity frequency

question is probably the best approach. The inclusion of
alcohol questions with other questions about other health-
related behaviour ensures that alcohol is put within the area
of normal health care, rather than anything special or outside
the proper concern of health staff and patients. Quantity
frequency questions can be used in interview, as part of a
questionnaire or by computer-based interview. Compared with
a seven day drinking history, the quantity frequency question
tends to underestimate the amount of alcohol consumed. This
is probably due to poor recall rather than lack of
truthfulness. There is some evidence that computer interview
gives a more accurate estimate of alcohol consumption than
face to face interview (Skinner et al, 1985a).

Use of the Instrument
1. At registration - many general practices obtain clinical
and social data from newly registered patients. This can be
by special appointment, by interview with nurses or other
staff, by questionnaire or by computer-based interview.
2. Health checks - in some practices, patients are invited to
attend for a formal health check as part of a screening and
health promotion programme.
3. Opportunistic screening - two-thirds of the practice
population consult within a one year period, and nine-tenths
within five years. If all individuals who attend the
practice are asked to complete a health questionnaire, with
time, most of the practice population could be screened.
4. Postal surveys - a health questionnaire can be mailed to
all patients enclosing a freepost return envelope. Although
costly, response rates of 75% can be achieved (Wallace and
Haines, 1985).

Screening for Harmful Drinking
A number of screening instruments have been developed in an
endeavour to separate harmful from problem-free drinking.
Many of these instruments have been developed for use in
specialist settings although some have been tried in primary
care. Such instruments have the major drawback that they
exclude individuals who, although they may not experience
current harm from their drinking, are at risk because of their
level of consumption. Some of the more widely used tests are
as follows:

Questionnaires
The Michigan Alcoholism Screening Test (MAST) is a 25-item
interview comprising questions relating to personal opinions
on drinking, opinions of family and friends and problems
arising from drinking. In a population of hospitalised
American "alcoholics" it was found to have a sensitivity of
98% (Selzer, 1971). It has been used principally in clinic
populations. Pokorny et al (1972) devised a shortened

version of MAST which extracted the 10 most discriminating items from the original. The questions asked are direct and unequivocal in their focus on alcohol, requiring the respondent to admit that drinking is a problem. Kaplan et al (1974) found that individuals self identified as having problems related to alcohol scored much higher on this test than did non-self identified individuals. Kristenson and Trell (1982) modified MAST by employing questions about attitude and customs rather than serious symptoms - which they felt would be more acceptable to a population of apparently healthy Swedish men. This instrument correctly identified 73% of known individuals with alcohol-related problems in their general population sample.

CAGE Instrument

This questionnaire consists of only four questions: (1) Have you ever felt you ought to cut down on your drinking? (2) Have people annoyed you by criticising your drinking? (3) Have you ever felt bad or guilty about your drinking? (4) Have you ever had a drink first thing in the morning to steady your nerves, or get rid of a hangover (eye-opener)?

Two or more positive replies are said to identify harmful drinking. In the original study of 366 American psychiatric patients (Mayfield, McLeod and Hall, 1974), 81% of known "alcoholics" answered positively to two or more questions compared with 11% of individuals without an alcohol-related problem. Most of the studies using CAGE involve clinical populations but Saunders and Kersham (1980) employed it with a sample of individuals identified in the community. In this particular study in Scotland, CAGE appeared more sensitive than the shortened MAST. Nonetheless, even CAGE failed to detect approximately half of the known active "alcoholics" and problem drinkers in that community.

Spare Time Activities Questionnaire (STAQ). This questionnaire was used in England in a primary health care setting by Wilkins (1974). Initially, he constructed an at-risk register based on some of the known predisposing factors discussed above. The STAQ attempted to disguise its alcohol focus by also asking about recreational pursuits such as watching TV and sports. It is longer than the instruments described above, requiring 7-8 minutes to administer to a heavy drinker. Wilkins reported a sensitivity of 76.5%. Saunders and Kershaw used it in a modified form in their community survey and found it had good agreement with CAGE but its power to detect known "alcoholics" was no better, identifying less than 50%.

Biological Markers

Biological indicators of alcohol consumption are likely to be more objective than questionnaires.

Gamma glutamyl transpeptidase (GGT) has proved to be one of the most sensitive tests for early liver disorder. The exact mechanism underlying this rise is not known but it is assumed to be related to enzyme induction. It has been reported raised in 60-80% of clinic sample populations (Rosalki and Rau, 1972). However, Kristenson and Trell (1982) showed that GGT did not prove a sensitive indicator of "alcoholism" in a health screening investigation identifying only one-third of "alcoholics". High levels of this enzyme may also be caused by barbiturate and other drugs or other non-alcohol-related forms of liver disease. An excess of false positive findings may, therefore, be observed in clinic populations. Raised levels begin to return to normal after 48 hours of abstention and this makes the time of sample collections critical.

Enlargement of the red blood corpuscles without anaemia is commonly found in excessive drinkers and a raised mean corpuscular volume (MCV) is now a widely used indicator of harmful drinking. The MCV is raised in 50-60% of clinic sample populations. It is an abnormality which is not corrected by folate supplements.

Table 3.4: Alcohol Problem Check

ACCIDENTS	OCCUPATIONS
work, home, road	catering,publicans,seamen
ALCOHOLIC SYMPTOMS	PHYSICAL SYMPTOMS
smelling of alcohol at	gastrointestinal upset - pain,
consultation	vomiting, diarrhoea, obesity,
morning shakes	especially in men
memory losses	
withdrawal fits	
known alcoholic	
BLOOD TESTS	PSYCHOLOGICAL SYMPTOMS
raised MCV, particularly	anxiety
above 98	attempted suicide
raised GGT, particularly	depression
above 50 IU/L	sexual problems
FAMILY	SOCIAL
psychological problems	criminal offences
in spouse	financial problems
psychological problems	work problems
in children	
battering of wife or child	

Neither of these tests are very reliable as screening tests as they are not particularly sensitive and lack power, having too high a false-positive rate. In a working population, excluding men with other causes of raised values,

50% who admit drinking over 56 units a week have a GGT more than 50 International Units per litre (IU/1) (false positive 15%) and 23-32% have an MCV of over 98 (false positives 5%) (Chick, Kreitman and Plant, 1981).

Alcohol and the Consultation

As a supplement to using screening instruments, it is also useful to have a check list of at-risk register to alert the possibility that alcohol is a cause for the reason for consultation (Table 3.4)

Using a similar register, Wilkins (1974) in Manchester noted that during one year, 5% of the registered adult population consulted in the practice with one of the at-risk characteristics. Of the 546 at risk, 28% were found to have problems associated with alcohol, compared to only 3% of those without any characteristics that had problems.

CLASSIFICATION

Having obtained information about the consumption of alcohol, it is useful to classify individuals into one of three boxes, Figure 3.1.

Figure 3.1: Classification Guidelines to Monitor the Risk from Alcohol

Classification	UNITS	Numbers (practice 2,000)
Low Risk	Women up to 15/week Men up to 20/week	700 500
Intermediate Risk	Women 16-35/week Men 21-50/week	75 140
High Risk	Women more than 35/week Men more than 50/week	15 40

The classification has as its purpose the provision of guidelines to monitor the risk from alcohol, for the assessment of that risk, and for suitable follow-up schemes.

The actual levels for the classification are based on the levels of risk referred to earlier.

Vulnerability

Not all people are equally vulnerable to the effects of similar intakes of alcohol. Women are at risk from liver disease at lower levels of consumption than men. Individuals in the following groups should be considered at higher risk than indicated solely by their alcohol consumption:

1. Age : children and the very old
2. Individuals with chronic conditions such as diabetes, epilepsy and raised blood pressure
3. Individuals with psychological difficulties such as anxiety and depression
4. Individuals taking medication that interacts with alcohol
5. Individuals living potentially harmful lifestyles, including being overweight and smoking cigarettes

ASSESSMENT

Individuals who are in the intermediate box and have one of the vulnerability factors listed above and all individuals in the high box require a fuller assessment. The primary objective of a fuller assessment is to obtain and share information and understanding, so that decisions can be made about management.

Fuller assessment should include a history, examination and investigations. It is useful to develop a pro forma for completing the assessment. Provision of such a structure ensures that a full assessment is completed.

The history should include information about drinking throughout the individual's life, information about present drinking to provide a base line, using a week's drinking diary, and information about potential social, psychological and physical harms from alcohol. Physical assessment should include measurement of height, weight and blood pressure and observation of any signs of liver disease. Investigations should include measurement of MCV, gamma GT and blood or breath alcohol.

RESPONDING

In this section, a model for intervention is offered. The response depends upon which particular box the individual is in.

Minimal Risk

Those assessed as being at minimal risk will for the time being require little or no further action so far as their alcohol is concerned. One must remember, however, that this may change. Individuals may become more vulnerable, even with no change in their alcohol consumption, as a result of changes in life events. For example, women may become pregnant, when different advice will need to be given.

As for all health-related behaviour, there is a need for review. This is best done by inviting individuals back for a further health check in five years time, when alcohol consumption is again assessed.

Moderate Risk
This group has a particular significance since it contributes the majority of the alcohol-related problems seen in society. Its members are also of particular importance to general practice since it is able to identify people at this level of alcohol consumption and offer them advice about reducing consumption. It is likely that such advice will be effective and prevent individuals from moving into a higher consumption category.

Advice needs to be given to reduce consumption to the levels regarded as safe, that is below 20 units (men) and 15 units (women) weekly. There are several components to this advice which may be helpful. The individual's health beliefs about alcohol consumption should be explored. It is useful to feed back information about levels of drinking and any findings of harm that their level of alcohol consumption may be causing. These include effects on physical health, as well as effects on life at home, and at work. It is particularly important to relate excess drinking to the individual's presenting complaint where this is applicable. It is useful to demonstrate that consumption is above the "normal range", even though it may appear quite moderate within the individual's own drinking circle. This can be done by using an alcohol histogram for men and women, which indicates the distribution of alcohol consumption within the population (Figure 3.3). It is useful to give information on the possible risks of increased drinking such as:

being overweight	anxiety and depression
stomach upsets	sexual difficulties
liver disease	difficulty sleeping
headaches, hangover	

Information also needs to be given about the advantages of drinking less, for example, saving money and safer driving. It is helpful to supplement advice with booklets such as the Health Education Council's "That's the Limit" booklet or the Scottish Health Education Group's "DRAMS" pack (see Chapter 4). Such booklets give further information on the risks of heavy drinking, how to calculate consumption in terms of units, sensible limits of consumption for women and men and suggestions on how to reduce consumption. It is important to recommend and reinforce these sensible upper limits (weekly: 15 units for women and 20 units for men) and to emphasise that this level of consumption should be spread throughout the week rather than concentrated into bouts or binges. Alcohol consumption should be recorded in the notes and also the fact that advice has been given. This group needs to be recalled

Figure 3.2: Distribution of Units Consumed Weekly by Men and Women in England and Wales

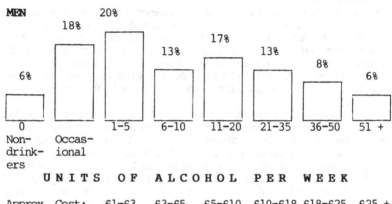

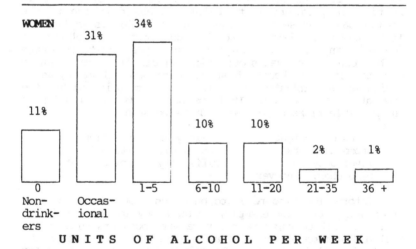

Source: Wilson, P. Drinking in England and Wales. HMSO, 1980.

after about one year to check on alcohol consumption. The notes can be tagged, or a manual or computer-operated recall system triggered.

HIGH RISK

The aim in responding to someone who is drinking heavily or with someone who has problems related to alcohol is to reduce consumption and to help with the harm that alcohol is causing.

Individuals may be in one of three phases related to their beliefs about drinking and the harm it might be causing them: pre-understanding, understanding, and action (Prochaska and Di Clements, 1984). Individuals in the pre-understanding phase have not thought about harmful drinking and need assistance in understanding the relationship between consumption and harm. Individuals in the understanding phase have thought about their drinking, but have not done anything about it. They need assistance in decision-making, weighing up and altering the balance sheet of the good and harmful effects of drinking. Individuals in the action phase are actually trying to do something about their drinking and may need assistance with this change process. The aim of therapy is to assist individuals in moving from pre-understanding and understanding to action. The exact response depends on which group the individual is in.

Pre-Understanding

The first part of understanding is to feed back information from the drink diary as to how much the individual is drinking. A drink diary is itself an important part of therapy. Many individuals are surprised at how a drink diary adds up and how much alcohol is actually consumed in a week.

The next thing to do is to list the problems possibly related to alcohol that the individual might be experiencing. Some of these problems will already be apparent or already documented in the notes. An individual may for the first time learn how some symptoms are related to alcohol and thus accept the need for adjustment of drinking habits; this is particularly so if these symptoms are immediately aggravated by drinking, acting as reminders of the need for change. It is useful to relate the presenting symptom to alcohol, when appropriate, since this will have immediate and powerful impact.

Understanding

Having reached understanding of the harm or potential harm that heavy drinking is causing, the individual may need assistance in deciding whether or not to do anything about it. It may be obvious to an outsider that drinking less would be beneficial, but the individual may have difficulties in deciding about this. Assistance can be given by drawing up a balance sheet of the advantages and disadvantages of drinking, discussing each of them in turn and attempting to shift the balance in favour of reducing consumption.

Action
The first thing is to discover from the patient what he or she wants and reach an agreement or contract on goals for change. Some individuals may need detoxification and this is discussed later.

The long-term goals will depend on the previous history, the amount that the individual is drinking and the extent of the alcohol-related problems. If the drinking is excessive, though hitherto harm-free, advice can be given about sensible levels of drinking, as mentioned above. Some drinkers with established problems will return to reduced drinking; however, there is some evidence that abstinence remains the preferable goal for those who demonstrate severe withdrawal symptoms from alcohol, have evidence of severe physical damage or who have systematically attempted controlled drinking without success (Heather and Robertson, 1983).

How to Change
The main aim of therapy is to reduce alcohol consumption. The way to reduce alcohol consumption is to encourage self-management and education, the first step being to start self-monitoring (Kanfer and Busemeyer, 1982; Kanfer and Grimm, 1980), that is, keeping a diary of how much is drunk, when, where and with whom.

The drink diary may identify risky circumstances or times when the individual has drunk more than was intended, or when drinking caused trouble. If so, the individual should be helped to anticipate such circumstances. Examples might be:

1. Times of the day or certain days of the week
2. People with whom drinking occurs
3. Whether hungry or thirsty
4. How the patient is feeling emotionally e.g. whether anxious, under stress, frustrated, angry or depressed
5. Conflicts with other people or rows within the family

The individual needs to try to avoid or find alternative ways of coping with these risky circumstances, since they may be associated with the urge to drink. For instance, if the patient has become used to a drink on the way home from work, in the future that patient may feel a strong urge to drink then. Thus individuals must learn to avoid situations where in the past they have drunk heavily and confine drinking to those situations where in the past they have drunk sensibly.

It is also useful to give advice on how to consume less alcohol (see Scottish Health Education Group, 1984; Robertson and Heather, 1986).

Having considered ways of reducing consumption it is necessary to set a realistic strategy for change. It is best to aim for specific short-term goals at first, rather than long-term goals and general intentions, allowing more immediate reinforcement from a sense of achievement.

Booklets and Further Reading
Literature has value in reinforcing advice and informing the patient (Miller and Taylor, 1980). Self-help manuals may be an alternative to professional advice (Heather, 1985).

Detoxification
Individuals who give a history of severe withdrawal symptoms, or who show signs of withdrawal at consultation, will need a period of detoxification and may need help to cover withdrawal symptoms. Detoxification can take place at home, in a general hospital or in an alcohol treatment unit. It is now clear that many individuals can be detoxified at home, provided that there is a reasonably supportive family. This is discussed in more detail in Chapter 10.

Maintaining the Reduced Drinking
In order to help maintain reduced drinking, it is essential to offer follow-up. At follow-up the individual's progress should be reviewed; continuing help should be offered and support as well as advice on managing difficulties given. Progress should be reviewed regularly over a year. The first six months of progress often give a good indication of longer-term prognosis.

Blood tests are a useful means of monitoring progress and the results and their implications can be discussed with the individual. GGT (normal range 15-40 IU/l) returns rapidly to normal with abstention and may return to normal if measured 48 hours after the last drink. A subsequent rise of 50% or more is strong evidence of further heavy drinking. The MCV (normal range 76-96) takes several weeks to return to normal after reduction in drinking. In health alcohol is removed from the blood at a rate of about 15mg per 100 millilitres/hour and detectable blood concentrations are present for over eight hours after three pints of beer in normal people. In patients with liver damage, concentrations may remain high for more than 24 hours.

Relapse Prevention
Many individuals will experience some form of relapse and will need to be warned about this. One needs to be aware of the sort of problems which are likely to cause relapse and systematically plan strategies either to avoid these problems,

to use alternative coping methods or even to undertake substantial changes to life style and family patterns (Marlatt and George, 1984). It is useful to draw up a list or inventory of relapse precipitants. Relapse should not be regarded as a loss of all that has been achieved. It should be viewed as an opportunity for the individual to learn more about self and problem.

Working with the Family

Many studies have stressed the importance of family support in helping individuals reduce their alcohol consumption (Harwin, 1982). Sometimes the general practitioner is able to help the family without ever seeing the drinker. Partners of excessive drinkers usually suffer greatly - psychologically, physically and socially. They often feel very guilty and are full of self-blame. Many therefore need counselling to help them cope with these feelings and to avoid drink-sustaining behaviour within the family. Both partners should be encouraged to accept responsibility for their own behaviour and thus their own symptoms and feelings, and should be helped to make whatever changes seem desirable for their own good and that of their partner.

Very often the partner has been behaving in such a way that the drinker has actively been prevented from seeing what problems the drink is causing; for example, he or she may have covered up by giving excuses for the drinker avoiding work, or by paying his debts.

The partner may be encouraged to follow the same lines as the doctor, for example by altering the balance sheet in favour of reducing drinking. He or she should reward non-drinking times, and be careful not to "reward" drinking times by giving in as an "easy option" when faced with an acute problem.

Referral to Specialist Agencies

The majority of heavy drinkers and individuals with alcohol problems can be helped by the primary care team. However, there are going to be some individuals whose care the team will need to share, particularly those who have severe problems, those who lack a supportive family, those with a severe psychological problem, and those for whom primary care has previously failed. When referral takes place it is important to maintain a relationship with the individual and give a further appointment after the initial referral to discuss what took place. Options for referral will depend on the locality. They include local councils on alcohol, community alcohol teams, Alcoholics Anonymous and alcohol treatment units.

AN AGENDA FOR CHANGE

Every general practitioner faces the consequences of the harmful effects of alcohol and has on his or her list of registered patients many more who will one day suffer such harmful effects and are therefore at risk. General practice has always coped with the results of excessive drinking as it has with so many other hazards to health; today's general practice is also closely involved with the preventive aspects of medicine, and the risks from alcohol should be seen as no different in conceptual terms from those posed by smoking, unwise diet or lack of exercise on the one hand, or by raised blood pressure and cervical dysplasia on the other. This chapter has presented a constructive view of the problems posed by alcohol, a view influenced by the idea that the harms which arise from its use are the inevitable results of its properties and effects, of the amounts consumed and the periods over which this consumption has occurred. Every general practitioner thus has the opportunity, and largely already possesses the skills and resources, to handle the task of helping patients to drink less and thus less harmfully.

However, for general practice to take on the challenge outlined in this review requires a change in attitude, an increase in confidence and the acquisition of new skills. How can this be achieved? One model that has been adopted locally is the employment of a facilitator, whose effectiveness in promoting change in the assessment and intervention of risk factors in the prevention of coronary heart disease has been well demonstrated (Fullard, Fowler and Gray, 1984). A similar approach is likely to be fruitful for alcohol. A facilitator can be based in a health promotion unit. Their task can be to liaise with general practice to provide information and to offer means of screening for alcohol consumption, and to teach skills of minimal intervention.

ACKNOWLEDGMENTS

I thank Mary Timbrell for typing the manuscript, and Oxford Regional Health Authority, the Alcohol Education and Research Council and the Mental Health Foundation for providing funds for studies referred to in this paper.

REFERENCES

Anderson, P. (1984) Managing alcohol problems in general practice. British Medical Journal, 290, 1873-5

Anderson, P. and Clement, S. (1986) The AAPPQ revisited – the measurement of general practitioners' attitudes to alcohol problems. British Journal of Addiction. In press

Anderson P., Cremona, A. and Wallace, P. (1984) What are safe levels of alcohol consumption? British Medical Journal, 289, 1657-8

Catford, J. and Nutbeam, D. (1984) Prevention in practice: what Wessex general practitioners are doing. British Medical Journal 288, 832-834.

Clement, S. (1986) The identification of alcohol-related problems by general practitioners. British Journal of Addiction, 81, 257-264

Chick, J., Kreitman, N. and Plant, M. (1981) Mean cell volume and gamma-glutamyl-transpeptidase as markers of drinking in working men. Lancet (i), 1249-51

Fullard, E., Fowler, G. and Gray, M. (1984) Facilitating prevention in primary care. British Medical Journal, 289, 1585-7

Fry, J. and Hasler, J. (1986) Facilitating prevention in primary care. British Medical Journal, 289, 1585-7

Gray, M. and Fowler, G. (1983) Preventive Medicine in General Practice, Oxford University Press, Oxford

Harwin, J. (1982) The excessive drinker and the family: approaches to treatment Alcohol and the Family Orford J. and Harwin J. (eds) Croom Helm, London

Heather, N. and Robertson, I. (1983) Controlled Drinking. Methuen, London

Heather, N. (1985) Change without therapists: the use of self-help manuals by problem drinkers. In Treating Addictive Behaviours: Processes of change. Ed. Miller W. R. and Heather, N., Plenum Press, New York

Jamrozik, R., Vessey, M., Fowler, G., Wald, N., Parker, G., and van Vinakis, H. (1984) Controlled trial of three different anti-smoking interventions in general practice. British Medical Journal, 288, 1499-1503

Kanfer, F. and Busemeyer, J. (1982) The use of problem solving and decision making in behaviour therapy. Clinical Psychology Review, 2, 239-66

Kanfer, F. and Grimm, L. (1980) Managing clinical change: a process model of therapy. Behaviour Modification, 4, 419-44

Kaplan, H., Pokorny, A., Kanes, T. and Lively, C. (1974) Screening tests and self-identification in the detection of alcoholism. Journal of Health and Social Behaviour, 15, 51-60

Kristenson, H. and Trell, E. (1982) Indicators of alcohol consumption: comparisons between a questionnaire (Mm-MAST), interviews and serum-gamma-glutamyl transferase (GGT) in a health survey of middle-aged males. British Journal of Addiction, 77, 297-304

Mant, D. and Phillips, A. (1986) Can the prevalence of disease risk factors be assessed from general practice records, British Medical Journal, 292, 102-104

Marlatt, G. and George, W. (1984) Can the prevalence of disease risk factors be assessed from general practice records? British Journal of Addiction, 79, 261-73

Marmot, M., Rose, G., Shipley, M. et al (1981) Alcohol and mortality: a U-shaped curve. The Lancet, 580-3

Mayfield, D., McLeod, G., and Hall, P. (1974) The CAGE questionnaire: validation of a new alcoholism screening instrument. American Journal of Psychiatry, 131, 1121-1128

Miller, W. and Hester, R. (1985) The effectiveness of treatment techniques: what works and what doesn't. In Cox, E.M. (ed) Treatment and Prevention of Alcohol Problems: a research manual. Academic Press, New York

Miller, W. and Taylor, C. (1980) Relative effectiveness of biblio-therapy, individual and group self-control training in the treatment of problem drinkers. Addictive Behaviours, 5, 13-24

Office of Population Censuses and Surveys (1979) Morbidity Statistics from General Practice 1971-2. Studies on Medical and Population Subjects No. 36. HMSO, London

Office of Population Censuses and Surveys (1984) General Household Survey 1982. HMSO, London

Pequignot, G., Tuyns, A. and Berta, J. (1978) Ascitic cirrhosis in relation to alcohol consumption. International Journal of Epidemiology 7, 113-20

Pokorny, A., Miller, B. and Kaplan, H. (1972) The brief MAST: a shortened version of the Michigan Alcoholism Screening Test. American Journal of Psychiatry, 129, 342-345

Pritchard, P. (1983) Patient participation. In Gray, D.P. (ed) Medical Annual. Wright, Bristol

Prochaska, J. and Di Clemente, C. (1984) The Trans-theoretical Approach. Dow Jones-Irwin, Illinois

Robertson, I. and Heather, N. (1986) Let's Drink to Your Health A self-help guide to sensible drinking. British Psychological Society, Leicester

Robertson, I., Hodgson, R., Orford, J. and McKechnie, R. (1984) Psychology and Problem Drinking. British Psychological Society, Leicester

Rosalki, S. and Rau, D. (1972) Serum-Glutamyl transpeptidase activity in alcoholism. Clinical Chimica Acta, 39, 41-47

Royal College of General Practitioners (1986) Alcohol - A Balanced View. Royal College of General Practitoners, London

Russell, M., Wilson, C., Taylor, C. and Baker, C.(1979) Effect of general practitioners' advice against smoking. British Medical Journal, 11, 231-235

Saunders, W. and Kersham, P. (1980) Screening tests for alcoholism: findings from a community study. British Journal of Addiction, 75, 37-41

Scottish Health Education Group (1984). _So You Want to Cut Down on your Drinking? A self-help guide to sensible drinking._ Scottish Health Education Group, Edinburgh

Selzer, M. (1971) The Michigan Alcoholism Screening Test: the quest for a new diagnostic instrument. _American Journal of Psychiatry_, 127, 1653

Sherlock, S. (1982) Alcohol related liver disease: clinical aspects and management. _British Medical Journal_, 38, 67-70

Skinner, H., Allen, B., McIntosh, M. (1985a) Lifestyle assessment: just asking makes a difference. _British Medical Journal_, 290, 214-16

Skinner, H., Allen, B., McIntosh, M. (1985b) Lifestyle assessment: applying microcomputers in family practice. _British Medical Journal_, 290, 212-14

Tether, P. (1984) Identifying and responding to problem drinkers in general practice the results of a British survey. Paper presented to "Alcohol Problems - Caring and Coping". Royal College of General Practitioners

Tether, P. and Robinson, D. (1986) _Preventing Alcohol Problems: a guide to local action._ Tavistock, London

Thom, B. and Tellez, C. (1986) A difficult business: detecting and managing alcohol problems in general practice. _British Journal of Addiction_, 81, 405-418

Turner, T., Mezey, E. and Kimball, A. (1977) Measurement of alcohol related effects in man: chronic effects in relation to levels of alcohol consumption. _Johns Hopkins Medical Journal_, 141, 235-48; 273-86

Vaillant, G. (1983) _The Natural History of Alcoholism._ Harvard University Press, London

Wallace, P. and Haines, A. (1985) Use of a questionnaire in general practice to increase the recognition of patients with excessive alcohol consumption. _British Medical Journal_, 290, 1949-1953

Wallace, P. and Haines, A. (1985) General practitioners and health promotion: what patients think. _British Medical Journal_, 290, 1949-1953

Wallace, P., Cremona, A. and Anderson, P. (1985) Safe levels of drinking: general practitioners' views. _British Medical Journal_, 290, 1875-6

Wilkins, R. (1974) _The Hidden Alcoholic in General Practice._ Elek, London

Wilson, P. (1980). _Drinking in England and Wales._ HMSO, London

Chapter 4

DRAMS FOR PROBLEM DRINKERS: THE POTENTIAL OF A BRIEF
INTERVENTION BY GENERAL PRACTITIONERS AND SOME EVIDENCE OF
ITS EFFECTIVENESS

Nick Heather

In discussion of the best means for the wholesale prevention
of alcohol problems, it is usually concluded that this can
only be achieved through political action aimed at fiscal and
other controls on per capita alcohol consumption (Kendell,
1979; Saunders, 1985). However, Skinner and Holt (1983) have
written that:

> A concerted application of early intervention by the
> medical profession could be more effective than any
> forseeable political action in reducing the prevalence of
> alcohol abuse (p. 790).

This is one of the boldest statements available of the great
potential of early identification and brief intervention for
alcohol problems carried out in medical settings, a potential
which is now internationally recognised (Grant, 1986).

Of all the medical workers who might become involved in
the response to alcohol problems, it is, of course, the
general practitioner from whom most is expected, and there are
good reasons for this. Babor et al (1986) have summarised the
advantages of the primary health care setting for this
response as follows:

1. Excessive drinkers suffer more ill health than others
   and make more than average use of health facilities.
2. Primary health care workers are usually accessible to
   the community and have an established credibility
   within it.
3. The primary health setting avoids the problems of
   stigma and labelling which typically arise when a
   patient is treated by special mental health or
   alcoholism services.
4. There is often an opportunity for family contact
   which is so important in helping the problem drinker.

Unfortunately, in spite of these obvious advantages
and despite ample encouragement, general practitioners have
shown a marked reluctance to become involved with problem
drinkers. For some commentators, this is simply a matter of
ignorance and prejudice, but more intelligent analyses
(Strong, 1980; Thom and Tellez, 1986) have suggested that
there may be more charitable explanations for this reluctance.
In the terminology of Shaw et al (1978), GPs may lack "role
adequacy", "role legitimacy" and "role support". In other
words, they do not know how to respond, are unsure whether to
respond or not, and feel unsupported when they do respond
(Clement, 1986).

THE DRAMS SCHEME

It was against this background that the Scottish Health
Education Group (SHEG) developed the DRAMS scheme for general
practitioners. DRAMS stands for "Drinking Reasonably And
Moderately with Self-control". The idea was to make available
to GPs a simple, interactive method which provides a clear
structure for intervening with problem drinkers, supported by
self-monitoring and self-help materials and aimed at reduced
alcohol intake. The DRAMS kit consists of a dispenser
containing the following elements:

1. A four-page introductory leaflet explaining to GPs the
   theoretical background of the scheme in current
   thinking on the need for early intervention and the
   use of the controlled drinking goal for this purpose.
   The detailed procedure to be followed in the scheme is
   also described.
2. A medical record card for use by the doctor, with
   spaces for patient details, results of blood tests
   (BAC, GGT, MCV), a record of weekly self-monitoring
   alcohol consumption, and a checklist of 10 adverse
   consequences of heavy drinking, including medical
   complications, social consequences and signs of early
   dependence (the medical questionnaire).
3. A two-week self-monitoring drinking diary card for
   use by the patient.
4. A 59-page self-help book which is a pocket-sized and
   an abbreviated version of the SHEG self-help manual,
   So You Want To Cut Down Your Drinking? (Robertson and
   Heather, 1985). The book contains an explanation of
   the concept of a unit of alcohol (= 8 grammes
   approximately pure ethyl alcohol), together with clear
   guidance as to weekly upper limits (= 35 units/week
   men; 20 units/week women), an elementary introduction
   to alcohol metabolism and the effects of heavy
   consumption, some suggestions for methods of cutting
   down drinking, including a brief, guided functional

analysis of drinking behaviour, and diary sheets for continued self-monitoring of drinking over a 13 week period. The book is attractively produced in full colour and contains numerous illustrations, charts and quizzes.

Suggestions to the doctor are that, if a drinking problem is suspected, the 10 items of the medical questionnaire are checked and the patient's responses entered on the medical record card. Any positive response suggests the possibility of a drinking problem and the doctor is advised to consider raising this with the patient. If the patient agrees, a blood sample is taken, the patient is handed the drinking diary card and asked to fill it in as honestly as possible, and a follow-up consultation in two weeks time is arranged. At the follow-up consultation, the results of the blood test and the drinking diary card are reviewed, and if the existence of a problem is confirmed, the doctor discusses this with the patient and advises him or her to try to reduce the amount consumed. The patient is then introduced to the self-help book and encouraged to decide on a realistic plan of action based on the guideline given in the book and using the supplementary diary sheets. Appointments for further consultations are made at which the patient's medical condition and progress at cutting down are reviewed, using the results of further blood tests and, in particular, feedback of GGT (cf. Kristenson et al, 1981).

THE HIGHLANDS AND ISLANDS PILOT PROJECT

The first step in the evaluation of DRAMS was a two-year pilot project conducted in the Highlands and Islands regions of Scotland by Dr Iain Glen and his colleagues (Glen et al, 1986). The DRAMS scheme was introduced to GPs in a series of eight area meetings at various widely spread locations, at the end of which 61% of all GPs in the region (n = 115) had received DRAMS kits and a full explanation of their intended use. It may be remarked in passing that this choice of region had both advantages and disadvantages for the application of DRAMS. An advantage was that, in the thinly scattered rural communities where GPs had their practices, it was likely that most of the excessive drinkers in a community would be known to the GP, including those who might be amenable to a controlled drinking approach, a situation much less likely in an urban setting. On the other hand, the disease model of alcoholism is firmly entrenched in the Highlands, where Alcoholics Anonymous is still the main treatment resource and Councils on Alcohol are at an early stage of development. Moreover, drinking in the Highlands tends to show the all-or-nothing character which is typical of areas with a strongly religious orientation (cf. Armor et al, 1978).

The effectiveness of DRAMS was assessed in various ways. Over a period of 21 months, 52 GPs were found to have used the kit in counselling a total of 161 patients and these doctors were asked for their own estimates of the success of the intervention. The results were that 55 patients (34% of the total) were considered to have had a successful outcome, 59 (36%) could be considered as unsuccessful and 47 (29%) could not be classified. An interesting finding was that the mean ages of groups of patients identified by GPs were all in late 30s to early 40s and thus similar to the mean age of clients attending specialised alcohol treatment centres. It was therefore disappointing that younger patients, presumably at an earlier stage of their problem, were not being identified more often.

Glen et al also examined four representative practices among those taking part in the study. Five surveys, consisting of a cohort of 500 consecutive patient contacts each, were carried out at each practice; a retrospective case-note study was followed by a survey before DRAMS had been put into effect and the cohort was then examined at six-monthly intervals. The results showed that a significant increase was not sustained after the project had ended. There was no evidence, however, of a decrease in overall alcohol-related morbidity during the period DRAMS was being used. The authors also looked at requests for GGT measurements made by GPs. Again, the number of such requests was found to increase substantially during the course of the project, suggesting a heightened awareness of the use of GGT in the treatment of problem drinkers; but there was no reduction in the mean value of GGT results, contrary to the authors' hypothesis.

In a more qualitative analysis of the acceptability of DRAMS, it was found that, on the whole, GPs agreed with the general approach and were glad to have an alternative to total abstinence to offer some of their patients. However, Glen et al report that the doctors who made use of the scheme took to it immediately following the briefing sessions and that there was little to be gained by pressurising reluctant GPs to become involved. Some GPs suggested that the use of the scheme should have been accompanied by a mass media campaign in order to sensitise the community to this type of approach. The authors were disappointed that very few of the GPs appeared to make use of the behavioural interaction element of the DRAMS method (i.e. GGT feedback and reviews of self-monitored consumptions) and felt that more emphasis should be placed on this aspect in future.

Although this study provided some useful information on the potential application of DRAMS, it was clearly not intended to be a controlled trial of its effectiveness. It was therefore decided to attempt this in a joint project between the Department of Psychiatry and the Department of General Practice at the University of Dundee. (It will only be possible to give a summary of this research here and for more detailed accounts, the interested reader is referred to Heather et al, 1986.)

A CONTROLLED EVALUATION OF DRAMS

A total of 16 general practitioner principals from 8 teaching practices in Dundee took part in the trial. The design called for the screening of all patients aged between 18 and 65 first attending their GP during a period which varied from 5 to 9 months, depending on the practice involved, between March and December, 1985. A one-page screening instrument entitled "Health Questionnaire", adapted from one used by Anderson (1984), was handed out by practice receptionists. The questionnaire asked about dieting, exercising, smoking and drinking, and enabled an estimate to be made of the total number of units consumed during the previous week.

At the consultation, the doctor dealt with the presenting complaint and then calculated the weekly units from the health questionnaire. If this was over 35 for men and 20 for women, the patient was eligible for the trial. Additionally, GPs were asked to use their clinical suspicion and knowledge of the patient to identify potential candidates. Such patients were given the medical questionnaire (MQ) section of the DRAMS kit and, if any item was positive, the patient became eligible. Thus, there were two grounds for eligibility for the trial - heavy drinking over recommended limits or the putative existence of an alcohol-related problem.

The next step was to exclude patients who gave evidence of late dependence on Chick's (1980) Brief Edinburgh Alcohol Dependence Schedule and also those who showed evidence of liver disease, severe mental illness, current anti-depressant medication, subnormal intelligence, opiate drug dependence or pregnancy. All those not excluded were then asked if they were willing to take part in research aimed at studying "the way people's drinking changes over time", a consent form was signed and randomisation envelope opened. The doctor stressed that the projct had nothing to do with "alcoholism".

Eligible and consenting patients who completed the initial assessment procedure were randomly allocated to one of three groups:

1. DRAMS (n = 34: M = 23, F = 11). The procedure here followed the full DRAMS scheme that the MQ had already been completed.
2. Advice (n = 32: M = 25, F = 7). In this group, patients were informed that their drinking could be harmful and were given strong advice, in the doctor's own words, to cut down drinking.
3. Non-intervention control (n = 38: M = 30, F = 8). Patients were told that the study would involve a

blood test and an assessment interview but no
reference to drinking or treatment was made.

Following the consultation, a blood sample was taken for
measurement of GGT and MCV, and the patient was asked to see
a research interviewer for an initial assessment. Whenever
possible, this was done immediately following the consultation
but, if not, the patient was asked to return to the surgery at
a time when the interviewer was available, usually within one
or two days. However, 15 patients, 5 from each group, did not
return at the appointed time or respond to further attempts at
contact and were lost to the research sample.

The initial assessment included the following areas:
demographic and other personal information, drinking history
and history of problem drinking, self-definition as problem
drinker or alcoholic, a detailed measure of consumption during
the last month, a similar measure of consumption in the
heaviest of the last 6 months, in cases where the last month
was not typical, the MAST (Selzer, 1971), a measure of
severity of physical dependence on alcohol (Ph. score; Miller
and Marlatt, 1984); frequency of mood distrubance during the
last 6 months; the Life Activities Inventory (LAI) - a self-
completion instrument giving standardised, scaled scores on
seven factors related to outcome of treatment for alcohol
problems, viz. I marital problems, II control of drinking
problems, III income/employment stability, IV physical health
and well-being, V residential stability, VI social
interaction, VII control drinking (see Heather et al, 1986b).

Blind follow-up assessments, the majority of which took
place in GP surgeries, repeated the measures of the initial
assessment, except for demographic data, drinking history,
MAST and Ph. score. In addition, a debriefing procedure was
added in which, after the study group to which the subject
belonged had been established, DRAMS, and advice group
subjects were asked how useful they had found the material
and/or advice given. Whenever possible, a further blood
sample was taken. Some subjects could not be contacted or
refused to be seen in person and these were sent through the
post a questionnaire which contained a self-completion version
of the last month's consumption measure and the LAI.

Subjects seen for the full follow-up interview were asked
to name a collateral source of information and this person
was approached and asked for an opinion on how the subject was
progressing, including any changes in drinking and drinking
problems which had been observed. Finally, when the subject's
follow-up had been completed, the relevant GP was sent a
patient attendance record requesting information on how many
consultations there had been during the follow-up period and
on how many of these drinking had been discussed. Details
were also obtained as to the compliance with the specific
components of the DRAMS scheme.

The Sample Size

A total of 119 subjects were admitted to the trial, of which 104 completed initial assessments. It should be said immediately that this was far fewer than we had anticipated. Based on list sizes, consultation rates and an estimate of heavy drinkers seen in general practice drawn from previous work (Wilkins, 1974), we had expected to reach a total of approximately 300 subjects during the intake period. With the benefit of hindsight, there are at least three reasons why this did not happen.

Firstly, our estimates included young adult males, who contain the highest proportion of heavy drinkers in the population, but who consult their GPs less often than others. Secondly, it is obvious that the proportion of heavy drinkers asked to fill in the health questionnaire would have under-reported their consumption. Given that the heavy drinking of many of these individuals would be unfamiliar to their GPs, an unknown number of heavy drinkers were missed by the screening procedure.

Thirdly, it must candidly be stated that some GPs were less enthusiastic about the project than others and contributed fewer subjects to it. From examining the frequency of GPs who entered given numbers of patients in the trial, it emerged that there was a group of six GPs who enrolled only two patients between them and, at the other extreme, that 28 patients (27% if the total) were enrolled by just two GPs. The reluctance of some doctors to make use of the trial may be related to some of the factors which have been described in the literature on the treatment of alcohol problems in general practice and this will be returned to. For present purposes, it should be noted that lack of interest in the trial may have communicated itself to the practice receptionist who would then be less diligent about handing out the screening instrument. All these factors no doubt contributed to a much lower rate of detection of alcohol problems than is typically reported in the literature. However, it should perhaps be emphasised that this research was not intended primarily as a screening exercise.

Sample Characteristics

The sample of 78 males and 26 females that we did obtain had a mean age of 36.4 years (s.d. = 12.2, range 18 - 63). Forty-seven subjects were under 30 years of age and it therefore appears that, in our study, younger individuals were being picked up. Forty-four were married or cohabiting, 33 were single and 27 were separated, divorced or widowed. Sixty-eight were in full-time employment, while 20 were unemployed. A total of 83 subjects lived either with spouse or family. Socio-economic status was as follows: I - 2; II - 11; III = 49; IV = 29; V = 11; missing = 2. Mean years of full-time education was 11.3 years (s.d. = 2.3). There were no

89

significant differences on initial measures between male and female subjects, although a higher proportion of females were single or divorced (65% vs. 36%) and a lower proportion in full-time employment (31% vs. 78%).

Thus the sample could be characterised as predominantly lower-middle class individuals of relatively high social stability. Comparing them on LAI factors scores with the sample of media-recruited problem drinkers studied by Heather et al (1986b), the present sample had fewer marital problems, higher income/employment stability and a higher degree of social interaction. The media-recruited sample showed a much higher level of alcohol-related problems, as measured by LAI Factor II, but, surprisingly perhaps, a similar mean score for physical health and well-being (Factor IV).

Twenty-one subjects, 18 males and 3 females, admitted to a current problem with drinking, but only one of these defined himself as an "alcoholic", with 4 males and 1 female replying "don't know". For those admitting a problem, the mean duration was 5.9. years (s.d. = 6.1, range 0 - 27). Table 4.1 shows frequencies of subjects, broken down by sex, falling into categories on the MAST suggested as guidelines by Miller and Marlatt (1984). There was a significant difference between male and female subjects on MAST scores (males, mean = 8.01 vs. females, mean = 4.73, p <0.05). Table 4.2 shows the corresponding data for Ph. score, the measure of physical dependence on alcohol. There was no significant difference between sexes for Ph. scores and means were similar in value (males = 4.67, females = 4.46). It is worth remarking that on each of the two instruments, four individuals scored over the levels which are suggested by Miller and Marlatt as indicating the need for abstinence treatment (MAST = 20; Ph. score = 10). One male subject scored over these levels on both instruments.

Table 4.1: Distribution of Alcohol-Related Problems (MAST) in the Initial Sample

Mast Score	Problem Category	Males n = %		Females n = %		All n = %	
0	None	5	6	8	31	13	13
1-4	Mild	18	23	7	27	25	24
5-10	Moderate	31	40	7	27	38	37
11-20	Significant	20	26	4	15	24	23
> 20	Severe	4	5	0	0	4	4
TOTALS		78	100	26	100	104	100

Thus, seven individuals seem to have slipped through the procedure designed to to exclude those who were more suited to an abstinence goal. However, these subjects would probably have received no attention to their drinking problem had they not entered the study.

Table 4.2: Distribution of Degree of Physical Dependence (Ph. Score) in the Initial Sample

Ph. Score	Dependence Category	Males n = %		Females n = %		All n = %	
0	None	2	3	1	4	3	3
1-4	Mild	43	55	12	46	55	53
5-10	Significant	2	2	12	46	42	40
11-14	Substantial	2	2	1	4	3	3
> 15	Severe	1	1	0	0	1	1
TOTALS		78	100	26	100	104	100

It is important to remember here that the subjects of the study had not attended their GPs to complain directly of problems with alcohol and that the intervention some of them received was purely "opportunistic". In fact, in a retrospective analysis of the presenting complaints of patients admitted to the study, it emerged that only three had come to see their doctors about a drinking problem. (A breakdown of these presenting complaints will be presented elsewhere.) It is therefore of considerable interest that, on closer examination, they displayed the levels of alcohol-related problems which they did.

Six Month Follow-Up Results
Follow-up information was obtained for 91 subjects (87.5% of the total), broken down into 29 (85.3%: M = 18, F = 11) in DRAMS, 30 (93.8%: M = 23, F = 7) in advice and 32 (84.2%: M = 27, F = 5) in the control group. Of these, 76 were seen for the full follow-up interview and 15 returned postal questionnaires. Of the 13 subjects lost to follow-up, 6 had moved away, 4 could not be contacted, 2 refused an interview or questionnaire and one had died. Collateral information was obtained for 47 subjects, blood tests for 56, and both collateral and blood tests for 35. There were no significant differences between groups in follow-up rates, type of follow-up information available or on any variable measured at initial assessment. However, it will have been noted that there was a higher proportion of women in DRAMS than in the other two groups and, although this imbalance was not

statistically significant, it may have affected the results obtained. There were also no significant differences on initial measures between subjects followed up and those lost to follow-up, and between those who received a follow-up by questionnaire.

It may be remarked at this point that the general level of correspondence between subjects' self-reports of consumption and collateral estimates of changes in drinking was good. In particular, there was only one case in which a reported reduction in drinking between baseline and follow-up of greater than 25% was accompanied by a collateral report of increased drinking.

Figure 4.1 shows means of last month's consumption for all three groups at intake and follow-up assessment. In the DRAMS group this was reduced from 170.3 to 136.8 units, compared with reductions of 178.0 to 147.5 units in the advice group and 231.1 to 195.2 units in the control group. There was no significant difference between groups in changes in last month's consumption (analysis of covariance, F = 0.45), although the reduction in mean consumption observed in the sample as a whole (194.4 to 160.9 units) was significant (t = 2.82, p <0.01, two-tailed). A similar pattern was observed for changes in the heaviest month's consumption in the last six: all three groups showed a reduction in mean consumption (see Figure 4.1) but there were no significant differences

Figure 4.1: Means for Last Month's Consumption in Units of Alcohol

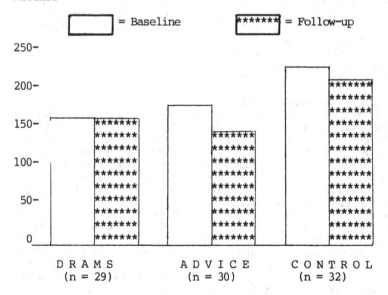

between groups. It was also noticeable that there was little change in any group or in the overall sample of alcohol-related problems (LAI Factor II). On LAI Factor VII, which is a measure of frequency and amount of drinking and number of drinking companions, there was a significant improvement in the overall sample (t = 2.02, p <0.05) but no significant differences between groups.

With respect to health-related measures, means for GGT in the three groups at intake and follow-up assessments are shown in Figure 4.2. In the DRAMS group mean GGT was reduced from 51.6 international units (IUs) to 30.1; in the advice group it was reduced from 29.1 IUs to 26.1; in the control group there was a slight increase from 40.0 IUs to 41.9. The distribution of GGT was markedly negatively skewed and it was therefore subjected to a log transformation to render the distribution approximately normal and suitable for parametric statistics. The difference between groups on log GGT was significant on an analysis of covariance (F = 2.52, p <0.05, one-tailed test). T-tests between separate groups showed that the difference between DRAMS and advice groups was significant (t = 1.83, p <0.05), but that there were no significant differences between advice and control groups (t = 0.05) or DRAMS and control (t = 2.17, p <0.05). There was no significant reduction in log GGT (t = 2.17, p <0.05). There were no significant differences between groups for MCV or physical health and well-being (Factor IV) but in the overall

Figure 4.2: Mean GGT (International Units) for Three Study Groups at Baseline and Follow-up

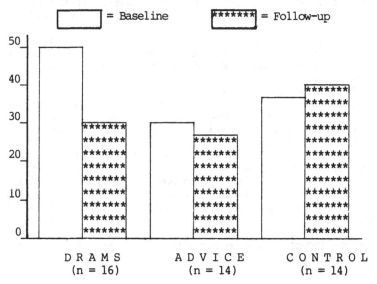

sample the improvements in both physical health and well-being
(t = 3.05, p <0.01) and MCV (t = 2.11, p <0.05) were
significant.

Data were also analysed using sex of subjects as the
independent variable. The sex difference in changes in the
last month's consumption approached significance (F = 3.43,
p <0.10), with males reducing from 228.9 units and females
from 92.3 to 73.4 units. The difference between sexes for
heaviest month's consumption was significant (F = 5.14, p
<0.05), with males decreasing from 263.5 to 240.8 units and
females from 126.5 to 108.6 units. However, there were no
significant differences due to sex for GGT, MCV, physical
health and well-being or control of drinking problems.

Contrary to expectations, there was no evidence of a
relationship between changes in drinking and the number of
consultations a patient received, either within the DRAMS
group or in the sample as a whole. This applied both to
consultations in which drinking was discussed and to the total
number of consultations during the follow-up period.

Analysis of Reduced Groups

When inspecting information from the debriefing at the end of
the follow-up interview and comparing it with the patient
attendance record, it became obvious that there had been many
departures from the procedure demanded by the design of the
study. For example, in the DRAMS group, 10 subjects had not
returned for the two week follow-up consultation and had not
therefore received the self-help book; in another three cases
the book had been given out incorrectly at the initial
consultation and the patient had not returned. In the advice
group, 13 subjects denied ever having received any advice to
cut down drinking, and in a further two cases the DRAMS
procedure appeared to have been followed. In the control
group, 6 subjects claimed that they had received advice and
another subject actually showed a DRAMS self-help book to the
interviewer.

These discrepancies were, of course, very disappointing
as far as the researchers were concerned, but there may be
understandable reasons for them (see also Neville et al,
in press). Most of the failure to conform to the design in
the DRAMS group can be attributed to lack of patient
compliance, which is only to be expected in this type of
study. On the other hand, some GPs may have been reluctant to
offer "strongly-worded advice" to some patients because of the
well-documented problems GPs have in raising the issue of
excessive drinking with patients they know well and do not
wish to offend (see Strong, 1980). In a few other cases, the
GP may have felt that it was ethically unacceptable not to
offer the DRAMS scheme to patients who patently had problems
with their drinking.

However understandable, these discrepancies created obvious problems for the analysis of results. We eventually decided that the only rational solution was to reduce the study group to cases where there was good evidence that the correct procedure described for each of the groups in the design of the study had been adhered to. Where there was any doubt, either from the debriefing or the patient attendance record, the subject was excluded. This meant that subjects in the DRAMS group who had not gone through the full DRAMS procedure (i.e. had not returned for the two week consultation or had not received the self-help book) were excluded. This left the following group sizes: DRAMS = 14 (M = 10, F = 4); advice = 15 (M = 11, F = 4); control = 25 (M = 21, F = 4).

Means of last month's consumption at intake and follow-up assessments for these "correct" groups are shown in Figure 4.3. This was reduced from 186.2 to 144.9 units in the DRAMS group, from 177.5 to 163.9 units in the advice group and from 225.4 to 211.8 units in the control group. In an analysis of covariance, the difference between groups in changes in last months consumption was not significant (F = 0.55). There was also no significant difference between groups for heaviest month's consumption in the last six (F = 0.37).

Figure 4.3: **Means of Last Month's Consumption at Intake and Follow-up Assessments for "Correct" Groups in Units of Alcohol**

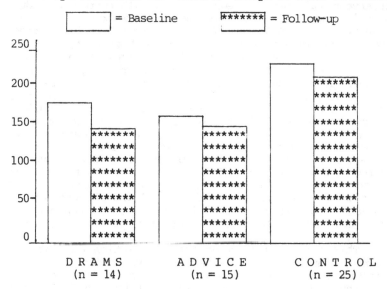

We also examined the proportions and percentages of subjects in these "correct" groups drinking above recommended limits at initial and follow-up assessment (men = 35

units/week, women = 20 units/week). For last month's consumption, this percentage was reduced in the DRAMS group (86% to 57%) but remained static in the advice group at 47% and in the control group at 68%. The difference in proportions drinking above recommended limits within the DRAMS group from initial to follow-up assessment was significant (t = 1.67, p <0.05, one-tailed test).

Interpretation of Results

The interpretation of the results of this controlled evaluation of DRAMS is equivocal and depends to a great extent on which outcome measure is used. In terms of mean monthly alcohol consumption, there was no evidence that patients given DRAMS fared any better than those given simple advice or no intervention. This remained true even when attention was confined to subjects for whom the correct procedure demanded by the design of the study appeared to have been followed and, thus, to those in the DRAMS group who received the full procedure and did not drop out. Although DRAMS subjects showed greater reductions in consumption than others when using "correct" groups, these differences did not reach statistical significance.

The only consumption measure to yield a significant change was the proportion of subjects within a group who were drinking above recommended levels either before or after the intervention. When the reduced groups with correct procedure were examined, this proportion was found to show a significant reduction in the DRAMS group but remained static in the other two groups. This occurred despite the fact that, as noted above, there were no significant differences between groups in changes in mean monthly consumption. This suggests that subjects in the DRAMS group, when they did succeed in reducing consumption, paid attention to the advice they had been given in the self-help literature and attained levels of drinking below the recommended upper weekly limits. Subjects in the other two groups had not received any specific advice about limits and therefore, even when they did reduce consumption, tended to remain above the drinking guidelines. Thus, it could be argued that DRAMS is an effective intervention if outcome is defined in terms of reduction of consumption to levels for subjects to experience all the elements of the DRAMS procedure (i.e. self-monitoring, return consultation, self-help book, GGT feedback) for this effectiveness to be realised.

This interpretation of the consumption data is, of course, complicated by the fact that the "correct" groups in question were not randomly assigned. Thus, subjects in the original DRAMS group who returned for the two week consultation, and who were thus included in the analysis of reduced groups, may have differed systematically from those who did not return and were therefore excluded from the analysis. Although these two kinds of DRAMS subjects did not show any significant differences on variables measured at initial assessment, there are clearly other, unmeasured variables on which they may have differed, chiefly those to do with motivation to cut down drinking. Thus, it can be argued that the finding under discussion merely demonstrates the difference between a selected group of more highly motivated DRAMS subjects and subsamples from the other two groups. Assuming for the moment the superiority of the reduced DRAMS group to be a valid result, it can also be argued that this is not enough to demonstrate the overall effectiveness of DRAMS. This is because it must be expected that, if DRAMS were in routine use in general practice, some patients would not comply with the full procedure. Thus, a consideration of whether or not DRAMS works must take this factor into account and show that DRAMS is superior to controls despite the tendency for some patients to drop out.

Taking changes in GGT as the measure of outcome, there was a significant tendency for the DRAMS group to show a greater mean reduction in a log measure of GGT than the advice group and a nearly significant superiority in this respect to the control group. Taken together, these findings are suggestive of a superiority for DRAMS even with drop outs included in the analysis. Given the significant finding for GGT, it is not clear why significant differences between groups did not also appear in the analysis of self-reported consumption. One possibility is that a change in GGT for an individual patient is a more valid and reliable measure of change in recent drinking than self-reports of consumption (cf. Trell et al, 1984). Indeed, there is a school of thought which proposes that self-reported consumption should be ignored in assessing the effects of interventions for alcohol problems (see, e.g. Watson et al, 1984). If this argument is accepted and attention is therefore confined to the GGT data, the present evidence suggests that the DRAMS scheme produced beneficial changes in the predicted direction.

A methodological problem concerns the fact that DRAMS subjects received more consultations during the follow-up period than subjects in the advice and control groups - both consultations in which drinking was discussed and consultations of all kinds. Thus, it is possible that it was this general factor, rather than any specific ingredients of the scheme, which was responsible for the putative superiority of DRAMS. However, the results provide no evidence of a relationship between the number of consultations and changes in drinking behaviour, both within the DRAMS group and in the entire sample. The only way to properly resolve this issue is, of course, to conduct another experiment in which the number of consultations in DRAMS and control groups is held constant as far as possible.

The reason for the lack of correlation between number of consultations and reduced consumption within the DRAMS group may be that there were far fewer consultations than expected. The mean number of further DRAMS contacts after the initial consultation, and including the planned two week consultation, was only 1.50 (s.d.= 1.29, range 0-5). Of these, the mean number at which a further blood sample was taken was 0.39 (s.d. = 0.58, range 0-2). This is partly due to the fact that 12 subjects in the DRAMS group did not return after the first consultation, but it is also true that, as in the Highlands and Islands pilot project (Glen et al, 1986), few GPs made full use of the interactive aspects of the scheme, especially the use of the GGT feedback, which was seen as an essential component.

Another potential difficulty for the interpretation of results is that there were somewhat more women in DRAMS than in the other two groups. However, this cannot have affected the evidence for the superior effectiveness of DRAMS since, as we have seen, male subjects showed significantly greater reductions on consumption measures than females, although males were at a much higher level of mean consumption at initial assessment. This finding is at variance with evidence from several studies showing that female problem drinkers fare better at controlling their drinking than males (Miller and Joyce, 1979; Duckert, 1983; Helzer et al 1985; Robertson et al, 1986). It may be that the kind of general practice intervention under the study here is not comparable with controlled drinking treatment per se, at least with respect to sex differences in response.

Since DRAMS is intended for use in a medical setting, it is naturally hoped that it would lead eventually to improvements in physical health. There was some improvement in health among DRAMS subjects, but this was not significantly different from the changes observed in the other two groups. However, in the follow-up sample as a whole and irrespective of which group subjects belonged to, there was a significant improvement in health as measured by LAI Factor IV, in addition to significant reductions in GGT and MCV.

One reason why it might have been difficult to discover a "treatment" effect of DRAMS in this study is the relatively intensive intervention received by subjects in the other two groups. Even in the non-intervention control group, subjects discussed the topic of drinking with their doctor, received a relatively long assessment interview dealing almost entirely with drinking and then agreed to a specially arranged blood test. Under these circumstances, it would not be surprising if some control group subjects had their attention drawn to the issue of excessive drinking and decided to attempt to cut down themselves. Thus it is possible to argue that all the subjects in this study received some form of "minimal was generally effective, as shown by significant improvements in health-related measures and a significant overall reduction in mean consumption. In order to substantiate this hypothesis, it would of course be necessary to have included a non-assessment control group and attempted a comparison between this group and the rest of the sample. As it is, this must remain a hypothesis which should be tested in future research.

The other important thing to bear in mind when considering these results is that few subjects of the study had attended their GPs to complain directly about an alcohol problem and that, when asked, only a minority (20%) reported that their drinking was causing problems. This kind of opportunistic intervention is very different from a situation in which people request treatment for a drinking problem or, for example, respond to newspaper advertisements offering help to cut down drinking. In this context, it would perhaps be unrealistic to expect large changes in drinking behaviour among a majority of patients. The most appropriate comparison is with the well-known study of GPs´ advice about smoking by Russell et al (1979), in which a large sample was needed to show a small but significant superiority of an advice plus leaflet group over various controls. Only 5% of patients in this group stopped smoking but, as the authors point out, if this effect were multiplied over all GPs in Britain, the results would be highly cost-effective compared with specialist smoking clinics.

The same may be true of DRAMS. Firstly, it would take a relatively large sample, larger than we were able to obtain in this study, to demonstrate a small but consistent effect when averaged over all patients given DRAMS. Secondly, if such an effect were demonstrated, the cost-effectiveness of the intervention would only become apparent when in widespread use among GPs. This must remain a hypothesis at present.

IMPLICATIONS FOR USE IN GENERAL PRACTICE

Apart from providing some evidence of its effectiveness, the study also yielded more qualitative information as to how DRAMS might profitably be modified for use in general practice. Firstly, the problems we had in conducting this this research - the reluctance of some GPs to participate in the trial, the slower than expected rate of recruitment of subjects, and some of the discrepancies between what was supposed to happen to subjects in different groups and what actually did occur - are not accidental phenomena. They are almost certainly connected with the difficulties that have been described in the literature as applying to the attempt to involve GPs in the treatment of alcohol problems (see e.g. Strong, 1980; Clement, 1986; Thom and Tellez, 1986). These difficulties include the unpopularity of working with "alcoholics", pessimism that anything effective can be done with them, a reluctance to raise the issue of drinking for fear of giving offence, and a feeling of insecurity about dealing with problems for which medical training had not provided the appropriate kind of skills. A questionnaire survey completed after the six month follow-up, which included doctors who declined to take part in the trial as well as those who agreed, provides evidence that some of these factors were involved in our study (Neville et al, in press).

It is clear that, in principle, the DRAMS scheme is able to overcome all these difficulties. Firstly, a clear distinction is made between the treatment of "alcoholics" and the kind of controlled drinking intervention used in DRAMS, which is more akin to health education - for example, to advice about giving up smoking. Secondly, the scheme should give GPs more confidence about dealing with problem drinkers by providing a clear structure for the intervention and guidance on how to raise the issue of drinking without confrontation. What therefore appears to be needed is more back-up for the intervention in the form of an expanded guide to the scheme for the doctor, and also more regular and on-going briefing and training sessions. The lesson is that DRAMS cannot simply be offered as a self-contained "package" which all GPs are supposed to use without further support. SHEG are now actively discussing how to improve DRAMS along these lines.

As well as more support for the GP, it may also be essential to sensitise the general public to the principles behind the scheme by means of local media campaigns, as suggested in Glen et al's (1986) report. If the message could be got across that the project had nothing to do with "alcoholism" and that the object was safer drinking and not total abstinence, this might remove some of the stigma associated with the issue of excessive drinking and make it easier for the GP to raise the subject during a consultation. One could also imagine a poster in the waiting room describing the DRAMS Scheme and saying something like: "Your doctor may ask you about you drinking .... This does not mean you are being regarded as an alcoholic .... It is simply that you may be drinking a little too much for your good health etc." This would give the GP a convenient pretext for introducing the topic of drinking without giving personal offence. Another possibility is to place the drinking intervention within a more general health education programme, aimed at cigarette smoking, exercise and diet as well as drinking. All these are means of attempting to reduce the sensitivity of patients and their GPs to discussions of alcohol consumption.

A further lesson concerns the disappointing use made by GPs of the interactive aspects of DRAMS, especially the use of GGT feedback. Perhaps more structure should be given to this feedback by arranging a series of monthly appointments at the initial consultation. Some of the load could be taken from the GP if the practice nurse were to take monthly blood samples and give the results of the previous month's GGT at the same time. The doctor could see the patient to review progress at less regular intervals, say every three months. This is the method used by Kristenson et al, (1981) in the Malmo study of heavy drinking in middle-aged men, and their results were very encouraging over the long term. Certainly, there is every reason to predict that GGT feedback, if properly structured, would have powerfully motivating and reinforcing effects on behaviour. Indeed, there is evidence from our study that GGT did show a significant decrease among subjects given DRAMS and a more structured intervention might increase this effect.

Apart from more structured GGT feedback, there are other lessons from our study for the design of an improved DRAMS scheme. With the benefit of hindsight, it is now patently obvious that a clear procedural distinction should have been made between patients who are ready and willing to reduce drinking and those who are not - in terms of Prochaska and Di Clemente's (1983) model of the change process, between those who have reached or are about to enter the action stage and those who are still in the contemplation or pre-contemplation stages. Patients could simply be asked whether, on the basis of the evidence presented to them about the harm caused could immediately enter a procedure similar to the existing DRAMS scheme. If not, or if they were unsure, they could enter a different procedure designed to increase their motivation to cut down, perhaps based on some of the "motivational interviewing" principles described by Miller (1983). Such a branching procedure might well reduce the number of patients who drop out of the scheme by making the intervention they receive more appropriate to the stage of change reached. More generally, attention could be paid to increasing patient compliance with the scheme by using the abundant information on this topic which exists in the literature (e.g. Di Matteo and Di Nicola, 1982). A revised DRAMS scheme which takes these factors into account is now being prepared.

To return to the optimistic tone with which this chapter started, in the short quotation from Skinner and Holt (1983), there are grounds for believing that forms of secondary prevention in medical settings, and especially in general practice settings, could have a dramatic impact on the prevalence of alcohol problems in our society. However, the difficulties inherent in this enterprise should not be underestimated. And, of course, it should go without saying that fresh developments in secondary prevention should always be accompanied by thorough evaluative research with adequate samples and by sufficient research funding to allow this to take place.

ACKNOWLEDGEMENTS

I am grateful to all the GPs who gave their precious time to this project, as well as to all the interviewer and coders who contributed to it and, of course, to the patients who agreed to take part. The DRAMS evaluation was a joint project between the Departments of Psychiatry and General Practice at Ninewells Medical School and was supported by a project grant from the Scottish Home and Health Department awarded to Dr P. D. Campion, Professor G. W. Fenton and myself. Thanks are also due Dr Ron Neville and David MacCabe for their invaluable contributions to the research.

REFERENCES

Anderson, P. (1984) personal communication

Armor, D., Polich, J. and Stambul, H. (1978) Alcoholism and Treatment. Wiley, New York

Babor, T., Ritson, E., and Hodgson, R. (1986) Alcohol-related problems in the primary health care setting: a review of early intervention strategies. British Journal of Addiction, 81, 23-46

Chick, J. (1980) Brief Edinburgh Alcohol Dependence Schedule, Alcohol Research Group. Department of Psychiatry, University of Edinburgh

Clement, S. (1986) The identification of alcohol-related problems by general practitioners. British Journal of Addiction, 81, 257-64

Di Matteo, R. and Di Nicola, D. (1982) Achieving Patient Compliance. Pergamon, New York

Duckert, F. (1983) Sex Differences in Control Training Program for Alcohol Abusers. Paper presented at World Congress of Behavioural Therapy, Washington DC, December

Glen, I., Hendry, J. and Milton, A. (1986) Drinking Reasonably and Moderately with Self-control: A pilot study of controlled drinking in individuals with alcohol abuse presenting to general practitioners in the Highlands and Islands of Scotland. Scottish Health Education Group

Grant, M. (1986) From contemplation to action: the role of the World Health Organisation. In W.R. Miller and N. Heather (eds), Treating Addictive Behaviours: processes of change. Plenum, New York

Heather, N., Campion, P., Neville, R. and MacCabe, D. (1986a) Evaluation of a controlled drinking minimal intervention (the DRAMS Scheme) in general practice, submitted for publication

Heather, N., Whitton, B. and Robertson, I. (1986b) Evaluation of a self-help manual for media-recruited problem drinkers: six-month follow-up results. British Journal of Clinical Psychology, 25, 19-34

Helzer, J., Robins, L., Taylor, J., Carey, K., Miller, R., Combes-Orme, T. and Farmer, A. (1985) The extent of long-term moderate drinking outcomes among alcoholics discharged from medical and psychiatric treatment facilities. New England Journal of Medicine, 312, 1678-1982

Kendell, R. (1979) Alcoholism a medical or political problem? British Medical Journal, 281, 367-371

Kristenson, H,. Trell, E. and Hood, B. (1981) Serum-GGT in screening and continuous control of heavy drinking in middle-aged men. American Journal of Epidemiology, 114, 862-872

Miller, W. (1983) Motivational interviewing with problem drinkers. Behavioural Psychotherapy, 11, 147-172

Miller, W. and Joyce, M. (1979) Prediction of abstinence, controlled drinking and heavy drinking outcomes following behavioural self-control training. Addictive Behaviours, 5, 13-24

Miller, W. and Marlatt, G. (1984) Manual of Comprehensive Drinker Profile. Psychological Assessment Resources Inc, Odessa, Florida

Neville, R., Campion, P. and Heather, N. (in press) Barriers to the recognition and management of problem drinking: lessons from a multi-centre general practice study, Health Bulletin

Prochaska, J. and Di Clemente, C. (1983) Stages and processes of self-change of smoking: towards a more integrative model of change. Psychotherapy Research, Theory and Practice, 19, 276-278

Robertson, I. and Heather, N. (1986) So You Want to Cut Down Your Drinking? a self-help guide to sensible drinking. Scottish Health Education Group, Edinburgh

Robertson, I., Heather, N., Dzialdowski, A,. Crawford, J. and Winton, M. (1986) A comparison of minimal versus intensive controlled drinking treatment interventions for problem drinkers. British Journal of Clinical Psychology. 25, 185-194

Russell, M., Wilson, C., Taylor, C. and Baker, C. (1979) Effect of general practitioners advice against smoking. British Medical Journal, 284, 231-236

Saunders, B. (1985) The case for controlling alcohol consumption. In Heather, N., Robertson, I. and Davies, P. (eds) The Misuse of Alcohol: crucial issues in dependence, treatment and prevention. Croom Helm, London

Selzer, M. (1971) The Michigan Alcoholism Screening Test: the quest for a new diagnostic instrument. American Journal of Psychiatry, 127, 1653-1658

Shaw, S., Cartwright, A., Spratley, T. and Harwin, J. (1978) Responding to Drinking Problems. Croom Helm, London

Skinner, H. and Holt, S. (1983) Early intervention for alcohol problems. Journal of The Royal College of General Practitioners, 33, 676-691

Strong, P. (1980) Doctors and dirty work: the case of alcoholism. Sociology of Health and Illness, 2, 24-47

Thom, B. and Tellez, C. (1986) A difficult business: detecting and managing alcohol problems in general practice. British Journal of Addiction, 81, 405-418

Trell, E., Kristenson, H. and Fex, G. (1984) Alcohol-related problems in middle-aged men with elevated serum gamma-glutamyl-transferase: a preventive medical investigation. Journal of Studies on Alcohol. 45,302-309

Watson. C., Tilleskjor, C., Hoodecheck-Schow, E., Pucel, J. and Jacobs, L. (1984) Do alcoholics give valid self-reports? Journal of Studies on Alcohol. 45, 344-348

Wilkins, R. (1974) The Hidden Alcoholic in General Practice. Elek, London

Chapter 5

EARLY INTERVENTION IN THE GENERAL HOSPITAL

Jonathan Chick

> **Gulliver to Houyhnhm:**
> I told him, we feed on a Thousand Things which operated
> contrary to each other; that we ate when we were not
> hungry, and drank without the Provocation of Thirst:
> That we sat whole Nights drinking strong Liquors without
> eating a Bit; which disposed us to Sloth, enflamed our
> Bodies, and precipitated or prevented Digestion.
>
> ("Gulliver's Travels", Jonathan Swift)

INTRODUCTION

It is not new to suggest that the general hospital is a point
at which therapeutic contact may be made with problem drinkers
(Chafetz et al, 1962). There is no dearth of evidence for the
association of alcohol consumption with physical illness and
injury. Indeed, there are numerous estimates of the number of
problem drinkers among general hospital patients. What is
less certain is whether intervention is justified - are such
cases merely occasional excess drinkers and unlikely to join
the numbers of chronic and seriously affected "alcoholics",
or to progress to serious alcohol-related illness? It is also
less certain whether such intervention would be effective,
though this chapter will argue that treatment can improve the
outcome, perhaps more consistently than intervention attempted
in other settings. First, the evidence showing that problem
drinkers can be identified in general hospitals will be
reviewed.

ALCOHOL, PHYSICAL ILLNESS AND INJURY

Individuals diagnosed as being dependent upon alcohol have two
to three times the death rate of the general population.
Accidents and physical illness account for most of the excess,
suicide, though increased among alcoholics, accounting for
only a small percentage of deaths. Death from cancer,
respiratory disease, cardiovascular disease as well as liver
disease are all more frequent than in the general population
(Adelstein and White, 1976). There is an association between
diagnosis of alcohol dependence and admission to hospital for
myocardial infarction, diabetes and strokes (Lindegard and
Langman, 1985). When the past histories of problem drinkers
attending for treatment are examined, general medical
conditions across the whole spectrum are more common than in
comparison groups. Kolb and Gunderson (1983) found that two-

thirds of naval personnel treated for an alcohol problem had had a prior medical admission for reasons other than for their alcohol misuse. By comparison, the rate for other sailors was significantly lower - around 50% having had a previous admission for a medical condition.

Even when alcohol dependence is not diagnosed, heavy drinking is linked with many medical conditions. Longitudinal general population studies show the links between alcohol consumption above 60 g per day (equivalent to 4 pints of beer) and subsequent death by stroke (e.g. Dyer et al, 1977), and, although the evidence is less clear cut, by coronary artery disease also (reviewed by Lindegard and Langman, 1985). Studies of drinking in general hospital patients and in general populations in the same district reveal that the likelihood of a general hospital admission for liver disease (Pequignot et al, 1978), myocardial infarction, other cardiovascular disease, and upper gastro-intestinal diseases begins to increase in men drinking above 30 g per day (Chick et al, 1986). Respiratory diseases are also common in this group (Chick et al, 1986) perhaps because of the prevalence of smoking among drinkers.

Attenders at hospital injury departments have what appear to be high rates of positive blood alcohol tests (Holt et al, 1980) and other markers of regular alcohol intake (Papoz et al, 1986). The available evidence suggests that many pedestrian injuries are probably caused by drinking alcohol. The counter-argument that it is only by chance that a drinking pedestrian is knocked down was examined by Irwin et al (1983). They obtained controls - age and sex matched pedestrians breathalysed at the same time of day and week - and found the controls to have on average much lower blood alcohol levels than the injured patients. Although the same type of case-controlled study has not been done, elevated blood alcohol levels are more common in road accident victims than would be expected on the basis of what is known of drinking among drivers (e.g. Vine and Watson, 1983). The deleterious effects of alcohol on driving skills have also been well established.

The blood test gamma glutamyl transpeptidase (GGT), which indicates heavy drinking, was used for screening middle-aged men in a Swedish population (Peterson et al, 1980). It was reported that alcohol consumption was the single most powerful predictor of premature death in this group.

DETECTION METHODS AND RATES

There is no tablet from the mountain giving the criterion for diagnosis of problem drinking. Numerous criteria and cut-off points have been used for deciding who to count as a case. Some studies use only self-reports, others use objective criteria (blood or breath tests, physical stigmata) as well (Martin et al, 1983) or instead (Holt et al, 1980). Some self-report methods include questions about past help-seeking (e.g. MAST: Selzer et al, 1971) or about attitudes of others (e.g. others criticising your drinking, CAGE: Mayfield et al, 1974). Other methods (e.g. Lloyd et al, 1982) avoid questions about the individual's or others' attitudes to drinking and concentrate on whether it is admitted that drink has caused an actual problem in either the health, personal or social domain. Studies vary in the time-frame used, that is whether only recent problems are counted (e.g. past year) or whether two years or even "ever" is the criterion.

Some approaches have included or have been restricted to questioning about consumption, employing an arbitrary cut-off (e.g. Jariwalla et al, 1979). The search for reliable information about quantities of alcohol consumed has itself lead to numerous different methods. In Britain, where drinking at least once per week is the norm, a preference has developed for asking about each drink consumed in the seven days prior to interview (or to admission), or if that recent seven days had been "untypical", to ask for a typical week's consumption. Lloyd et al (1982) used 400 g/week as a cut-off in male patients or a maximum day's consumption of more than 100 g. Barrison et al, (1980) in London asked about frequency of drinking at or above a criterion of 80 g/day (for men) and 40 g/day (for women), classifying those who did so "every day or most days" as excessive drinkers, as did Williams et al (1978) in Sydney.

To use as the sole indicator whether or not the patient has been admitted for a classically alcohol-related diagnosis such as liver cirrhosis or pancreatitis will miss some severe and many milder "cases", since as will be described, problem drinkers are found in almost all diagnostic categories (Williams et al, 1978; Lloyd et al, 1986).

As well as varying in the methods of detection, and the criteria or cut-off points within those methods, studies also vary in the population sampled. Some studies have surveyed only specific specialities, such as medical, or orthopaedic; some have included, others have excluded, patients admitted with drug overdose or self-injury among whom excessive drinking is common (Varadasaj and Mendonca, 1986); some have included day-attenders, for example at casualty departments; some have excluded the very ill, the elderly or those with poor ability to communicate. These are some of the reasons why comparison of rates for problem drinking between studies would seem on the whole meaningless, as is also the search for a consensus (McIntosh, 1982). It is therefore perhaps surprising to find that in surveys in the English-speaking developed countries, predominantly in urban-serving general hospitals, rates for "problem drinking" variously defined, almost always fall between 15% to 30% for men and 8% to 15% for women. A few studies producing higher rates have been in hospitals serving homeless or skid row communities. Rates may be higher in the high alcohol consuming countries of Europe.

Rates in Specific Hospital Services

Services for drug overdose and self-injury include a high proportion of problem drinkers. Not only are high blood alcohol levels frequently recorded on admission (29% above 80mg/100 mls in recent Canadian study - (Varadasaj and Mendonca, 1986) but also the histories of these patients reveal a high rate of longstanding alcohol-related problems (Kessel, 1965). Medical wards contain a higher proportion of problem drinkers than surgical services, except surgical services dealing with accident victims, especially head injuries. Among evening attenders at a Scottish casualty department, 32% had a blood alcohol concentration of over 80 mg per cent (Holt et al, 1980). In an English casualty department, the comparable rate was 11% (Backhouse et al, 1986). In Sweden, where an alcohol offence or evidence of alcohol abuse can place an individual on a register, 28% of casualty department attenders are registered as abusers (Rydberg et al, 1973). In the English study just mentioned (Backhouse et al, 1986) 11% of attenders were deemed by research interviews to be attending because of an alcohol-related difficulty, though an assessment of whether a chronic problem was present was not made. Attenders at French casualty departments may have a higher rate. At least among accident victims, chronic heavy drinking sufficient to elevate the serum GGT or MCV (mean cell volume of red blood cells) present in 27% (Papoz et al, 1986).

Obstetric patients have been surveyed to identify women at risk of alcohol-related foetal damage. In the United States of America, Rosett et al (1983) selected women for counselling who were drinking more than 25 g of alcohol per day. These accounted for 9% of the surveyed patients. Plant (1984) interviewed women attending an antenatal clinic in Scotland and found much less heavy drinking, only 6% reporting as much as 12 g per day.

In some cities general hospitals offer health screening to selected age cohorts. At Malmo General Hospital in Sweden since 1974 men in their late forties and early fifties have been invited for screening. Intervention has been offered to excessive drinkers and this will be described later. The prevalence of excessive drinking, defined as a raised serum gamma glutamyl transpeptidase (GGT) attributable at subsequent interview to alcohol intake, was 12% (Kristenson et al, 1980).

Lloyd et al (1982) and McIntyre (1979), in their surveys of problem drinkers in general medical wards of Scottish hospitals, noted those whose problem was already identified to the extent that a specialised treatment initiative had occurred. Problem drinkers who had no previous treatment were termed newly identified cases. Using a criterion based on heavy self-reported consumption and/or self-reported problems, plus a repeat interview in those with an unexplained elevation of MCV or serum GGT, rates in the Edinburgh study were as follows:

Males: 27%, of whom 5% had had previous treatment
Females: 11%, of whom 8% had had previous treatment
Patients who had overdosed, were of no fixed abode, were too ill to be interviewed or over 65 were omitted from this study.

The result is of interest because the proportion of newly identified to already treated cases was much lower in women than in men, despite a lower consumption criterion being used to detect female cases. It suggests that unobtrusive markers of drinking such as blood tests may in some cultures be more important for detecting new female cases in whom interview alone may not reveal the problem. The Glasgow study which also excluded overdose patients, but included only males, found that out of 56 current problem drinkers the ratio of newly identified cases to those with previous treatment was much less - less than 2:1, compared with 4.5:1 in the Edinburgh study. However, the Glasgow consumption criterion was 90 g/day compared to Edinburgh's 80 g/day and a ward physician made the assessment, while in Edinburgh a separate "research" nurse conducted the screening interview, probably detecting more new cases.

Do Routine Admission Procedures Detect Problem Drinkers?

The level of awareness among physicians and nurses that excessive drinking is a health hazard has probably increased in many countries in the past decade, though this has not been established empirically. However, inclusion in the routine history of questions which would detect problem drinking is still not commonplace.

One English hospital study found that alcohol consumption was noted accurately in only a third of case-records (Barrison et al, 1980). In a Scottish hospital recording of consumption was superior to this and was recorded quantitatively in 25 of 34 newly identified problem drinkers, but the physician's records more than half the time failed to note a history of adverse consequences of drinking and withdrawal symptoms (Lloyd et al, 1982).

The history is important: if physicians relied excessively on blood tests they would miss at least a third of patients who are defined as problem drinkers by interview. For example, only 61% of the newly defined cases in the Edinburgh study quoted had a serum GGT over 40 international units (IU) and only a quarter had an MCV over 98. In the Sydney study (Williams et al, 1978), in which a global assessment of whether or not an alcohol problem was present was the case criterion, serum GGT was raised (over 55 IU for men, over 40 IU for women) in 46%, and MCV was over 95 in 24%.

109

Both serum triglycerides, and serum uric acid were raised in 30%, but for all these tests the rate of false positive tests (positive results in-patients without alcohol problems) makes them too unreliable to use on their own; but they can be useful pointers to the need for a more probing history.

Blood alcohol level on admission, not a routine test, may be helpful in that false positives are less common than with the above tests all of which are altered by other pathologies. However, false negatives (problem drinkers with zero blood alcohol levels) are common. In one study in a medical service only 29% of cases positive on examination plus questionnaire had a blood alcohol-level present at over 100 mg/100 ml on admission (Martin et al, 1983).

The routine physical examination includes inspection of the skin of the face, the tongue, the eyes, the hands and the liver. The recent World Health Organisation (1986) study of screening methods has shown that signs in the skin and eyes and tremor of the hands and tongue can be used to discriminate excessive drinkers, a finding already demonstrated in the French medical literature (e.g. Berchet et al, 1979) and much used by physicians in French alcohol clinics.

In summary, however, even in screening general hospital populations, where it is more commonly physical harm from alcohol that is the cause for admission as opposed to social or personal harm in psychiatric clinics, physical tests and examination are no substitute for an enquiry into drinking habits and history of problems from drinking. The screening questionnaires such as MAST whose use originated in psychiatric or specialised alcoholism clinics and is successful in such populations, often miss cases in general hospitals - only 29 of 81 "cases" in Glasgow General Hospital study were MAST-positive (McIntyre, 1979). The best approach is a non-judgemental enquiry into recent alcohol consumption and a set of questions about dependence symptoms and social and physical harm associated with drinking. The simple question, "Do you think you have an alcohol problem?" should be included.

CHARACTERISTICS OF PROBLEM DRINKERS IDENTIFIED IN GENERAL HOSPITALS

Having identified problem drinkers in the general hospital, what typifies their drinking or their symptoms?

In the Edinburgh study quotes, of newly identified male problem drinkers, only 42% were daily drinkers, though most (78%) were drinkers who at least monthly drink heavily (more than 7 pints of beer or equivalent) in a session. The mean maximum day's consumption in a typical week was 20 units (180 g). Nevertheless, there were drinkers who reported problems in the last year from their drinking and typically drank what many would regard as not excessive quantities: 25% admitted less than 39 units (350 g) per week (Lloyd et al, 1987).

Classical symptoms of dependence were uncommon in this sample with a prevalence intermediate between that observed in a community sample of drinkers and that seen in patients attending a psychiatric hospital clinic for alcohol problems.

In the Edinburgh sample, over half the male problem drinkers had been admitted for an illness not classically related to alcohol.

Psychiatric symptoms are not a prominent feature of such a group: 35% reached the criterion on a screening questionnaire for possible minor psychiatric illness. This is similar to rates found among the physically ill groups of patients.

The Natural History of Problem Drinking Identified in the General Hospital

As shown in the previous section, a broad range of individuals are recruited when the criteria are extended to include those who have only had one or two possibly isolated problems from their drinking, or who are simply drinking at a level which, on epidemiological evidence, puts them at risk. Little is known about the future drinking habits, illnesses or social and personal problems of such a group. As with problem drinkers identified in door to door surveys, a future enquiry will reveal that some are now free of problems (Chick et al, 1984). Many drinkers will move in and out of periods of problems, having some years free, other years not free of difficulty arising out of their drinking. Chick et al (1985) found that without special counselling while in hospital, a third of newly identified problem drinkers were problem-free after one year. Furthermore, those who were without problems and only "at-risk" drinkers at the time of their hospital admission also had reduced their consumption by 50% or more. McIntyre (1979), while offering specific counselling to a few patients, in general only gave medical advice and found that slightly over a third had probably sustained a reduction in consumption for the six months after discharge. However, periods of 6 to 12 months are very short in the evolution of a drinking problem. There is a great need for longer follow-up studies of these hospital-identified groups. That there is an increased mortality in such groups, however, is suggested by the work of Peterson et al (1980) and of studies on other heavy drinking groups quoted in the first section of this chapter. The consumption band above 80 g per day is well beyond the range of light drinking that has been found in some studies to have a protective effect in cardiac illness (e.g. Marmot et al, 1983). There are numerous influences that may affect a problem drinker's consumption pattern as the years unfold - some exacerbating, some decreasing his or her intake e.g. pressures from employers, friends, family, financial constraints, poor physical health, greater or lesser access to alcohol, periods of institutionalisation, change of drinking

friends and aging. It is thus extremely difficult to predict
the outcome in any individual case. All that can be specified
is the risk, i.e. the odds, with which an individual drawn
from a particular group is likely to have a certain outcome.
It is, of course, premature to use the term "early problem
drinker" for an individual simply drinking, say, 90 g per day.
He or she is, however, at a greater risk of dying of an
alcohol-related cause, or inflicting serious harm on himself
or his family than someone drinking less. However,
statistically, it is more likely that he or she will escape
such serious consequences. A middle-aged man identified as a
problem drinker in the general population screening project in
Malmo (Peterson et al, 1980), has at least a 30 to 1 chance
that he will still be alive four years later. The next
section looks at how that chance can be improved by
intervention.

**INTERVENTIONS APPROPRIATE FOR PROBLEM DRINKERS IN THE GENERAL
HOSPITAL**

There is evidence for a tendency among problem drinkers
attending a hospital psychiatric clinic to expect an approach
of the type used in physical medicine. Davies (1981),
interviewing problem drinking patients before and after
consultations with psychiatrists, found that their
expectations were more often met if they had been physically
examined, had blood tests taken, and had been offered
"treatments" such as deterrent pills (e.g. Antabuse) or
admission to hospital, or at least clear simple advice.
Potamianos, Gorman and Peters (1985), found that problem
drinking patients admitted to both psychiatric and medical
clinics tended strongly towards an "organic" as opposed to a
"psychosocial" expectation of treatment.

General Hospital Staff
Staff will naturally tend to adopt a physical approach,
hopefully explaining to the patient the relation between his
or her physical pathology and excessive drinking, and offering
advice about safe drinking or abstinence as indicated.
However, there are two difficulties. First, in the general
ward the problem drinker has often not yet begun to see his
problem as alcohol-related or accept that it would be
advisable to alter his drinking habits; he may be very
resistant to the physician's advice. The second difficulty is
that research has shown there to be a lack of interest as well
as pessimism about treating "alcoholics" amongst general
nursing and medical staff (Potamianos et al, 1985; Mogar,
1969). Training of medical and nursing staff in the
management of the problem drinker should therefore be aimed
at:

1. Dispelling negative stereotypes as well as improving detection rates.
2. Teaching and conducting the initial dialogue with the patient about his drinking in a manner that will lead him to decide to do something about it rather than increase resistance. The model might be the "motivational interview" of Miller (1983) or the "balance sheet" in which the patient draws up lists of the advantages and disadvantages of his drinking to help him make a decision about the changes he will make.
3. Enhancing communication skills, so that explanations given about the role of alcohol are understood (1).

An alternative approach might be to use a designated specially trained staff member to counsel problem drinkers. In the study of Chick et al (1985), a nurse with specialised experience of alcoholism visited the wards wearing a white coat, with a lapel designation giving her Ward Sister rank. She was acquainted from the medical and nursing notes with the results of investigations and the medical history. In addition to an hour's dialogue and self-help booklet with advice on cutting down consumption, she attempted to see the patient with the spouse on one occasion. Self-help literature at varying reading levels is available (e.g. Scottish Health Education Group, 1985) and should be available to patients without their having to search in booksellers. Miller and Taylor (1980) have demonstrated that in mild cases, self-help literature can be as effective as a course of out-patient therapy.

Voluntary lay counsellors including recovered alcoholics have been invited to counsel problem drinkers identified in hospital. Their efficacy will clearly be greatest if their approach to the patient is given the full weight of the physician's authority, and if the physician has already begun a dialogue with patients about their drinking. In some British hospitals a successful link exists between the wards and the Local Alcohol Advice Centre, or Council on Alcoholism. The casualty department should ideally have an attached worker who can take referrals from the busy casualty staff. In city centre departments a social worker in the casualty department can have a valuable role in assessing individuals with alcohol problems and whether utilising the opportunity provided by the attendance to commence a dialogue with the individual, or making a referral.

Follow-up is likely to be important. In some cases, the general practitioner will be the appropriate person. Regular feedback about blood test results over the coming months can be offered, as in the Malmo screening and treatment project (Kristenson et al, 1983).

Early Intervention in the General Hospital

EFFICACY STUDIES

It has proved difficult to conduct randomised controlled
studies in problem drinkers to compare the effect of
intervention versus no intervention. In alcohol clinic
populations, there are few studies which have demonstrated an
effect of treatment (reviewed in Chick, 1984). It is
practically and ethically difficult to have a control group
receiving no treatment. However, in populations who would
otherwise not be treated were a study not in progress, a no-
treatment control group is possible. In a male general
hospital sample Chick et al (1983) found that half the
counselled patients but only a third of the controls were
definitely improved a year later. In a hospital-based general
population screening project in men, subsequent morbidity was
reduced three-fold, and mortality halved compared to controls
(Kristenson et al, 1983). As with all studies showing
positive treatment outcome they should, ideally, be repeated.
      Turning to uncontrolled studies, Rosett et al (1983)
found that of 49 heavy drinking pregnant women attending antenatal care, 33 (67%) reduced their consumption by the third
trimester. Katz et al (1981), in patients with alcohol-
related liver disease, found 17 out of 36 attained at least 4
months abstinence after discharge and with regular
counselling. Patek and Hermos (1981) found a proportion
(unfortunately unspecified) of patients with alcoholic
cirrhosis reduced or stopped drinking simply on medical advice
and maintained good progress for years with minimal help.
      These results have been encouraging. If it is shown that
results in these settings are better than in special alcohol
clinic populations there may be a number of reasons. It has
been shown that patients with fewer psychiatric problems
respond better to treatment (McLellan et al, 1983). Better
results may also be expected if intervention takes place
before cerebral or irreversible psychological damage has
occurred. However, it would seem likely that advice linked to
health, given in a medical setting at a time when an
individual is concerned about his health, has an important
chance of success.

NOTE

      1. Medicine International (1985), Volume 2, contains
papers which would contribute to a course for medical staff;
see also Medical Council on Alcoholism Handbooks for students
obtainable from 1, St Andrews Place, London NW1 4LB.

REFERENCES

Adelstein, A. and White, G. (1976) Alcoholism and mortality.
    Population Trends, 6, 7-13

Backhouse, M. Gurevitch, T. and Silver, V. (1986) Problem
    Drinkers and the Statutory Services: data bases, economic
    costings and service responses. Unpublished report to
    the DHSS. Addiction Research Centre, Institute for
    Health Studies, University of Hull
Barrison, I., Viola, L. and Murray-Lyon I. (1980) Do housemen
    take an adequate drinking history? British Medical
    Journal, 281, 1040
Berchet, J., Blin, G. and Carraz, M. et al (1979) GGT et
    grille de Le Go. Bulletin d'Information sur l'alcoolisme
    de l'haut comite d'Etude et d'information sur
    l'Alcoolisme. Suppl. Scientifique et Technique, June,
    7-37
Chafetz, N. (1962) Establishing treatment relations with
    alcoholics. Journal of Nervous and Mental Disease, 134,
    395-409
Chick, J. (1984) Drinking Problems: patterns of recovery
    and the effect of treatment. Institute for Studies on
    Alcohol, London
Chick, J., Lloyd, D. and Crombie, E. (1985) Counselling
    problem drinkers in medical wards: a controlled study.
    British Medical Journal, 290, 965-967
Chick, J., Duffy, J., Lloyd, G. and Ritson, B. (1986) Medical
    admissions in men: the risk among drinkers. Lancet, (in
    press)
Davies, P. (1981) Expectations and therapeutic practices in
    out-patient clinics for alcohol problems. British
    Journal of Addiction, 76, 159-173
Dyer, R.. Stamlec, J. and Paul, O. (1977) Alcohol
    consumption, cardiovasular risk factors and mortality in
    two Chicago epidemiological studies. Circulation, 56,
    1067-1074
Holt, S., Stewart, J., Dixon, J., Elton, R., Taylor, T. and
    Little, K. (1980) Alcohol and the emergency service
    patient. British Medical Journal, 281, 638-40
Irwin, S., Pullerson, C. and Rutherford, W. (1983)
    Association between alcohol consumption and adult
    pedestrians who sustain injuries in road traffic
    accidents. British Medical Journal, 286, 522
Jariwalla, A., Adams, P. and Hore, B. (1979) Alcohol and
    acute general medical admissions to hospital. Health
    Trends, 11, 95-97
Katz, A., Morgan, M. and Sherlock, S. (1981) Alcoholism
    treatment in a medical setting. Journal of Studies on
    Alcohol, 42, 136-143
Kessel, N. (1965) Self Poisoning. British Medical Journal,
    1265, 1336-1340
Kolb, D. and Gunderson, E. (1983) Medical histories of
    problem drinkers during their first twelve years of naval
    service. Journal of Studies on Alcohol, 44, 84-94

Kristenson, H., Trell, E., Fex, G. and Hood, B. (1980). Serum gamma glutamyl transferase: Statistical distribution in a middle-aged male population and evaluation of alcohol habits in individuals with elevated levels. Preventive Medicine, 9, 108-119

Kristenson, H., Ohlin, H., Hutten-Nosslin, M., Trell, E. and Hood, B. (1983) Identification and intervention of heavy drinking in middle-aged men; Results and follow-up of 24 - 60 months of long term study with randomised controls. Alcoholism, 7, 203-209

Lindegard, B. and Langman, M. (1985) Marital state, alcohol consumption and liability to myocardial infarction, stroke, diabetes, mellitus or hypertension in men from Gothenburg. British Medical Journal, 291, 1529-1533

Lloyd, G., Chick, J. and Crombie, E. (1982) Screening for problem drinkers among medical in-patients. Drug and Alcohol Dependence, 10, 355-359

Lloyd, G., Chick, J., Anderson, S. and Crombie, E. (1987) Problem drinkers in medical wards, consumption patterns and disabilities in newly identified male cases. British Journal of Addiction, in press

McIntosh, I. (1982) Alcohol-related disabilities in general hospital patients: a critical assessment of the evidence. International Journal of the Addictions, 17, 609-639

McIntyre, D. (1979) Alcohol-related problems among male patients admitted to a general mdical ward - their identification and follow-up. Health Bulletin, 37, 213-217

McLellan, A., Luborsky, L., Woody, G., O'Brien, C. and Druley, K. (1983) Predicting response to alcohol and drug abuse treatment: role of psychiatric severity. Archives of General Psychiatry, 40, 620-625

Marmot, M., Rose, P., Shipley, M. and Thomas, B. (1983). Alcohol and mortality, a U-shaped curve. Lancet, 580-583

Martin, B., Northcote, R., Scullion, H. and Reilley, D. (1983) Alcohol related morbidity in acute male medical admissions.Health Bulletin, 41, 263-267

Mayfield, D., Mcleod, G. and Hall, P. (1974) The CAGE questionnaire: validation of a new alcoholism screening instrument. American Journal of Psychiatry , 131, 1121-1123

Miller, W. and Taylor, C. (1980) Relative effectiveness of bibliotherapy: individual and group self-control training in the treatment of problem drinkers. Addictive Behaviours, 5, 13-24

Miller, W. R. (1983) Motivational interviewing with problem drinkers. Behavioural Psychotherapy, 11, 147-172

Mogar, R. (1969) Staff attitudes towards the alcoholic patient.Archives of General Psychiatry, 21, 449-454

Papoz, L., Weill, J. and L'Hoste, J. (1986) Biological markers of alcohol intake among 4796 subjects injured in accidents. British Medical Journal, 292, 1234-1237

Patek, A. and Hermos, J. (1981) Recovery from alcoholism in cirrhotic patients. American Journal of Medicine, 70, 782-785

Pequignot, G., Tuyns, A. and Berta, J. (1978) Ascitic cirrhosis in relation to alcohol consumption. International Journal of Epidemiology, 7, 113-120

Peterson, B., Kristenson, H., Sternby, N., Trell, E., Fex, G. and Hood, B. (1980) Alcohol consumption and premature death in middle-aged men. British Medical Journal, 280, 1403-1406

Plant, M., (1984) Alcohol consumption during pregnancy: baseline data from a Scottish prospective study. British Journal of Addiction, 79, 207-214

Potamianos, G., Winter, D., Duffy, S., Gorman, D. and Peters, T. (1985) The perception of problem drinkers by general hospital staff, general practitioners and alcoholic patients. Alcohol, 2, 563-566

Potamianos, G., Gorman, D. and Peters, T. (1985) Attitudes and treatment expectations of patients and general hospital staff in relation to alcoholism. British Journal of Medical Psychology, 58, 63-66

Rosett, H., Weimer, L. and Edelin, K. (1983) Treatment experience with pregnant problem drinkers. Journal of American Medical Association, 249, 2029-2033

Rydberg, U., Bjerver, K. and Goldberg, L. (1973) The alcohol factor in a surgical emergency unit. Acta Medicine Legalis et Socialis, 22, 71-82

Scottish Health Education Group, (1985) So you want to cut down your drinking? Scottish Health Education Group, Edinburgh

Selzer, M.L. (1971) The Michigan Alcoholism Screening Test: the quest for a new diagnostic instrument. American Journal of Psychiatry, 127, 1653

Varadasaj, R. and Mendonca, J. (1986) Blood-alcohol survey in patients with self-poisoning. British Journal of Psychiatry, 148, 615

Vine, J. and Watson, T. (1983) Incidence of drug and alcohol intake in road traffic accident victims. Medical Journal of Australia, 612-615

Williams, A., Burns, F. and Money, S. (1978) Prevalence of alcoholism in a Sydney teaching hospital: some aspects. Medical Journal of Australia, 2, 608-611

World Health Organisation (1986) Collaborative project on the identification and treatment of persons with harmful alcohol consumption. Report on Phase 1: The development of a screening instrument. WHO, Geneva

PART TWO

SUPPORTING OTHER COMMUNITY AGENTS

Chapter 6

THE SALFORD EXPERIMENT: AN ACCOUNT OF THE COMMUNITY ALCOHOL
TEAM APPROACH

Sue Clement

INTRODUCTION

The need for community services for problem drinkers and for a
greater awareness of the importance of alcohol-related
problems was formally recognised by the DHSS in 1973 in their
circular Community Services for Alcoholics (DHSS, 1973). The
Kessel Committee report of 1978, The Pattern and Range of
Services for Problem Drinkers (Advisory Committee on
Alcoholism, 1978) specified the direction in which the DHSS
Advisory Committee on Alcoholism felt that community services
should be going and reinforced the emphasis on community care
for problem drinkers found in the 1976 report Priorities for
Health and Personal Social Services in England (DHSS, 1976)
and the 1975 report Better Services for the Mentally Ill
(DHSS, 1975).
    In The Pattern and Range of Services it was recognised
that the provision of specialist care to all problem drinkers
in the community was neither possible, because of the size of
the problem, nor particularly appropriate. It emphasised the
importance of involving primary care workers in the helping
process and it specifically identified a variety of primary
care workers, social workers, GPs, probation officers and
community nurses who "should be prepared to identify problem
drinkers and manage many themselves" (Advisory Committee on
Alcoholism 1978). It also recognised, however, that there were
problems attached to expecting primary workers to carry out
such a role, in that primary workers often failed to recognise
the alcohol misuse that lay behind their client's presenting
problem and when they did recognise it, they were often
hesitant to deal with it because they lacked the necessary
confidence, training and resources. The need for adequate
training of primary workers in the identification and
management of alcohol problems was taken up in the Advisory
Committee Report on Education and Training (1979). The
Services Report, however, went beyond advocating training by

recognising the need of primary care workers for the support
of a multi-disciplinary team of specialists to advise and help
them in the management of problem drinkers.

THE WORK OF THE MAUDSLEY ALCOHOL PILOT PROJECT

Many of the recommendations in The Pattern and Range of
Services had sprung from the research findings of the Maudsley
Alcohol Pilot Project which began in 1973 and ended in 1977.
In their 1974 general population survey the MAPP found that
those respondents who reported the heaviest alcohol
consumption and the most problems from drinking had a contact
rate with primary care workers which was three times higher
than the rest of their sample, yet as far as could be
detected, none of them had received any help specifically for
their drinking problems (Shaw et al, 1978). The MAPP report
hypothesised from their studies that there were three major
factors underlying the inadequate response of primary care
workers:

1. Anxieties about **role adequacy** through not having the
   information and skills necessary to recognise and
   respond to drinkers.
2. Anxieties about **role legitimacy** through being
   uncertain as to whether or how far drinking problems
   came within their responsibilities.
3. Anxieties about **role support** through having nowhere
   to turn for help and advice when they were unsure how
   or whether to respond.

The MAPP team adopted an overall theoretical term which
conceptually combined these three interacting components.
Workers who did not know how to respond, who were unsure
whether they should respond or not and who felt unsupported in
making any response were defined as experiencing "role
insecurity". All three aspects of role insecurity were seen
as being basically caused by deficiencies either in the
workers' training or in their working situation. It was felt
that, whereas role insecurity was caused initially by agents
feeling unprepared both intellecutally and situationally to
respond, ultimately it was manifested by them being unprepared
emotionally to respond. This emotional expression of role
insecurity was termed "low therapeutic commitment".

THE COMMUNITY ALCOHOL TEAM APPROACH

Workers who expressed a high degree of therapeutic commitment
were found by the MAPP to be distinguished from others by four
major characteristics:

1. They were experienced in working with drinkers.
2. They were working, or had worked in the past, in a situation in which role support was available.
3. They had received a training in counselling.
4. They had clinical knowledge about alcohol and alcohol related problems, for instance, how to recognise acute withdrawal symptoms and the likely physical, psychological and social consequences of excessive drinking.

An examination of how these factors interacted to produce high levels of therapeutic commitment identified role support as being the crucial factor which could be provided for inexperienced workers and be expected to make some improvement in their response. The addition of clinical information and counselling training was found to make no impression on role insecurity if support was unforthcoming. However, if it occurred in conjunction with role support it was found to facilitate the development of therapeutic commitment (Cartwright, 1980). In order to test the hypothesis that providing role support would increase workers' therapeutic commitment and hence improve their response, two of the MAPP researchers took on full-time responsibility for providing such support and adopted the name "Community Alcohol Team" (CAT).

> The CAT was referred to as a **community** team because its focus of operation was in the community, not in hospitals.
> The CAT was called an **alcohol** rather than an alcoholism team, because it was attempting to help agents respond to a variety of problems associated with alcohol ...
> The CAT was called a **team** because it involved agents from different professions. The two full-time members were a consultant psychiatrist and a senior social worker.
>
> (Shaw et al, 1978)

The function of the CAT was to provide role support for groups of primary care workers, whilst simultaneously providing them with information, training in skills and helping them gain experience in working with drinkers. They attempted to do this in two ways: by training courses and by a consultation service. Thus, the major difference between the CAT approach to encouraging workers to respond to drinking problems and the pre-1978 attempts via official circulars was that it was recognised that merely giving agents a rational account of the size of the problem and their responsibility to respond was not sufficient. The Maudsley CAT experiment was based on research conclusions that workers must be given active help, that their rights and responsibilities must be clarified, that

The Salford Experiment

they must be given information about the specific problems
involved in actual cases, that they must be given concrete
proposals as to how to translate this information into
therapeutic responses and, most important of all, they must be
supported and supervised when carrying out their response
(Shaw et al, 1978).

THE SALFORD COMMUNITY ALCOHOL TEAM

The MAPP consultation service and training courses were pilot
experiments to see whether the response of primary workers
could be improved through offering training and role support.
The work of the Salford Community Alcohol Team described in
the rest of this chapter was an attempt to take this model and
adapt it to the requirements of a district-based community
alcohol service. In the transition from a pilot project to a
district-based service the way in which the model was applied
underwent some change. In essence, however, the aim of the
Salford project was similar to that of the MAPP CAT: to
improve the response of primary care workers to clients with
alcohol-related problems through the provision of role support
and training.

Salford is an urban area with a population of around
240,000. The area is served by three probation teams of
approximately 25 officers in total and ten Social Services
patch teams containing approximately 80 social workers and
social work assistants (social service officers). There are
eight health centres with attached CPNs, health visitors and
district nurses and around 50 of Salford's 128 GPs are health
centre-based. Secondary resources include a large psychiatric
hospital within the grounds of which is based a regional
alcohol treatment unit (ATU) called the Kingswood Clinic;
there is another psychiatric unit attached to the district
general hospital. There are several hostels available to
problem drinkers from the area but day centre facilities for
drinkers are limited. The Greater Manchester and Lancashire
Council on Alcoholism (GMLCA) offers a counselling service to
Salford residents. Compared to many other areas then, there
were a number of specialist services for problem drinkers
already in existence when the development of a CAT was first
thought of, which meant that it was possible to consider
developing a service which did not involve the provisions of
direct client care. At the same time it was clear that the
majority of problem drinkers in Salford were not coming into
contact with existing secondary level services. It was
estimated that in 1981 there were approximately 2,500 adults
in Salford with drinking problems, which was a conservative
estimate. In the same year data from the Salford psychiatric
case register showed that only 355 people with a primary,
secondary or tertiary diagnosis of alcohol problems came into

124

contact with either psychiatric or specialist alcohol
services.

Research done in Salford in 1980 (personal communication,
1980) had found that 35-40% of patients referred by primary
care workers failed to keep their first appointment at the
ATU. A subsequent survey initiated by ATU staff found that
primary workers wanted to see a number of changes in existing
service provision: (1) a more rapid response to referrals;
(2) a move by specialist staff from the hospital setting into
the community.

The development of a CAT was seen as a a way of meeting
these needs, which would also begin to tackle the identified
problems of low service uptake combined with the high
attrition rate when specialist referral did occur. It hoped to
address these latter problems by promoting the early
identification and management of problem drinkers in the
community by primary care workers themselves.

In 1983 funding was made available to finance a three
year experimental project to evaluate the effectiveness of the
CAT approach as described by the Maudsley group. Two full-
time CPN posts and one social worker post were funded, two by
the DHSS and one by SHA. These posts comprised the
establishment of the CAT. In addition, two research posts
were funded through health authority/Local Authority finance.
Part-time secretarial help was funded from a combination of
DHSS and joint finance monies.

SELLING THE SERVICE

The three members of the CAT were appointed at different times
between July and August 1983. Their first step was to try to
"sell" the service to primary workers, which at this point was
seen as promoting an assessment service and on-going support
to primary workers in their subsequent case management. All
assessments would occur jointly with the worker wherever
possible and there was a commitment to respond within 24 hours
to requests for help when necessary.

Selling this service was done through the distribution of
leaflets and posters and through extensive personal contact.
In the first few months the CAT attended team meetings of all
the probation officers, social workers, CPNs, health visitors
and district nurses involved in the project and followed up
these meetings by less formal visits to workers' bases.
Information about the service was sent out to all GPs via the
FPC mailings, several Section 63 meetings attended and GPs
were visited personally at their surgeries. It was a period
when the CAT assumed a very high public profile and it was
also a time when it received a lot of feedback from primary
workers themselves about the kind of service which was
proposed.

Adaptation Following Primary Worker Feedback

Previous experience of specialist community teams had produced amongst some workers, particularly social services staff, conflicting concerns about getting involved with these services. Firstly, there was the view that the sudden growth of such teams would leave generic workers "nothing to do but give out bus passes" and, somewhat paradoxically, there was also resentment towards teams who "never got their hands dirty", offering a consultative service.

> They come in and advise us on how it should be done, that's all very well but it is us that has to do it! What we need is people who will actually see our clients and do something for them.
>
> (Salford social worker)

Probation officers and CPNs were the least likely to express such views and tended to be very positive about the service offered. Other workers, however, were much more ambivalent, many seeing it as an irrelevance, because they said they never saw any clients with alcohol problems. Other workers saw it as an attempt to foist extra work on them at a point when their resources were already stretched.

It became clear to the CAT that they needed to be seen as offering more than consultation if the service was to become extensively used. The initial shift from the consultative model came when the team agreed to carry out assessments plus short-term intervention if required, during and after which the primary worker would continue to see the client with CAT support. The shift in emphasis, then, was from advising workers on good practice to actually modelling that good practice. Throughout CAT contact with the client, however, the primary worker was to be kept closely involved and the ultimate responsibility for the client remained with the primary worker. The service which evolved, therefore, was seen as an acknowledgement of the differing levels of therapeutic commitment amongst primary workers, which was shown by the fact that some workers appeared to be requiring much more support than others before they would even begin to engage with the service. The flexibility of the service which evolved meant that the team was able to steer a middle course between "taking clients over" and "never getting their hands dirty".

Even given the greater degree of client involvement than was originally envisaged, the service model described above remained unacceptable to GPs. While very welcoming of the idea of a rapid response to their patients, the GPs unanimously argued that they had insufficient time to become involved in the on-going management of problem drinkers. Having already established the precedent of adapting the

service to meet workers' needs and with the anxiety that the
group thought most likely to come into contact with problem
drinkers would not use the service otherwise, the decision was
taken that the team should offer a direct referral service to
GPs. This resulted in a two-tier model of service delivery,
with direct client referrals being accepted from GPs and a
more consultative service being offered to other primary care
workers.

The emphasis on meeting the primary care workers was an
important one because it enabled them to define what "role
support" meant to them. The team had started with a
preconceived notion of what such support should entail. It
was only through consultation with the workers themselves that
they came to realise that their idea of support was not, in
fact, what many workers felt they required.

THE EDUCATION AND TRAINING PROGRAMME

In order to evaluate the impact of training plus the clinical
service offered, only half the primary workers were actually
offered educational input (the "CAT and ED" group). The
others were offered the clinical/consultation service alone
(the "CAT" group).

In their initial contacts with primary workers, the CAT
tried to assess the workers' perceptions of their own training
needs. Although the majority of workers were unclear as to
their needs they did express a desire for information about
the problems associated with heavy drinking, indicators of
problem drinking and treatment approaches. They were also
more inclined to favour multi-disciplinary training over
single-discipline events, many workers commenting that it
would be useful to see how other agencies dealt with drinkers
and feeling that such events would promote inter-agency co-
ordination.

There were differences between the training events run by
the Salford CAT and those run by the MAPP team. The first was
the multi-disciplinary nature of the events run in Salford and
the other was the different emphasis placed on the group-based
discussion of on-going cases and workers' associated problems.
This was the primary teaching mode adopted by MAPP but played
only a relatively small part in the Salford training
programme. The Salford programme was based around a number of
short, one-day repeated courses, which was found to be the
format most acceptable to primary workers' line managers.
Nine day-events were held in all in the first two years of the
project. Four of these enabled the majority of workers to
attend an "Introduction to Alcohol-Related Problems" day,
three covered "Local Facilities" and two were on "Case Work
Skills". Table 6.1 shows the percentage of workers attending
different types of training events. Overall, 86% of the

workers offered training (with the exception of GPs) attended at least one day-event.

The experience of the CAT in offering training to GPs paralleled that of many other projects. Attempts were made to attract GPs via the medium of Section 63 meetings and drug company lunches but the attendance was always small. These separate events were planned when GPs expressed their unwillingness to attend multi-disciplinary training events; experience, however, showed them to be of limited usefulness. The question of the best way to input training to GPs remained unresolved during the period of project evaluation.

Table 6.1: **Percentage of Workers Offered Training Attending Particular Types of Training Days in the First Two Years of the Project**

	Introductory % Days	Facilities % Days	Case-Work % Days
Probation	40	60	20
Social Workers	84	42	58
SSOs	55	46	36
CPNs	100	67	83
Health Visitors	79	90	37

THE CLINICAL AND CONSULTATIVE ROLE OF THE CAT

The Clients

The CAT received 411 referrals in its first two years (Clement 1987). The term "referral" here describes any person about whom a primary worker consulted the CAT. It does not necessarily mean that they were seen by the CAT, although as it will be seen later, the majority were. Of the 388 clients for whom records were available, 72% were men and 28% women. Nearly all the clients referred were themselves problem drinkers, rather than members of drinkers' families. They ranged in age from 16-82 years, the average of the men being 38 years and of the women 43 years. A greater percentage of the men were single whereas over 55% of the women were living in a stable relationship. Over half the clients referred were unemployed.

Most clients had a long history of problem drinking, the median duration being 8 years, but the range reported was enormous, from one month to 50 years. Men were significantly more likely to report a longer history of problem drinking than were women. Eleven per cent of referrals had been drinking problematically for less than a year. The majority of clients, however, were experiencing a broad range of other problems at the point of referral to CAT and 17% were already in touch with more than one helping agency. There were very few differences between the clients referred at the beginning and at the end of the two year evaluation period.

Table 6.2: Referral Agent Profession

Referral Agent	% Total Referrals	Mean No. of Referrals per Worker *
General Practitioner	43	1.6
Probation Officer	20	3.9
CPN	19	5.7
Social Worker	9	.6
Health Visitor	2	.3
District Nurse	1	.1
Psychiatrist	3	-
Other	3	-

* Based on the number of all such workers in the area for whom the service was available.

The Referral Agents
GPs made 43% of all referrals, with an additional 6% of referrals being made by agents not defined as primary workers. Thus 51% of referrals were made by workers offered the advice

129

and support service. Probation officers and CPNs were much
more likely to use the service than were social workers and
health visitors and referrals made by district nurses were
negligible in number (see Table 6.2).

Workers offered education and training (the CAT and ED
group) were found to be more likely to use the service
initially than workers who were not (the CAT group). However,
the service use of CAT and ED workers was found to steadily
decline over the first two years of the project whereas the
referral rate of CAT group workers stayed relatively stable
(see Table 6.3). The initially higher service use of CAT + ED
workers was not a result of educational input as it was
apparent before the first training events occurred. It
appeared as though simply being told that training would be
offered was enough to facilitate service use.

Table 6.3: Number of Referrals to CAT in its First Two Years

Worker Group	Sept 83 – March 84	March – Sept 84	Sept 84 – March 85	March – Sept 85
CAT	76	58	45	33
CAT + ED	32	41	31	43
OTHER	6	7	5	9

* Missing data N=2

The CAT Service

Rapid Response. The evaluation showed that the team's
commitment to a rapid response to workers requests was
successfully met, with 84% of all assessments being carried
out within seven days of the workers getting in touch with the
CAT. Thirty per cent of all assessments were carried out
within 36 hours of referral.

Joint Assessments. One of the ways in which the CAT had hoped
to model good practice to workers was by conducting joint
assessments of the client at which the primary worker was
present. In offering a joint assessment the CAT was
emphasising that responsibility for the client remained with
the primary worker and that the CAT expected the worker to
remain involved with the client. In 13% of cases referred no
assessment at all occurred. Of the remainder, when GP and
non-primary worker referrals were excluded, 26% of all
assessments carried out were found to have occurred jointly
with the primary worker.

Degree of Client and Primary Worker Contact. There were marked differences between the professional groups in the mean number of contacts per case between the CAT and the primary worker's client (see Table 6.4). There was less contact per case between the CAT and probation clients than for the clients of any other worker. The greatest degree of contact occurred between the CAT and social service clients. As would be expected from the different forms of service offered there was less contact per case between the CAT and GPs than for other workers and those contacts they had were of a shorter duration. The mean duration of contact between the CAT and GPs was 12 minutes compared with 20 minutes for other workers.

Table 6.4: Contact with the CAT by Primary Workers and their Clients

	Mean Number of Contacts per Referral[*]			
	GPs	SWs	CPNs	POs
Between CAT + and Client	6.9	8.2	5.9	3.8
Between CAT and + Primary Worker	1.8	3.6	3.1	3.2
Between CAT and + Other Resource	2.6	5.3	1.8	2.2

[*] Administrative contacts and those of less than 10 minutes duration are excluded.
+ These categories are not mutually exclusive e.g. a client and worker may both have been present at the same contact with the CAT.

Table 6.5 shows the number of contacts between the CAT and workers per case, expressed as the percentage of cases where workers had a particular number of contacts. If the figures for workers other than GPs are examined it can be seen that in 55% of cases there were fewer than three contacts between the CAT and the worker making the referral. In 10% of these cases assessment of the client did not occur, either because the contact had been for advice and information only or because the client was unobtainable. This leaves 45% of cases where assessment occurred but where the workers themselves were not in contact with the CAT on more than two occasions (excluding administrative contact). In only 15% of cases were there more than five contacts between the worker making the referral and the CAT. The extent of contact necessary before consultation and/or support can be said to have taken place will vary depending on the needs of the worker and the viewpoint of the reader. Bearing in mind that the mean duration of all these contacts was 20 minutes, and establishing an arbitrary cut-off point at three worker/CAT contacts, it can be said that in at least 45% of cases some meaningful degree of consultation about the client occurred between the CAT and referring agent.

Table 6.5: Number of Contacts Between the CAT and Workers

	Number of Contacts					
	1	2	3	4	5	5+
% GP Cases	56	25	10	3	3	2
% Other Cases	29	26	14	10	7	15

Referrals to Different CAT Members. In the initial stages of the project it had been questioned whether the professional background of the CAT workers was important. Would nurses prefer to refer to another nurse and social workers to a social worker? Although the evidence suggests that workers were more likely to refer to their own profession in that the CAT social worker (who had also had probation experience) was found to have carried out a greater percentage of social work and probation referrals than either of the CPNs, the data also show that one of the CAT CPNs carried out 66% of the CPN client assessments, whereas the second CPN carried out little more than the social worker. This suggests that personality factors are also important variables to consider.

THE EVALUATION OF THE CAT's IMPACT

Research Design and Measures

For the purpose of the evaluation the primary care workers were divided into three groups, a group to whom the team made no input, a group designated "CAT" which had access to the clinical/support service and a group designated " CAT + ED" which, in addition to the clinical/support service, was also

offered education and training. The practical problems in
allocating workers to these groups have been described
elsewhere (Clement, 1987). Workers operating from the same
base were all allocated to the same group and an effort was
made to ensure they served roughly similar populations
demographically. There were no significant differences
between the groups on any of the baseline measures taken. By
comparing the group with the CAT and the CAT + ED groups, it
was hoped to isolate changes which could be attributed to the
team. By comparing the CAT and CAT + ED groups it was hoped to
isolate the additional impact of the provision of education
and training.

Two main measures of change were used, the AAPPQ (Version
4), used by the MAPP to measure changes in the levels of
therapeutic commitment of primary workers, and semi-structured
interviews. The AAPPQ was distributed to all the primary
workers in Salford at the beginning of the CAT project and at
12 and 24 months into the project. Baseline interviews were
not able to be conducted but a stratified random sample of
primary workers were interviewed between 6 to 9 months into
the project and again a year later. The interviews used
"vignettes" in an attempt to assess the identification and
management skills of workers in relation to problem drinkers.
They also looked at how workers dealt with the last problem
drinker they had seen (Clement, 1987). Because of anticipated
compliance problems, a shortened version of the AAPPQ was
developed for use with GPs. Because this necessitated a
separate analysis of their responses, the impact of the team
on GPs will be discussed separately and the following findings
relate only to other workers.

Knowledge of Alcohol and Alcohol-Related Problems

This was measured by a multiple choice scale which comprised
Section C of the AAPPQ. It was anticipated that workers
offered the CAT service would increase their scores on this
measure to a greater extent than the group and that workers
offered formal educational input would do better than workers
who only had access to the consultative services. Although
there was found to be a trend in this direction, the
differences observed were not great enough to reach
statistical significance.

Changes in Therapeutic Commitment

This was measured by Section B of the AAPPQ. The degree of
therapeutic commitment expressed by the group remained
unchanged over the period of project evaluation. There were,
however, significant increases in the expressed therapeutic
commitment of workers to whom the CAT offered a service (see
Table 6.6).

Whilst in the first year educational input did not
significantly affect this overall increase, its impact was

noticeable in the second year of the project when workers
offered training continued to gain in therapeutic commitment
whilst the other workers' scores remained stable.

Table 6.6: Difference Scores on Therapeutic Commitment Scale
Between the Three Occasions the AAPPQ was Administered

	Mean Difference Scores		
	1983 - 84 *	1984 - 85	1983 - 85 **
CONTROL (N=18)	- 3.83	+ 3.67	- 0.17
CAT (N=25)	+ 4.80	+ 0.08	+ 4.88
CAT + ED	+ 8.86	+ 4.55	+ 13.41

* $F = 8.899$, $p < .001$ ** $F = 10.769$, $p < .001$

Further analysis of these data showed that unlike the other
professional groups, social workers did not show an increase
in therapeutic commitment following training. This possibly
supports the MAPP's original contention that separate training
should be offered to each profession. It certainly supports
the contention that educational input needs to be sensitive to
the needs of different professional groups.

An interesting finding was that changes in therapeutic
commitment were not influenced by the number of referrals
workers had made to the CAT. To some extent, however, this is
an artefact of the further finding that workers who made more
than one referral had higher levels of therapeutic commitment
to begin with, and the implications of this are discussed
later.

Changes in Feelings of Role Support
The MAPP had indicated that a feeling of being supported when
working with drinkers was a necessary pre-condition to the
development of therapeutic commitment. The provision of role
support had been one of the main aims of the Salford CAT.
Whereas workers in the group reported a small decrease in
feelings of support, as measured by the AAPPQ, workers offered
the CAT service showed an increased experience of such
support. Workers in the CAT and ED group showed a slightly
greater, but non-significant, increase over workers in the CAT
group. These positive changes were restricted to the first

year of the project and no further increases were observed in
the second year of the project.

Identification of Drinking Problems Among Clients

The interview data showed that the number of problem drinkers
whom workers (other than GPs) identified on their case loads
increased between 1984 and 1985 (see Table 6.7). This
increase was not apparent amongst those workers who were not
offered the CAT service. Amongst those workers who were,
there was an overall increase of 38% in the number of
drinkers identified. Although for each individual worker the
increase was small, taken together it represents a substantial
increase in the number of problem drinkers identified.

Table 6.7: Percentage of Problem Drinkers among Combined Case-
Loads

	1984		1985	
	CONTROL	CAT/CAT+ED	CONTROL	CAT/CAT+ED
	N=17	N=33	N=17	N=33
Total no. of cases	627	1,507	659	1,336
Total no. of problem drinkers	60	160	71	220
% of problem drinkers	10	11	11	17

This increase in identification did not appear to result from
an increased knowledge of the indicators of an alcohol
problem. When measured by the interview vignettes such
knowledge was shown to be relatively stable and already
reasonably extensive. It seems more likely to have been due
to the increased frequency with which workers were found to be
discussing drinking with their clients at an early stage of
their involvement with them. The implications of this for
training packages are clear.

Changed Patterns of Management of Problem Drinkers

It has already been stated that data from the interviews showed that primary care workers were more willing to discuss drinking with clients and at an earlier stage of their involvement with them. This was found to be reflected as an increased awareness of how much alcohol their clients were consuming (see Table 6.8) which was not apparent amongst the control group (Clement, 1987). There was no firm evidence, however, that this resulted in workers being more willing to offer advice on changing consumption to their clients. What was shown, in the AAPPQ data, was an increase in the use of specialist services in almost all cases accounted for by referrals to the CAT. The interview data also showed that primary workers were likely to spend substantially more time with clients who accepted referral than with problem drinkers whom they did not refer or who rejected referral. This could be argued to suggest that referral to the CAT did facilitate workers' involvement with problem drinkers, although not necessarily in terms of focusing directly on the drinking.

Table 6.8: **Percentage of Workers having a "Clear Idea", "Some Idea" or "No Idea" of the Alcohol Consumption of the Last Problem Drinker they have Seen**

Worker Response	1984 (N=27)	1985 (N=27)
A Clear Idea	22%	44%
Some Idea	15%	22%
No Idea	63%	33%

Impact of Education and Training

It has already been noted that primary workers offered education and training in addition to access to the clinical/support service continued to increase in therapeutic commitment over the two years studied, whilst workers only offered access to the clinical/support service ceased to improve after the first year. This increased therapeutic commitment was manifested by an increase in a variety of positive attitudes amongst workers offered training whilst the other workers showed a narrower range of attitude change.

While the number of CAT referrals from primary workers not offered training remained stable at 73 or 74 per annum,

referrals from workers offered education decreased by 42% from
134 in the first year to 78 in the second year (see Table
6.3). Unfortunately, the number of workers lost to second
interview made it impossible to analyse the interview data in
terms of the small numbers involved. There is no firm
evidence, therefore, to support the hypothesis that this drop
in referral rates shows that workers offered training were
beginning to deal with more problem drinkers themselves. This
hypothesis, however, would be consistent with the increased
therapeutic commitment shown by these workers, given that they
were still receiving some support from the CAT on other cases.
Other explanations of this trend towards decreased referrals
such as disillusionment with the service, increased
utilisation of other referral points or a decrease in the
number of problem drinkers on caseloads are not backed up by
the available evidence. Comments made by some workers during
interviews support the view that workers offered education
were increasingly prepared to work with problem drinkers on
their own, while continuing to utilise the service in some
cases!

> Initially I used them to get a second opinion for the
> joint assessment and so on, but now I feel I would only
> need their advice if it was really complicated.
>
> (CPN)

The Identification of Early Problem Drinkers
There was no evidence that over its first two years the CAT
received an increasing number of referrals of earlier problem
drinkers. Neither was there any indication that the CAT had
changed workers' perceptions of problem drinkers themselves.
When asked during interview to spontaneously generate words
which they felt described problem drinkers, around half the
workers overall generated words which were predominantly
negative. No change was observed in this pattern between 1984
and 1985. Probation officers were far less likely than other
groups to view problem drinkers negatively, with only 27% of
POs generating negative words compared with 46% of social
workers, 48% of GPs and 54% of CPNs. Although workers had
shown themselves to be more willing to engage with problem
drinkers, there was no evidence that this had resulted in a
changed perception of these clients.

A survey carried out in the first six months of the
project (Clement, 1987) showed that the median duration of
drinking problems identified amongst primary worker clients
ranged between 5 and 10 years depending on the profession of
the worker. It may well be that the association of problem
drinking with certain negative client characteristics will
tend to remain unchanged until workers start to gain
experience of working with clients with less well-established
histories of alcohol misuse. The many referrals made to the

CAT service, however, was more indicative of the large number of people with serious drink problems in the population who had not been offered help previously than it was of a "new" client group coming into contact with services. There were no indications that the CAT was successful in facilitating the identification of earlier problem drinkers by workers.

There remains the question of whether the clients referred to the CAT contained a higher proportion of earlier problem drinkers than would usually be found among a treatment population. Although the median duration of problems among clients referred was eight years, 11% of clients had been drinking problematically for less than a year and 24% for less than three years. Unfortunately, no recent comparative data are available. It is impossible to say, therefore, whether the provision of the CAT service, which was reported to be more acceptable to many clients than hospital-based services, resulted in people being more likely to accept specialist input earlier in their drinking careers, or whether the knowledge of more acceptable services made it easier for workers to suggest referral to them at an earlier stage.

The Impact of the CAT on General Practitioners

GPs made 43% of referrals to the team. There was considerable variability in the number of referrals individual GPs made, with some practices being particularly heavy service users and others making few referrals. The potential of GPs in facilitating the treatment of problem drinkers, however, is illustrated by the fact that two group practices (not health centre-based) were responsible for a greater percentage of referrals to the team than the entire Social Services Department.

All the GPs interviewed were extremely positive about the CAT service because of its community orientation and the rapidity with which patients were seen. They reported experiencing a much greater degree of support in dealing with patients with alcohol problems and increased feelings of role adequacy following the CAT's inception. As with other workers, however, there was no indication that the CAT had changed GPs views of what constituted an alcohol problem, nor their perception of problem drinkers as being "difficult" and "frustrating" patients.

There was some evidence, however, of an improved response from the interview data which showed that GPs had become more likely to run routine blood tests on patients they felt were problem drinkers and some indication of a decrease in the prescription of psychotropic medication unless detoxification was required. Changes in therapeutic commitment, however, were restricted to GPs within the CAT + ED group, which was a somewhat puzzling finding in the light of the fact that this group had, in fact, received little in the way of educational input. One possible explanation might be that it was the experience of working with more therapeutically committed colleagues in the primary health care teams which produced this effect and that GPs need to experience role support from their immediate colleagues as well as from an external agency before their degree of therapeutic commitment will change.

No attempt was made by the CAT to influence GPs through the kind of approach outlined by Anderson in Chapter 3 and, in this instance, the work of the CAT was clearly closer to that of an "alcoholism" than an "alcohol" team. The service offered, however, did appear to lead to some beneficial changes and the relationships formed between the CAT and GPs during this period could be said to have laid the foundations upon which new initiatives could be built.

LIMITATIONS OF THE COMMUNITY ALCOHOL TEAM APPROACH

District midwives, health visitors and social workers were the groups who made the least use of the CAT consultative/support service. They were also the groups with the lowest levels of expressed "therapeutic commitment". Analysis of the AAPPQ data showed that regardless of professional group, workers with the lowest initial levels of therapeutic commitment were less likely than other workers to use the CAT service. The fact that whole professional groups expressed less therapeutic commitment than others, however, can be attributed to a number of factors:

1. Low levels of education and training regarding alcohol and alcohol problems.
2. Low levels of recognition of clients with alcohol problems on case-loads (low role adequacy).
3. Low levels of motivation attributed to clients who were identified as problem drinkers (low role adequacy).
4. Uncertainty about whether or not working with drinkers was part of their job (low role legitimacy).
5. Low priority given to involvement with problem drinkers by workers' management (lack of role support).

All these factors were brought out by workers during the interviews and are very similar to those variables described by the MAPP. The theory argues that the provision of education and role support will increase workers' therapeutic commitment through improving their feelings of role adequacy and role legitimacy. The CAT was seen as the vehicle through which training and support could be delivered. The Salford research findings showed that although the CAT was effective in improving workers' feelings of role adequacy, it did not produce significant changes in workers' feelings of role legitimacy. The interview data showed that professional

groups who made limited use of the CAT service were those
whose management assigned a low priority to involvement with
problem drinkers. Two conclusions can be drawn: (1) role
legitimacy cannot be significantly influenced by an agency
(e.g. the CAT) which is external to the professional groups
own management, (2) role legitimacy is related to the priority
which workers´ managers place on involvement with problem
drinkers.

Role support from an external agency, therefore, will not
be significantly utilised unless workers are confident that
their management is supportive of their becoming involved with
clients´ drinking problems and, in a situation of scarce
resources, attaches a degree of priority to such work. There
did, however, appear to be an exception to this general rule
in the case of Salford CPNs. Although manifesting a
relatively high degree of therapeutic commitment and making
good use of the CAT service, these nurses did not feel that
their management gave much priority to involvement with
problem drinkers. The AAPPQ data, however, showed that
significant numbers of other primary care workers, in
particular GPs, saw CPNs as agents to whom they themselves
could refer problem drinkers. The referral practices of other
workers, therefore, created a situation in which CPNs were
being required to deal with significant numbers of problem
drinkers, despite this being assigned a low priority by their
management. This externally assigned role legitimacy meant
that they made good use of the CAT service. However, if one
compares their pattern of service use with that of probation
officers, a group who also manifested relatively high
therapeutic commitment and made good use of the CAT, some
interesting differences emerge.

Probation officers were the one group of primary care
workers who felt that their management assigned a relatively
high degree of priority to working with problem drinkers.
They were also the group with the lowest rate of contact
between the CAT and their clients. Although the average
number of discussions per case about clients referred to the
CAT was roughly the same for both CPNs and POs, CPN clients
received much more direct input from the team than did
probation clients (see Table 6.4). It can be argued
therefore, that POs were more likly to use the CAT in a
consultative fashion whilst CPNs were more likely to obtain
the kind of service for their clients which GPs were offered,
although remaining more closely involved with the process.
These differences in their pattern of service use appear to
reflect the priority their management placed on their
involvement with problem drinkers.

IMPLICATIONS OF THE RESEARCH FINDINGS FOR THE CAT MODEL

The evidence suggest that the CAT facilitated the management of problem drinkers by primary workers in the community in those cases where the worker had received training in doing so, from the CAT or elsewhere, and was employed by a service which assigned some priority to working with problem drinkers. In cases where the worker was expected by other primary care agents to work with problem drinkers there was a high rate of use of the CAT service, but workers were less likely to remain involved in on-going client care without high levels of role support, in terms of CAT/client contact. In cases where there was no expectation, whether from management or other professions, that the worker had a role to play in the management of alcohol problems, there was a much lower rate of

Figure 6.1: Factors Affecting Degree of Service Use and Degree of Involvement with Problem Drinkers

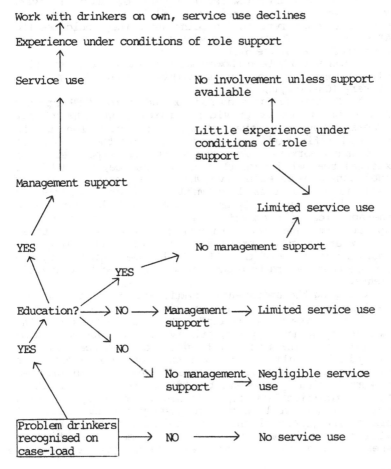

141

service utilisation and workers were even less likely to become involved in managing the problem without extensive support. Thus, there were organisational constraints on the degree to which the CAT was able to develop the therapeutic commitment of primary workers. It succeeded in so far as those constraints allowed. It could do little, however, to alter the priorities imposed on workers by their management. Lack of management priority, however, did not appear to have an impact on training uptake, with the exception of district nurses where management priority was so low that training was seen as irrelevant and the opportunity to participate was refused. Training appeared to be important in that it raised therapeutic commitment to a level where the evidence suggests that workers began to work with an increasing number of drinkers themselves, without, in some cases, CAT support.

When workers had a low level of role legitimacy, however, even given training, they were unlikely to increase in therapeutic commitment to the point where they would use the CAT service except when faced with a problem which could not be ignored (see Figure 6.1).

It has already been shown that training without effective role support will not increase involvement with problem drinkers (Cartwright, 1980).

The Salford findings do not contradict the MAPP emphasis on the importance of providing training and support for workers. They do, however, show that the provision of role support has first and foremost to come from the managers of the primary workers before the additional expertise of an external team will be utilised. In essence, the MAPP CAT model can only be effective when the primary care agency itself is therapeutically committed. The problem, then, is not the "therapeutically uncommitted agent" but rather the "therapeutically uncommitted agency". In the absence of support from management in working with drinkers in those cases where alcohol problems are being identified, the consultative role of the CAT will become minimised by the pressure from workers to engage in working directly with their clients.

Changing the therapeutic commitment of agencies is not something which the CAT alone can achieve. To do so it needs itself to receive "role support". It is fairly clear that the low priority attached by many primary care agencies to working with problem drinkers is due to a lack of resources which is making it difficult for many of them to carry out even their primary role effectively. Unless working with problem drinkers is clearly relevant to their central role, as it is for the Probation Service, it is highly unlikely that hard pressed managers will be able to justify the involvement of workers with these clients. When district nurses have 20 calls to make in one day, to expect them to have time to assess for alcohol problems is expecting a lot. For social

intervention to become involved themselves in working with
problem drinkers clearly has resource implications which need
to be addressed by the Local Authority. The "role support"
which the CAT needs in tackling the problem of the
therapeutically uncommitted agency, then, can be seen to
be evidence of political will in dealing with problems of
alcohol misuse, in terms of resources available to primary
care services. One lesson from DHSS circular 21/73 (DHSS,
1973) is that such political will at the local level is
unlikely to come into being without support from central
government (Arbery, 1984).

The arguments about the problems of implementing a
comprehensive community response, then, appear to have come
full circle. While lack of political will was identified many
years ago as the barrier to development in the non-statutory
sector, the Maudsley project argued that within the statutory
sector much could be done to implement community care within
existing resources by tackling the low therapeutic commitment
of individual workers. The Salford experiment has shown this
to be only partially true. Although the success that the CAT
has achieved with some groups of workers argues for the
integration of such a service into the overall network of
alcohol services, it is also apparent that such an approach
alone cannot facilitate a comprehensive community-based
service. Until sufficient resources are made available to
primary care agencies for them all to be able to take on board
working with drinkers, the CAT can only be seen as an
additional tier of specialist services, bringing specialist
services into the community rather than facilitating a truly
community-based response at the primary care level.

REFERENCES

Advisory Committee on Alcoholism. (1978) The Pattern and Range
    of Services for Problem Drinkers. DHSS and Welsh Office,
    London
Advisory Committee on Alcoholism. (1979) Report on Education
    and Training. DHSS and Welsh Office, London
Arbery, B. (1984) Community Care or Financial Expediency - A
    Critical Appraisal of Non-Hospital-Based Services for
    Problem Drinkers in England and Wales. Proceedings of
    the 30th International Institute of the Prevention and
    Treatment of Alcoholism, Athens, ICAA
Barker, R. (1982) An Investigation of the Effects of a CAT on
    Problem Drinkers, Primary Workers and existing fac-
    ilities in Salford. Research proposal to DHSS
Cartwright, A. (1980) The attitudes of helping agents towards
    the alcoholic client: the influence of experience,
    support,training and self-esteem. British Journal of
    Addiction, 75, 413-431
Cartwright, A., Harrison, J., Shaw, S. and Spratley, T.

The Salford Experiment

Cartwright, A., Harrison, J., Shaw, S. and Spratley, T. (1977) Implementing a Community Based Response to Problems of Alcohol Abuse. Report to DHSS by MAPP

Clement, S. (1987) An Evaluation of the Salford CAT. DHSS and SHA

DHSS (1973) Community Services for Alcoholics. Circular 21, London

DHSS (1975) Better Services for the Mentally Ill. HMSO, London

DHSS (1976) Priorities for Health and Personal Social Services in England. HMSO, London

Owens, E. Personal communication

Shaw, W., Cartwright, A., Spratley, T. and Harwin, J. (1978) Responding to Drinking Problems. Croom Helm, London

Chapter 7

CONSULTANCY AS PART OF COMMUNITY ALCOHOL TEAM (CAT) WORK

Terence Spratley

INTRODUCTION

My interest in consultancy work has a long history. In 1975,
Alan Cartwright, Stan Shaw and myself wrote our report to the
Department of Health and Social Security called Designing a
Comprehensive Community Response to Problems of Alcohol
Abuse. We suggested the development of CATs and listed
their possible functions. Our 1978 book, Responding to
Drinking Problems indicated that two of the main functions of
CAT's were to train primary care workers or general community
workers, and to support them in their work with drinkers.
These two functions of training and support can be carried out
in many different ways, but the way that has interested me the
most is using the "consultation process" in which it is
possible to carry out both these functions simultaneously.
The opportunity occurs for this when a worker in a general
community agency (general practitioner, social worker,
probation officer, community psychiatric nurse, etc) asks a
CAT worker for help with a client, and where the CAT worker
does not see the client but works indirectly.
    Learning consultancy skills is not easy. I believe that
consulting, and being consulted, by members of my own team has
been extremely useful for training me. Observing consultancy
and discussing with the consultants concerned what they were
thinking and saying has also helped me. I recognise that
others are not so fortunate as I am inasmuch as they do not
have easy access to other people's consultations. It is with
this in mind that I write this paper. I describe what I try
to do in my consultations. I have tried to reveal what is
going on in my head by listing some of the questions I ask
myself, and then explaining the reasons for the questions.
    Although I describe my own approach in the hope that
others may learn from it, I do not believe that other people
can assume my approach. My approach is based upon a
combination of beliefs, values, life experiences, preferences

and prejudices which are unique to me. The choice of language I use to express my ideas and actions will raise difficulties. I use words that derive from religion, psychotherapy and behaviour therapy and systems theory - words that will provoke strong reactions in different readers. Whereas in the actual consultation I try to use the words that workers use themselves wherever appropriate, here I have used words that are most significant to me and which help me to make best use of the consultation.

My object in consultation is to increase the therapeutic commitment of workers by increasing their feelings of role security - that is by helping the workers to think that they have the right to help alcohol clients (role legitimacy), and that they have the appropriate knowledge, understanding and skills for this task (role adequacy). Helping the worker to be as effective as possible with an actual client of itself increases therapeutic commitment. The concurrent training that I give is doubly helpful. It is hoped that workers go away from the consultation not only more effective with the client discussed but also with any future alcohol clients. I hope that they also recognise this. In my consultation work, I place special emphasis on the nature and quality of the "therapeutic relationship". This is to individual work what the "therapeutic ethos" is to an Alcohol Day Unit (see Alan Cartwright's chapter). Although there are many different forms of treatment which can help drinkers, in my opinion they will be more successful when they are offered in the correct context. This context for one-to-one work I call the therapeutic relationship, and it is a context which is created by the worker in order to help the client feel safe to change, to understand how to change, and perhaps even to want to change. It is a context in which the worker supplies accurate information relevant to the clients' needs to enable them to make their own choices for the future. It is a context in which clients may experience themselves as belonging, having value and being cared about. In my experience drinkers fail to change more often because of a failure of the therapeutic relationship than a failure of the actual treatment offered.

The style of consultation I am describing is appropriate only for one-to-one worker/client contact. When acting as consultant for family work I operate from a systems theory basis in which we use live team consultancy with a one-way screen. I do not act as consultant for group work as other members of the team are much better qualified to do this. I must stress again that my method of working is a personal one and cannot be entirely appropriate for others, but I hope that it may stimulate others to consider their own techniques. I should also state that most of my experience is of being consulted by agents of special interest rather than totally naive general community workers. This will perhaps not be true of most CAT workers.

THE PROCESS OF CONSULTATION

To save time, I like to have written information about the client beforehand. This includes a full history, the progress of treatment and the present problems. I like to have studied the material before the consultation. I usually start by asking workers to tell me about the client, not merely repeating what they have written, but highlighting important points. I may interrupt occasionally to clarify or investigate certain points. I also use all appropriate opportunities to promote discussion - my main teaching tool - to give knowledge, ideas, understanding and to correct misunderstanding. When they have finished, I ask them, what they think are the problems. Sometimes, I do the reverse, namely, I start by asking what are the problems before learning about the case, especially if I know the worker.

When workers presents their problem to me in a consultation, they usually say something like this: "Mr X keeps relapsing", or "Mrs Y does not recognise that she has an alcohol problem", or, "Mr W does not believe that he should be totally abstinent". Now I am sure that all these problems are real enough but I know from hard experience that for me to help the worker with this particular case I should try to understand **what is the worker's problem with this client.** My task in consultation is to help workers to understand and to overcome the factors which prevent them being more useful to the client. If I succeed, they will be in a better position to help their client. If I know them very well, I may at the beginning directly even ask, "What is your problem with this client?" If they are prepared to look at this then, before we discuss the client, we can go into their difficulties with the client. Workers may be well aware of difficulties and be only too happy to discuss them. They may say something like, "I have got to do well with this client as I am very worried about suicide, violence to children etc", or "I find it difficult working with a client who is so old". Sometimes workers may not recognise that they have a problem with the client or have identified the wrong problem for themselves. I do not usually persist in questioning them at this stage, but wait until I have a greater understanding myself.

Whilst the worker is talking to me about the client I am trying, of course, to learn about and understand the client. However, that is the simplest part of my task. In order to carry out a useful consultation I am also trying to understand many other things. I will list some of the questions that I may ask myself to gain understanding in the following rather arbitrary categories:

1. The client
2. The worker
3. The therapeutic relationship between the two
4. The practical aspects of the therapeutic setting
5. The relationship between worker and myself
6. The consultation setting
7. My own reactions

I do not need to ask all the questions. I select the key questions intuitively as the situation unfolds itself. The following is a selection of questions under each heading that I frequently find relevant and useful.

THE CLIENT

1. **Is a client under the influence of alcohol or drugs, or is his/her mental state affected by withdrawal or brain damage when seeing the worker?**
If this is the case then the information that the worker is obtaining may not be accurate especially if, as is often the case, the worker is unaware of these distorting factors.
2. **Why is this client in contact with this particular worker at this particular time?**
I find it very helpful to understand the exact process whereby the client and worker first came into contact. Many workers naively assume that clients make contact because they wish to change or "get better". Of course this may be the case but often it is not. Clients may be in contact to persuade an employee or a spouse that they are "doing something" about their drinking when in fact they are not doing anything to change this at all.
3. **Why do they drink like this, i.e. what factors are operating to increase and reduce drinking?**
Of course, it is never simple. All clients have many different factors operating both on and within themselves which will tend to maintain the drinking unchanged or increase or diminish it. These factors will inform the worker's drinking hypothesis for this client which should eventually influence the choice of therapy to be offered to the client.
4. **Does this client drink to the extent of causing harm? If not, why is the worker concerned about drinking?**
Some workers lack proper access to consultation for their non-alcohol clients. In consequence, they can attempt to use CATs for consultations where alcohol is not the most relevant issue.
5. **What harm physically, socially and psychologically is the client experiencing?**
I include here the degree of tolerance and severity of withdrawal symptoms. These latter will in my opinion be major factors in determining which clients will do better by becoming totally abstinent and which will be able to just

reduce their consumption. In my experience, it is very unlikely that those with severe withdrawal symptoms will successfully maintain reduced drinking without harm. Frequently the drinker may need help with the alcohol-related harm in its own right. This may even become a goal of treatment, e.g. to reduce the risk of alcohol-related violence.

6. **What other relevant facts of the client's personal, social and drinking history will enable me to develop a drinking hypothesis and assess what is an appropriate treatment contract?**

I find I can most easily understand people in terms of their history. People's present behaviour can be influenced by their earliest experiences as well as their most recent ones. Many workers fail to recognise how some clients are acting out past problems in their present drinking. A client's parenting experience is especially important.

7. **What is this client's present family and social situation?**

Apart from the obvious factors in a person's family and social life which affect drinking there are many very subtle dynamic situations, especially in families, which can be powerful influences for maintaining the status quo. Many workers fail to understand the nature and power of these homeostatic processes. In contrast, the potential within some families for facilitating change is also very great and can be mobilised if recognised.

8. **What is the client's own assessment of his/her drinking?**

A problem? Not a problem? I find it to be particularly vital to discover this. So often workers have no real idea of the client's own assessment, and operate on their own definition of the problem which maybe totally different from that of their client. For example, they may be working on the basis that the client should either cut down or stop drinking, whilst the client has not yet got as far as holding that drink causes any problems.

Clients go through many stages in a drinking career and it is important to ask how they assess their drinking and its consequences. Of course, their own description may not accord with reality nor even with their own inner beliefs. Nonetheless, their own "public position" is the best basis for any treatment contract that is negotiated between worker and client. The client can only honestly negotiate with the worker from the position that has been stated to the worker.

The earliest stage in a problem drinking career exists when clients state that they have no problems. This is followed by the stage where they acknowledge problems but do not attribute them to their drinking. The third stage starts with the client owning problems from his/her drinking; but of course this does not mean that the client judges that there is a need to change his/her drinking. The client may judge that on balance the benefits and problems of continuing to drink in the same manner outweigh the benefits/problems of changing. The next stage is when clients state that they want to change their drinking. For many clients this stage is the final stage, but for others, extra stages are necessary. These include the stage when clients say that they want to be totally abstinent as they have failed to successfully reduce their drinking by less radical measures. There may be stages of "relapse prevention" or of "sobriety maintenance". Of course, clients can rapidly change their position in either direction, but nonetheless a worker can only start from the client's present stated position. A crucial part of all therapy is to give the opportunity to clients to progress along the stages to a point which accords with the facts of their situation. If the worker does not know the client's stated view of their position, then all attempts at therapy are likely to be confused. I believe that helping a worker to recognise what the client's stated position is, and then forming a treatment contract on that basis, is one of the most important tasks of my consultation.

9. **Is the client a danger to self or others?**

It is important to recognise those who are actively suicidal or those who are likely to injure others. It is easy for workers to fail to recognise the morbidly jealous male who, in particular, can be very dangerous to his female partner. It is also important to be aware when small children are at serious risk from either the drinker or the drinker's partner. Recognising if severe withdrawal is likely and undertaking appropriate treatment with Diazepam and vitamins is necessary.

10. **Does the client also have a drug problem, a gambling problem or other serious problem that will materially affect the treatment of the drinking problem?**

Many clients have multiple problems. Decisions may have to be taken regarding problems other than the alcohol ones.

11. **What are the client's resources?**

What kind of physical, social, psychological and intellectual resources do clients possess which can be used to help them? What has been successful and what has failed, and why? It is clearly vital to match the help offered to the client's ability and to use that type of help. It is usually unwise to persist with treatment that has previously failed but I find that some workers lack the knowledge or skill to provide alternatives more in keeping with the client's resources.

THE WORKER

Whilst workers are talking to me about their client I am also observing them for a variety of verbal and non-verbal clues about themselves and their relationship with the client and also with me.

1. What are their levels of knowledge, understanding, skills and attitudes in working with drinkers?

Clearly, severe lack of knowledge and skills give the consultant great opportunities for education, but on the other hand, some workers bring great skills from other disciplines, and these skills can be directed to help the drinking client.

Understanding, of course, is not just intellectual; it needs to come from the heart. Some would use the word empathy to describe this. This type of understanding comes with experience, openness and compassion, and is not easily taught. Skills take time to develop. Role play and observing others are useful methods of teaching skills but in consultations one is often limited to a detailed description of "how it could be done".

2. How do they conceptualise alcohol problems and therapeutic processes and what therapeutic techniques do they prefer?

Some workers have limited ideas and models which need to be expanded to help understand the behaviour of alcohol clients.

Certain models can mitigate against appropriate work with a particular client. For example, an Alcoholics Anonymous disease model may not be useful to a client who has not got as far as acknowledging that the drink causes problems. Similarly, a worker who conceptualises all "depression" or "anxiety" as illness to be treated by drugs, is not likely to be helpful to a patient whose only real hope lies in learning other ways to cope with negative feelings. Prescribed drugs can prevent a client from recognising those life situations and attitudes which are mainly responsible for negative feelings. I try to provide workers with a simple alternative framework for conceptualising drinking problems and responding to them. If they accept this framework then consultation is easier. If they are either unwilling or unable to use my framework then I try to help them as far as possible using their own framework but sometimes that will not be possible if I believe that their framework is actively harmful. For example, GPs may believe their patient is ill, and that they ought to give long-term diazepine tranquillisers "to treat the anxiety of a drinker". I would hold that this is actively harmful to drinkers and that a double addiction could result. In these cases, I can only state my case and then say that if this treatment fails they may then like to consult me again when there might be a willingness to try alternative techniques. Of course, some clients put enormous pressures upon doctors to prescribe drugs and the consultant may need to strongly support a doctor who chooses to resist these pressures.

3. What ability does the worker have to learn and develop new skills?
Some workers are very open, flexible, intelligent and keen to learn. Others are not. It is important to recognise potentials and limitations and not to threaten but to make the consultation very safe and to set realistic objectives for training.

4. What are the inconsistencies and contradictions and significant omissions in the account given by the worker?
These usually give me clues to the worker's difficulties with the client or with me. Some workers seem repeatedly to get into the same difficulties and examples from previous clients can help them to recognise a pattern in their behaviour, providing this is done with tact and sensitivity. Some workers have particular problems with, for example, the young or the elderly, or with men or women. It is for this reason that I believe CAT workers should keep files on workers as well as clients; it can save a lot of time.

THE THERAPEUTIC RELATIONSHIP

I must repeat that in my opinion more workers fail to help their clients because of problems in this area than for any other reason. Many alcohol clients have great difficulties in forming relationships. It is vital for workers to understand their clients' difficulties in this regard and to act positively to assist them in overcoming their difficulties. But, of course, a relationship is between two people and I often discover that it is the worker who is preventing the development of a therapeutic relationship. I am firstly guided by Mother Teresa of Calcutta on the four general principles for helping others, which are as follows:

1. Is the worker giving the client the truth, as much truth as the client can understand, accept and assimilate at that time?
So often I find that workers are not being frank with their clients. Some workers try to cover up their mistakes rather than be open with the client. Other workers are unwilling to admit their uncertainties about therapy. I am also interested to discover how workers handle dishonest statements, contradictions and evasions by clients. Do they collude with these or do they bring them into the open at the right time? Confronting issues is very helpful and is a key to growth. Understanding the reasons for lack of frankness and helping clients to become more open is vitally important.

2. Does the worker love the client?

By this I mean are they working for the welfare of the other person. Sadly, workers are sometimes more concerned to have a quiet life than to work properly. Working with drinkers takes time, effort, commitment and courage. Very often workers are working primarily for someone else's welfare, not the client's. To keep their manager satisfied, to keep themselves busy, to obtain funds for the agency - these are common ways in which client's interests are sabotaged.

3. Is the worker serving the client?

Serving clients is the opposite of controlling or manipulating them. Service implies offering skilled help which the client may choose to accept or reject.

Many workers have a tendency to control clients and, of course, many clients are only too happy to collude with this. To take away responsibility from clients, or to collude with them in their reluctance to take responsibility for their choices, is, in my view, a critical mistake. I try to be very alert to the use of words and phrases such as, "he can't pass a pub without going in", "he needs good accommodation before he can stop drinking", "his wife must come back before he will change". These phrases usually indicate that the focus of control has passed from client to worker and the relationship has ceased to be one of service.

Some workers use threats to manipulate the client. Threats are incompatible with a good therapeutic relationship - they represent coercion not cooperation.

4. Is the worker happy to be with the client?

To be an effective helper one has to be fulfilled and satisfied by the work. If workers have persistent negative feelings with a client, then something is wrong. If they cannot understand and alter this situation, their emotional responses could result in them harming not helping the client. It is for this reason that I often directly ask a worker, "How do you feel about this client?" Workers may sometimes know exactly how they feel and be prepared to honestly discuss these feelings. Sometimes they may not openly express their feelings to me or may actually be totally unaware of their own feelings. They may express verbally feelings which are in total contradiction to non-verbal signs. Powerful feelings in workers undoubtedly affect the therapeutic relationship, especially when they are unaware of their true feelings. Happiness is not a guarantee of an effective relationship. Some workers fail to recognise when they are in trouble with a client. This can be due to simple inexperience, a lack of knowledge, or of worker counter-reactions (the emotional reactions triggered off in workers by their clients). A classic example of the latter is when workers so strongly want to be successful that they are unable to recognise all the indications that therapy is failing.

153

I am always very attentive when workers use superlatives about a client - "he is the best/worst", "the least/most", etc. Any extreme statement nearly always indicates such a counter-reaction. It is vital to discuss the counter-reaction. "Who in your past does this client most remind you of?" is a question I ask workers to help them understand their reaction to the client. Of course, workers cannot avoid bringing their own past into the situation. If they can understand this they can be helped to avoid unhelpful reactions to the client. I am fortunate in having colleagues with psychotherapy training who can help workers to work through their counter-reaction problems.

Broadly speaking the counter-reactions result whether from role insecurity, or from past and present problems in the worker's own life, i.e. counter-transference (see Alan Cartwright, Chapter 13).

5. What are the stated goals of the contract and are they appropriate?

Without a good therapeutic relationship it is not possible to negotiate a therapeutic contract with clients. I sometimes find that workers are attempting to help drinkers on the basis of dishonest, unloving, manipulative, unhappy relationship - a hopeless task.

As part of a good therapeutic relationship there needs to be an explicit mutually agreed contract. Of course, I am particularly interested in whether the goals chosen are total abstinence or reduced drinking - but also whether any chosen goal is appropriate and compatible with the client's stated position.

6. What are the agreed means of achieving those goals and are they appropriate?

The means agreed upon should be within the resources of both client and worker.

7. What rules of therapy are there?

I believe that workers should set down their rules and their limits which their clients should be free to accept or reject. No rules and no limits result in an insecure client. Workers must be realistic about the conditions they can cope within the particular setting in which they work.

PRACTICAL ASPECTS OF THE THERAPEUTIC SETTING

Is the worker's working situation interfering with treatment?

It is important for consultants to gain as much understanding of a worker's working situation as possible. I refer not just to the physical setting where the work takes place, but also the rules regarding the work within the agency, agency expectations of the worker and management and hierarchical problems. I have often discovered that workers are being sabotaged in their work with clients by members of their own agency; this may be deliberately done or unconsciously brought about. I often find that managers and high status people, like doctors, disrupt potentially successful therapy of workers because of envy or threats to their own ways of working. Helping workers to understand this can allow them to attempt to re-negotiate more favourable circumstances. I have known workers deciding to leave their agencies when, after several consultations, they recognise that their working setting makes good work impossible for them.

THE RELATIONSHIP BETWEEN THE WORKER AND MYSELF

What is the quality of the consultation relationship - am I being truthful, loving, serving and joyful?
The dynamics between a worker and consultant can be complex at times. Consultants may feel role insecure or need to boost the reputation of their agency. It is easy for workers to assume childlike roles and for consultants to assume parental roles in consultation. These counter-transferences may emerge as excessive attempts to please or even to rebel.

THE CONSULTATION SETTING AND EXPERIENCE

1. **How much time do we have at our disposal?**
   I try to be realistic about what can be achieved in support and training in the time available.
2. **Is this the best available setting in which to conduct this consultation?**
   Privacy and the freedom from distraction and interruption are helpful to us both.
3. **What is the emotional impact of the consultation upon the worker?**
   Exposing one's work to others can be very threatening, especially to experienced workers. It is important for consultants to accept their own mistakes and misunderstandings without loss of self-esteem. I find that I have already made most therapists' errors myself and sharing my experience of similar errors can sometimes be valuable to workers, and help them with any feelings related to role insecurity.
   At the University of Kent Alcohol Interventions Training Unit Diploma Course in Alcohol Counselling and Consultation, I facilitate consultations in multi-disciplinary groups. I use the group process to bring all members' knowledge and experience into the consultation and I also use the group to develop the consultation skills of its members. However, group consultation is very complicated and I value the presence of another experienced colleague with me in these groups. It should not be forgotten how threatening group consultations can be and how easy it can be to damage another worker's sense of role security.

MY OWN REACTIONS

What are my reactions in this consultation?
I try to watch myself carefully to pick up my own counter-reactions to both client and worker. My counter-reactions, like the worker's, may be due to role insecurity or counter-transference problems. Strong negative emotions in the consultation are an indication that something is happening to me. I try to become aware of the causes so I do not pass my problem onto the worker. Getting jokey or exaggerating or showing off are all behavioural cues I ought to notice and understand. I personally try to be careful not to be "successful" in the consultation, as that could lead me to control or manipulate the worker and thus harm both worker and clients in the long term.

CONCLUSIONS

Finally, I would like to give you this advice as potential consultants:

1. As consultants you should not forget that you are modelling patterns of behaviour to the worker.
2. You should keep good records of the session and ideally send a report to the worker. I ask them to record any advice that I have given.
3. You should separate consultancy from supervision which carries management responsibility.
4. Any CAT should carefully plan how it sets up its consultancy services. There are many different ways in which these can be developed and carried out.
5. You should be a competent experienced alcohol worker and have a comprehensive understanding of alcohol problems and case management which can be adapted and modified to cover different types of worker. Psychotherapy training or personal awareness training, even if limited, is very useful to consultants.
6. You should ideally have access to a therapeutic system such as the one we have at Mount Zeehan, which can respond rapidly to any client who is beyond the ability of the worker to help. Resist the tendency to take clients unnecessarily.
7. You should be part of a team whose members you can consult regularly when you have problems in working with clients or in consultation work. The best training for consultancy is consulting and being consulted by members of one's own Community Alcohol Team. I am extremely grateful for and to my team of colleagues here in Canterbury. The debt I owe them is enormous.

REFERENCES

Cartwright, A., Shaw, S. and Spratley, T. (1975) <u>Designing a Comprehensive Community Response to Problems of Alcohol Abuse</u>. Maudsley Alcohol Pilot Project, London
Shaw, S., Cartwright, A., Spratley, T. and Harwin, J. (1978) <u>Responding to Drinking Problems</u>. Croom Helm, London

Chapter 8

OLD WINE IN OLD BOTTLES: WHY COMMUNITY ALCOHOL TEAMS WILL NOT WORK

Stephen Baldwin

INTRODUCTION

The formation of Community Alcohol Teams (CATs) has been a focus of alcohol services development across Great Britain, since the intitial Maudsley Alcohol Pilot Project (MAPP) experiment (Cartwright et al, 1975). It will be argued here that the validity and utility of the CAT approach is questionable and that it will have only limited success in establishing and maintaining high quality services for people who have alcohol problems. This conclusion is based on the experiences of other forms of Community Team, in particular, Community Elderly Teams and Community Mental Handicap Teams.

THE EARLY DEVELOPMENT OF THE CAT MODEL

The Maudsley research made specific recommendations about the proposed functions of CATs including: development of comprehensive services, creation of a centralised network of resources, inter-agency cooperation, educational provision for generic agents, identification/training of generic agents with a special interest in alcohol problems, provisions of support services to all agencies involved with drink problems, installation of new day services, research and monitoring. It also made some specific recommendations about the way in which subsequent CATs might be developed in the United Kingdom.

CAT Membership
The 1975 MAPP report emphasised the inclusion of particular professional groups in the team (i.e. doctors and social workers) and also hinted at the usefulness of excluding others: "representatives of the nursing profession, the Probation Service, the local Council on Alcohol ... might impair the cohesion and effectiveness of the team" (Cartwright et al, 1975).

Catchment Area
It was suggested that catchment areas should coincide with National Health Service (NHS) districts, with an average of 250,000 residents per district. One social worker from each NHS district should develop a full-time commitment to the CAT. If medical personnel were not available full-time, it was suggested that a psychiatrist would provide input to more than one CAT.

Physical Siting
Minimal recommendations were made concerning physical facilities, ancilliary services, financial support or organisation/management for CATs. Administrative and managerial costs were seen as coming from existing NHS/Local Authority (LA) funding. Despite this lack of attention to implementation, however, establishment of a formal base was recommended on the grounds that it would confer advantages of joint finance, improved access, day care services, centralised record-keeping and provision of a focal contact point for other agencies.

Individual Casework
There was a recognition of the potential conflict between a high volume of casework commitments to clients and time available to provide support to other agents. The MAPP report suggested a balance between development of casework and other support services, with the emphasis placed on the provision of support services.

CATs and Councils on Alcohol
Some overlap between the function of CATs and Councils on Alcohol (CAs) was expected, although CAT members were assigned prime responsibility for support and advice to other agents. CATs were expected to exert a considerable influence over the activities of CAs, and the report recommended CAT control of training, support and coordination of CA counsellors and integration into statutory services.

CAT Responsibility
Various options for CAT responsibility were suggested, incuding the DHSS and community physicians. Although the danger of an increased medical orientation was recognised, responsibility to an appropriate social or medical group was recommended.

CAT Finance
In contrast to the funding for the MAPP research, it was suggested that finance for CATs ideally should be shared by combined medical, social and voluntary sources.

Although the 1975 report examined the role of the CAT in developing a comprehensive network of alcohol services, subsequent reports and <u>Responding to Drinking Problems</u> (Shaw et al, 1978) de-emphasised the role of the CAT in enhancing liaison between specialist alcohol services. Instead it focused on the role of support for primary care workers, in order to increase therapeutic commitment to people with alcohol problems.

Certain organisational problems remained unresolved. Finance and accountability of CATs were both dismissed as "not the important points".

Continued investment in specialist services was ensured with the emphasis on CAT members (i.e. psychiatric/social workers) assuming responsibility for the training of other non-hospital agents. The focus was on second-level interventions, with teaching, training and consultation services. First-level intervention (client casework) and third-level interventions (service development work) were assigned lower priority. CATs were seen as a component of specialist psychiatric services with psychiatrists and social workers as key members

ESTABLISHING COMMUNITY ALCOHOL TEAMS (CATs)

A recent survey of CATs in the United Kingdom (UK) (Clement, 1986) showed the extent to which these teams had evolved from the original formulation. CPNs were the dominant professional group amongst CAT members, followed by social workers. Only 6 out of 14 teams had access to a psychiatrist. Non-statutory agencies were represented in some of the larger teams, but overall the emphasis remained on NHS and social work personnel, with only 6 teams receiving Probation input. The size of the resident population of catchment areas varied widely from around 124,000 to 455,000 showing a departure from the concept of the NHS district-based CAT. Of more than 80 non-administrative, non-secretarial staff attached to CATs, only 25% provided a full-time input. Another quarter provided less than 5 sessions per week to the CAT.

Only 5 out of 14 CATs had been established in traditional NHS settings (e.g. day centres, regional treatment units). This development has not been consistent with the MAPP report, which recommended strong links with NHS buildings and staff. In contrast, 6 CATs have been established in their own unattached premises and 3 others have been sited in CA offices. This has been a shift of emphasis, and a small decrease in direct NHS links with CATs.

Examination of the survey data indicated that 6 CATs were established with the primary aim of first-level interventions (client casework). This represents another shift from the MAPP proposals which emphasised second-level interventions (teaching, training and support of other agents). Eight other CATs indicated a primary aim which included working with other agents. Data collected to record current activities indicated

that all CATs provided support or education to other agents,
12 CATs provided direct services to clients, 10 CATs indicated
service development work, half of the CATs provided public
education (e.g. schools), 4 CATs promoted industrial alcohol
policies.

No evidence of CAT control of training, support and
coordination of Councils on Alcohol was found in the survey.
In contrast, it was clear that where CATs had been established
in premises, teaching training and workshop provision was
viewed as the province of CA staff, and not of CAT members.
This suggests a reversal of the relationship originally
envisaged by MAPP.

Administrative and clinical accountability of teams were
to a variety of sources (management committees, line managers,
project managers) and clinical accountability was often to
non-administrative staff. No single model of management was
clear.

Funding came from a variety of sources such as jointly
from NHS sources and the local Council on Alcoholism (CA),
District Health Authority (DHA), Regional Health Authority
(RHA), Department of Health (DHSS), Local Authority (LA) and
Home Office. As with management structure, no dominant
patterns were apparent.

The survey revealed no standard CAT model and that there
has been substantial variation from the original MAPP
guidelines. Despite the lack of uniformity, however, many
CATs have experienced similar problems. Failure to specify
management roles and lines of accountability have produced
difficulties for most CATs. The absence of individual
responsibility for specific roles and functions has also
created problems. Some CAT members have reported difficulties
in the transition from a casework to a consultative role.
Confusion among clients about the function of the CAT has been
recorded when expectations about direct service provision have
been generated. Many CAT members felt unsupported by the
structure in which they work.

The emphasis on second-level intervention amongst some
CATs has also produced difficulties. Some non-hospital agents
have not always readily accepted the consultative role of the
CAT, expressing reservations about the creation of more
specialist teams that were not prepared to accept casework
with clients (see Chapter 6). The evidence for behaviour
change amongst these agents beyond an increased number of
identified problem drinkers remains scant, despite attendance
on training courses.

Many primary care workers, despite completion of training
courses, have expressed doubts about the legitimacy of their
involvement with clients who have drink problems. There is a
lack of consensus among professional groups about their role
in working with people who have drink problems (see Chapter
6).

In addition, despite more than a decade since the appearance of the original MAPP proposals, recent reports still advocate further discussion of critical points such as roles of professional groups, decisions about routes of referral, training policy, support mechanisms for other workers (Clement, 1987). Failure to specify these points as clear aims, goals and objectives has impeded the development of alcohol services. The implementation of the original CAT model has been difficult.

LESSONS FROM OTHER SPECIALIST SERVICES

A major shortcoming ... is their close identification with ... hospital and the health services. There is very limited involvement. The limited membership ... makes them less effective in performing a coordinating function for clients and families. This is especially difficult for teams only having a community nurse and social worker who will possibly not have the necessary authority to obtain cooperation from the other services ...

All too often the services available to ... people ... are dependent on the area in which they live. This is now the situation in respect of multidisciplinary teams. Some areas do not have any. Even where they do exist, the service differs widely. The guidelines ... leave ... too much scope for local variations. They do not ensure that all ... people have an equal chance to benefit from an integrated service.

(Campaign for Mental Handicap, 1982)

These statements could have been written about CATs; they were written, however, in 1982 about the development of community mental handicap teams (CMHTs). Whilst clear differences exist between the client populations of CATs and CMHTs, equally clear similarities exist in the structures generated to provide services for these two groups.

A review of the evolution of CMHTs indicates some surprising parallels with the development of CATs. The first recommendation for the formation of CMHTs was made after the investigations during 1976 and 1977 of the National Development Group (NDG, 1977). Establishment of CMHTs was suggested to promote and coordinate services for people with mental handicap: NHS and Local Authority (LA) staff were to be recruited to establish one CMHT for each local population of 60,000 to 80,000 persons, each NHS "district" would require three to four teams to provide services. Each CMHT would include a social worker, a consultant psychiatrist, a psychologist and a community nurse to provide local services (Development Team, 1982). The role and function for the CMHT was to develop and coordinate services, using specialist staff both from NHS and LA sources. CMHTs were designed to enable joint planning and joint finance between local health and social services. A national survey of services for people with mental handicap suggested that 71 CMHTs had been established by 1982 (Campaign for Mental Handicap, 1982).

Even a brief inspection of specialist services for other client populations reveals a similar trend. The design of services for elderly people has been changed to include provision of Community Elderly Teams or CETs (Baldwin, 1986). Similar trends have been evident in other specialist services such as rehabilitation and physical disability.

The evolution of CATs should be viewed within the context of national development of services for a range of client groups. Comparisons between CATs and CMHTs allow some conclusions about the probability of successful establishment of these community services in the UK. In particular, it is implausible that sufficient specialist staff exist to expand CAT services according to the original model. Assuming a CAT in every health district, it would require around 200 further specialist social workers and 200 specialist psychiatrists to staff them. Whether these staff currently exist is doubtful. Even given the dubious assumptions that they might exist or could be trained, it would still mean, taking a constant rate of expansion of alcohol services (in itself doubtful) that establishment of a notional network of CATs would not be achieved until the year 2157.

There are both practical and logistic problems in the implementation of the CAT model. The original proposals may have been useful in drawing the attention of service planners to the need to expand alcohol services. Comparisons with other "community team" initiatives, however, demonstrate many problems and restrictions which reflect more fundamental themes within the "community care" approach. It is these wider themes which require reappraisal and re-evaluation.

The Myth of "Care in the Community"

Repeated failures to achieve successful relocations of hospital services in non-hospital settings has produced understandable suspicion about any new initiatives to establish so-called community services. Attempts to shift services to non-hospital settings for various client populations in the 1960s and 1970s have yielded only limited success by most standards. Evaluation studies, where available, have suggested a rather limited range of services available to clients whose services have been transferred to new locations (e.g. Landesman-Dwyer, 1981). Indeed, the recent reactions to so-called community care initiatives by consumer groups, advocacy organisations, trades unions, voluntary organisations and pressure groups have been such as to necessitate a fundamental reappraisal of the concept.

Old Wine in Old Bottles

The single major difficulty with community care initiatives has been definitional. Such services have often failed to specify (1) number, quality and intensity of individual programmes for clients; (2) necessary support services; (3) staff training requirements; (4) staff recruitment policies; (5) pay scales; (6) size of client population; (7) costs of services to clients; (8) location of services; (9) mechanisms of transfer to new settings; (10) consumer participation; (11) criteria for a successful programme, and (12) targets for completion.

These deficiencies in conceptualisation of provision have been evident in a wide range of specialist services including rehabilitation, mental handicap, physical handicap, alcohol and drug abuse, forensic, children and adolescents, gerontology and "adult mental health". In each of these specialist services, there has been a shift in emphasis since 1970 to decrease institutional service provision in favour of services in non-hospital settings. Formation of "community teams" to provide these services has been a key feature of these services in transition.

In addition to definitional problems with community initiatives, the concept of "community" itself has been widely criticised as vague, imprecise, inaccurate and liable to exploitation. This has been due partly to a failure to agree on the concept of "community": some reviews have identified more than 90 definitions (Hillery, 1955). Most recently, "community care" has become synonymous with non-hospital service (Zigler, 1977), although there is no reason to suppose that either one is inherently preferential or of higher quality. Clearly neither the fabric of buildings nor location of staff offer guarantees about quality of care or life experiences by clients (Baldwin et al, 1984). There are certainly plenty of examples of non-hospital services which have provided quality of life inferior to their institutional counterparts (e.g. Baldwin, 1986a).

A necessary objection to the continued usage of the concept of community care is the ease with which the concept has been employed by successive administrations with opposing political ideologies (Finch, 1984). The failure to specify meaning and provide operational definitions of the term has perpetuated a concept which has been embraced equally by the political right and left. Thus, pluralistic policies of expansion, diversity and increased costs have been successively juxtaposed with policies of contraction, homogeneity and decreased costs; both have been afforded the status of "community care". Some critics have urged the whole abandonment of "community" as an ideological concept which is oppressive, gendered, reactionary and conservative (e.g. Stacey, 1969; Wilson, 1982).

Notwithstanding intractable definitional problems to an understanding of "community" services, the existence of other major conceptual barriers has rendered the concept useless for effective service planning and provision in the 1980s. All "community care" initiatives have been based on assumptions about shared costs between health and social services. The establishment of CATs, CMHTs and CETs are all examples of attempts to provide comprehensive local services via joint planning, joint finance, joint management and, sometimes, joint accountability. Indeed, the transfer of NHS clients, staff and resources to local authority settings is a key feature of most de-institutionalisation initiatives. In particular, the successful establishment and maintenance of CATs was based on the principle of cooperation between NHS and

Table 8.1: Organisation and Management Problems in Psychiatric Hospitals (DHSS, 1981)

Theme	Health Service	Social Service
Accountability	To DHSS	Local Control
Membership	Appointed	Elected
Finance	Exchequer	Two-thirds raised locally
Control/Public Accountability	DHAs and CHCs separately*	Elected members perform both roles
Geographical boundariess	DHA catchment area*	Based on traditional neighbourhoods
Internal structures	a) Regional and District HAs* b) Confined to health	a) Social Services with wider functions b) Other duties (e.g. delinquency)
Dominant skills	a) Medical/nursing b) Long history of training	c) Social work b) Many staff not trained
Responsibility	a) Individual clinical responsibility b) Dispersed	a) Most responsibilities to LA leading to more member involvement* b) Managerial control more specific

NB. * HA = Health Authority; CHC = Community Health Council; LA = Local Authority.

Local Authority staff, with specific recommendations about service development based on joint finance, joint planning and joint responsibility (Cartwright et al, 1975).

A close inspection of the fabric and true function of health services and social services, however, reveals these assumptions about any meshing of goals to be fundamentally flawed. Comparison of key themes within these two services indicates clear tension (see Table 8.1). Moreover, it is evident that differences in health and social services ideologies have produced ends (goals) and means (methods) which are mutually exclusive and frequently in opposition.

Definition of the key themes identified in Table 8.1 reveal that NHS and LA systems do not merge easily. Major differences in history, policies, mechanisms and goals illustrate barriers to successful integration of the two services.

In practice, attempts to initiate such integration between health and social service systems have been problematic. Establishment of so called "multidisciplinary" teams, so often favoured in joint strategy planning documents, has been largely unsuccessful due to domination by traditional disciplines. Whilst some hopeful examples of true interdisciplinary team work have been reported (e.g. Parham, Rude and Bernanke, 1977; Baldwin et al, 1984), this has required prior rejection of the traditional "teamwork" model. In reality, most attempts to transfer services from NHS to LA settings have been unrewarding experiences both for clients and staff. The need to close institutions and abolish inefficient or harmful interventions should remain a priority in all human services. Targets to shut hospitals may help local initiatives to implement a joint strategy (e.g. Korman, 1984). There is accumulating evidence, however, that key features of these strategies have been ill-concieved and implemented with great difficulty. Joint planning and joint finance, in particular, clearly have not been successful (e.g. Wistow, 1983).

The provision of local, comprehensive services for individual clients in non-hospital settings remains a priority for service development. Most high quality services do not require a hospital base, and it is appropriate that service planners continue to set closure dates for large centralised institutions which tend to segregate, isolate and stigmatise their client populations. A danger exists, however, that the methods have not yet been identified to effect transfer of services into local settings. Closure of NHS facilities in the absence of appropriate non-hospital local services has produced justifiable suspicion and concern; some data have indicated that UK services have been closed without suitable relocation of client populations (e.g. Smith, 1984). Other reports have indicated that this phenomenon is not confined to the UK. Parallel data indicating failure of similar de-institutionalisation attempts have been reported in Italy (Ramon, 1984) and the USA (Bassuk, 1984).

In summary, there is a need to re-think ideas about de-institutionalisation of services staff and clients. Specialist "community teams" will never be able to resolve fundamental ideological problems of service design and delivery. Continued investment in such teams risks damage to clients.

SERVICE DESIGN

A reveiw of the progress of CATs since 1975 necessitates the conclusion that a fundamental reappraisal of the concept is now required. The historical development of CATs is understandable, given the political and economic climate since 1979. It is now vital, however, to examine whether the CAT model can ever provide the mechanism to provide a comprehensive local range of services for people who have drink problems.

The formation of CATs should be seen within the context of a wider de-institutionalisation movement which has urged institutional closures and promoted life in the local settings. There is no evidence to support the belief that this policy decision was based either on a moral argument to improve quality of life, or on data which indicated improved services. Rather, it seems that "community care" initiatives had their origins in economics and the need to reduce capital and revenue costs (Salzinger, 1981; Zigler, 1977). The establishment of CATs within this context might be seen as a panic response by NHS staff to the wider movement which threatened loss of control of services. In a zeitgeist which promoted "multidisciplinary teams", physicians and social workers took up the "community cudgels" to establish non-hospital services. The effectiveness of the second-level intervention focus of many CATs so established remains unproven.

CATs share many of the problems experienced by other specialist teams. An appreciation of these problems and possible solutions requires a fundamental re-think about service design and structure.

1. **Generic Services.** These services are required by all persons, irrespective of age, sex, race, ability or impairment. By definition, they represent general needs for services such as education, health, accommodation, employment, leisure and mobility which are shared by everybody. (An example of a need shared by all clients is the requirement for GP services at a health centre or clinic.) In principle, generic services should be available to all client groups, although in practice this does not occur.

2. **Specialist Services.** These services duplicate generic services, and are provided to particular specialist groups of

clients. These groups have been identified due to some shared common characteristics (e.g. age, disability, infirmity, social problems, legal transgressions). Specialist services duplicate many of the functions of generic services, but provision is limited to a particular group of clients. (For example, a hospital ATU provides for needs such as accommodation, health, education but required temporary admission to an institution.) Specialist services tend to accumulate large numbers of similar clients with shared characteristics in a single location. This frequently produces congregation, isolation, social rejection and stigmatisation of both clients and staff.

    3. **Special Needs Services.** These services are by definition distinct from generic services. Provision of special needs services indicates some additional requirement which cannot be made available by generic services. In principle, special needs services are available to all clients who require them. In practice, however, special needs services tend to be expensive due to provision for small numbers and only a restricted number of clients obtain such services. For example, some clients, by virtue of chronic drinking, require detoxification from alcohol. This is a special needs service, not required by most people. Other restrictions are frequently imposed on access to special needs services due to limited availability. In practice, clients in specialist services do not enjoy equal access to special needs services and may be disqualified by virtue of age or impairment.

    If services are conceptualised in this way it can be argued that most people who have drink problems require equal access to a combination of generic services, and special needs services. Further provision of specialist services may be against the best interests of both clients and staff.

THE FUTURE OF CATs - TOWARDS NEIGHBOURHOOD SERVICES

Comparisons with other specialist services have revealed that the problems identified with attempts to establish a national network of CAT services have been experienced by staff working in these other fields. For this reason, a constructional approach should be adopted in the appraisal of current alcohol services. It should be questioned whether most people who have drink problems require specialist intervention, which may be stigmatising and duplicate what is already available. The needs of most clients can be met through a combination of generic and special needs services. At the heart of specialist service provision is the destructive phenomenon whereby limits imposed on funding and resources inevitably force managers to define priorities for channelling to one group of clients at the expense of another. The failure to resolve this central problem of service design results in continued imbalances between provision for populations, whereby one client group can only benefit from increased resources or a simultaneous decrease occurs for another client group (Rose-Ackerman, 1982).

There are some hopeful signs of the recognition of the need to reappraise definitions and understanding of how local, flexible comprehensive services might be provided for clients in non-hospital settings. One new model (Orford, Chapter 1 of this volume) requires that people with drink problems increase their use of generic services in such a way as to reduce the risk of stigmatisation. This view of future services has recognised the requirement for "special needs" services (e.g. detoxification) and has also recognised the fundamental principle of non-institutionalisation. As a rule, detoxification should occur with appropriate support in the client's own residence (Stockwell, Chapter 10 of this volume).

There have been other recent recognitions of unmet client needs which suggest the importance of re-thinking the concept of specialist services. Examination of the needs of elderly people has supported the conclusion that existing specialist alcohol services have not provided a comprehensive response to drink problems within this client population (Zimberg, 1978). Elderly clients with drink problems do not conform to stereotypic images as the aging process produces different responses to alcohol. Older clients may require a balance of careful re-integration into both generic services and special needs services.

The recognition that there will never be enough specialist services produces the conclusion that fundamental change is required in human services planning and implementation. In addition, consideration of any single professional group yields the conclusion that further expansion in numbers of specialist workers will be limited and that a different adaptive professional response is required (e.g. Lickorish, 1970; Bender, 1976). Moreover, it may be against the best interests of clients to receive specialist services. Detailed needs assessments with clients has usually produced requirements based upon both generic and special needs services (e.g. Harding, Baldwin and Baser, 1987). This approach, however, represents a departure from existing provision for services targeted at groups, to a service based upon individual needs.

One possible response to the problems posed by the discrepancy between present specialist services and actual client needs has been to re-think radically the services response. Attempts have been made to initiate interdisciplinary teams in local neighbourhoods (e.g. Baldwin, 1987). These teams have been able to target generic/special needs services to smaller client populations ranging from 50,000 to 100,000 users. This style has required specialists to re-deploy their skills in novel ways to respond more

efficiently to actual client needs. Some neighbourhood
workers have also developed new skills to adopt a multi-level
approach to client casework, with concurrent training of other
support staff and service development work. Neighbourhood
services have been established which reflect a value system
based on integration, non-discrimination, equality of access
and consumer participation.

The recognition that existing services cannot function
effectively for people who have drink problems demands an
imaginative and pioneering response. Some specialists will no
doubt grasp this uncomfortable, but important, nettle before
the year 2157.

Until primary care services are radically restructured,
Community Alcohol Teams can only remain a component of
"specialist" services facilitating service delivery to a
"problem drinking" client group.

REFERENCES

Baldwin, S. (1986a) Systems in transition: the first 100
elderly people. International Journal of Rehabilitation
Research, 9, (2) 139-148

Baldwin, S. (1986b) Problems with needs. Disability, Handicap
and Society, 1, (2) 139-145

Baldwin, S. (1987) From communities to neighbourhoods - I.
Disability, Handicap and Society. In press

Baldwin, S., Baser, C. and Pinka, A. (1986) The emperor's new
community services. Nursing Times Community Outlook,
February 12, 6-8

Baldwin, S., Robins, J., Harker, B. and Robb, P. (1984) The
place invaders: establishing neighbourhood teams for
people with mental handicap in Sheffield. Journal of
Community Education, June 3, (2) 19-25

Bassuk, El (1984) The homelessness problem. Scientific
American, July 25, 1 (1) 28-33

Bender, M. (1976) Community Psychology. Methuen, London

Cartwright, A., Shaw, S. and Spratley, T. (1975) Designing a
Comprehensive Community Response to Problems of Alcohol
Abuse. Report to the DHSS by the Maudsley Alcohol Pilot
Project. DHSS, London

Cartwright, A., Harwin, J., Shaw, S. and Spratley, T. (1977)
Implementing a Community Based Response to Problems of
Alcohol Abuse. Final Report to the DHSS by the Maudsley
Alcohol Pilot Project. DHSS, London

Clement, S. (1986) Personal communication

Clement, S. (1987) Chapter 6 of this volume

CMH (1982) Teams for Mentally Handicapped People. Campaign
for Mentally Handicapped People, London

Development Team (1982) Development Team for the Mentally
Handicapped. Third Report 1979-1981. HMSO, London

DHSS (1981) Organisation and Management Problems of Mental Illness Hospitals: Report of a Working Group. DHSS, London

Finch, J. (1984) Community care: developing non-sexist alternatives. Critical Social Policy, 9, Spring, 6-18

Harding, K., Baldwin, S. and Baser, C. (1987) Towards multi-level needs assessments. Behavioural Psychotherapy. In press

Hillery, G. (1955) Definitions of community: areas of agreement. Rural Sociology, June 20, 111-123

Korman, N. (1984) Paying for community care. Health and Social Services Journal, October 18, 1238-1240

Landesman-Dwyer, S. (1981) Living in the community. American Journal of Mental Deficiency, 86 (3), 223-234

Lickorish, J. and Sims, C. (1971) How much can a clinical psychologist do? Bulletin of the British Psychological Society 24, 27-30

NDG (1977) National Development Group for the Mentally Handicapped. Pamphlet series - No 2. Mentally Handicapped Children: A Plan for Action. HMSO, London

Parham, J. Rude, C. and Bernanke, P. (1977) Individual Programme with Developing Disabled Persons. Research and Training Centre in Mental Retardation, Texas Tech, Lubbock, Texas

Ramon, S. (1982) Psychiatrica Democratica:an overview of an Italian community mental health service. Unpublished paper, London School of Economics, University of London

Rose-Ackerman, S. (1982) Mental retardation and society: the ethics and policies of normalization. Ethics, 93, 81-101

Salzinger, K. (1981) Remedying schizophrenic behaviour. In Turner, S., Calmoun, K. and Adams, M. (eds) Handbook of Clinical Behaviour Therapy. Wiley, New York

Shaw, S., Cartwright, A., Spratley, T. and Harwin, J. (1978) Responding to Drinking Problems. Croom Helm, London

Smith, J. (1984) Stuck on the transfer list. Health and Social Services Journal, 6 September

Stacey, M. (1969) The myth of community studies. British Journal of Sociology, 20, 134-146

Wilson, E. (1982) Women, the community and the family. In Walker, A. (ed) Community Care: the family, the state and social policy. Blackwell/Martin Robertson, Oxford

Wistow, G. (1983) Joint finance and community care: have the incentives worked? Public Money, September, 33-37

Zigler, E. (1977) Twenty years of mental retardation research. Mental Retardation, 15 (3), 52-53

Zimberg, S. (1978) Psychosocial treatment of elderly alcoholics. In Zimberg, S., Wallace, J. and Blume, S. Practical Approaches to Alcoholism Psychotherapy. Plenum, New York

Chapter 9

ALCOHOL AND DRUG DEPENDENCE: THE CASE FOR A COMBINED COMMUNITY RESPONSE

Brian Arbery

INTRODUCTION

If there is one fact that should be taken as read in the broad area of substances, it is that the substance user will almost inevitably confound the ideas and plans of so-called specialists. The history of services for drug and alcohol users is littered with an underused inheritance of well intentioned proposals whose chief failing was that they attempted to classify clients into neat, well defined categories based on the prevailing presenting substance. The delay in implementation of policies and proposals throughout health and social care has often meant that the services established meet the original requirements of a group of customers whose needs have themselves changed in the meantime. The failure of the treaters and policy makers to either predict or respond rapidly to modifications in alcohol and drug user behaviour has resulted in services which meet the needs of ten years ago rather than the present day. Nowhere is this more obvious than in their failure to meet the needs of the growing and significant group of individuals who are using substances on a multiple basis or who practice substance substitution.

The administration of services, their funding and aims, too frequently delimit themselves to providing for the user of a specific substance, either alcohol or other drugs or solvents. It is argued here that these divisions are no longer appropriate, not simply due to the fact that current theoretical perspectives define close commonalities between addictive behaviours, but primarily because the client constituency itself has changed significantly since the mid-1970s. This chapter looks at why we should be thinking now of combining services for alcohol and other drug misusers, some barriers to implementing this approach and a model of the way forward based on an analysis of these difficulties.

PROBLEMS WITH SINGLE SUBSTANCE SERVICES

Whatever our theoretical basis for looking at the broad "addictions" field, it is client choice and not treater's preconceived opinions which should determine the pattern of services. Failure to do this has resulted in the wasteful development and maintenance of underutilised resources which maintain methods of working inappropriate to the needs of the majority of substance users. Examples of this are the slavish commitment to the disease model of alcoholism manifested by some voluntary bodies, and the "concept"-based therapeutic communities for the residential rehabilitation of drug "addicts".

It is interesting to note that despite the general lack of residential resources for drug users there has been underutilisation of concept houses due, it could be argued, to their failure to relate to predominant client needs. Similarly, it seems that the maintenance of single substance services results in many potential clients not making contact because they do not identify that substance as problematic in their lives and no other services are available, or because they do not see themselves as fitting the stereotypical definition of the clients with whom the service suggests it is working. The projection by an agency of narrow definitions of what is or what is not an "alcoholic" or "drug addict" effectively debars potential service users from access to services.

The inappropriateness of dividing substance users into distinct populations based on substance is illustrated by the almost random way in which some people will be brought into contact with the service provider. For example, a person arrested for possession of an illicit drug will be defined as a drug user by law. The fact that they may be consuming well in excess of the recommended level of alcohol intake per day at the same time will not be taken into account in an assessment of their future needs for personal assistance. They are defined as having a drug problem and will thus be processed as a drug user. A similar situation may well arise with an alcohol user who is arrested on a drink-related offence, who is also regularly using prescribed and/or illicit drugs but does not have them on their person at the time of arrest. He or she will be assumed to have a drink problem. Equally a voluntary (self-presenting) client can sometimes ignore part of the total substance usage in the selection of appropriate agency, i.e. alcohol problems are more socially acceptable than drug problems, therefore presentation to an alcohol agency may be less damaging to self-esteem. This would not necessarily cause difficulties were it not for the attitude of the treatment agencies themselves. Whether health service, social service or voluntary sector based, the division between the substances is generally tightly drawn and the practitioner is frequently seen both by the agency and client (and self for that matter) as a substance specific specialist. In many services, particularly those for drug users, the issue of substance use apart from that for which primary referral has taken place is not even recorded or questioned. The client who has been initially channelled to the "wrong" agency then may have little chance of receiving the broader range of help which is needed.

At the other end of the spectrum there also exist agencies where the client is seen as a chemically dependent person for whom the use of all substances is dangerous. This approach is equally limiting and ignores the fact that many can continue to use a substance without developing further problems.

In both cases the substance used is emphasised rather than the factors underlying use, and very often the real needs of the client will remain unmet.

COMMONALITIES BETWEEN THE ADDICTIVE BEHAVIOURS

Over the last 20 years, there have been a number of attempts by practitioners and researchers to define umbrella models which offer a satisfactory explanation of "addictive behaviour". The problem with many of these theories is that they have tended to focus on either the individual or the substance without having regard to social or economic factors. Perhaps the most useful model so far which avoids this trap has been that provided by Jim Orford in his book Excessive Appetites (1985) which defined a range of "addictive" behaviours as falling into the same broad spectrum. Orford includes excessive eating, gambling and sexuality in the definition as well as substance use. The model provides a method of understanding the determinants which could cause individuals to be involved to a greater or lesser degree in one or more appetitive activities and enables the introduction of the significant social and economic variables. If this approach is taken, it is possible to identify similarities between apparently different groups of substance users which enable common treatment methods to be pursued.

Orford's view of appetitive activities relies heavily on the fact that the experience of those who engage in all types of excessive behaviour is often similar even though the activities may superficially appear to be quite different. It allows us to look both at the individual as a determinant in the development of such behaviour patterns, and the factors of the social and physical environment encompassing both permissive and restrictive influences which develop or restrain such behaviour. Within a single society, the way in which the activities under consideration are carried out will vary considerably between individuals dependent upon age, sex and social class and that these may well be more significant factors than substance-based variables. Characteristics of appetitive behaviour are seen to include increasing attachment to the behaviour of choice in conjunction with the existence of risk or negative consequence which might either be physical, social, immediate or long-term and will affect either the individual or others relating to them. The individual will often have feelings of ambivalence towards the behaviour, thus explaining the feelings of restraint, moral dilemma and suffering so frequently found in substance users. Changes in behaviour (either increasing or reducing) come from personal decisions but it is recognised that there are multiple factors, internal and external, which influence the way in which those decisions are made. The role of "treatment" therefore becomes the facilitation of the clients' decisions to change in conjunction with helping them develop strategies to maintain that decision in the long term. None of these factors argues for a substance specific approach.

Orford's approach has certainly enabled us to look at the range of appetitive activities in a more rational and less stigmatic way. Once one accepts that there are similarities between the addictive behaviours and that the significant variables are not necessarily substance of use or predispositions to a particular behaviour, the focus then shifts to social/environmental factors in determining the basis for service planning. It may be more appropriate to look at clients by age group, by sex, by ethnic background or social class instead of attempting to view all clients as having the same problems within each individual substance area.

THE CLIENT POPULATION

In so far as the specific areas of alcohol and drugs are concerned, it is reasonable to ask if there really is a homogeneous group of substance users. There is no doubt that there has been a significant change here in the last 20 years. Prior to the mid-1960s the use of opiates and other illicit drugs was generally seen as being confined to a small number of "deviant" groups. Since then most individuals in the country have been exposed to or are certainly aware of the use of non-legal substances and the acceptance of the use of illicit drugs (particularly cannabis) has become far more widespread. The increased availability and acceptance of illicit drugs, then, has made it more likely that people who would formerly have been solely alcohol misusers will develop problems associated with multiple substance misuse. The widespread use of benzodiazepines and other prescribed psychotropics amongst the population as a whole has also contributed to this picture. Consequently, it can be argued that the problem drinker today is likely to have quite different attitudes towards the use of other substances than

has hitherto been the case. Similarly the illicit drug user
has moved out of the mystical pseudo-political sub-culture
which predominated during the 1960s. There may still be a
small number of 40-year old regular drug users who feel that
they are personally making a commitment to an alternative
society, but such opinions are no longer seen as widely
associated with, or a justification for, drug usage.

The coming together of the two populations may be
illustrated by an analysis of 166 clients referred to the
Salford Community Alcohol Team between September 1983 and June
1984. This revealed that 50 were using alcohol and drugs
(Murphy 1985)- 30% of all male clients and 29% of all
females. As shown in Table 9.1, the group included users of
both illicit and prescribed drugs. Among the latter, about one-
third were using prescribed drugs at the same time as drinking
while the other two-thirds were alternating their alcohol and
drug use.

Table 9.1: Drug Use among Problem Drinkers Referred to Salford CAT

	Men	Women	All	(%)
No Drug Use	82	34	116	(70%)
Illicit Drugs	12	3	15	(9%)
Prescribed Drugs	24	11	35	(21%)
Totals	118	48	166	(100%)

A recent study of prisoners in Pentonville, London has
also shown a significant level of multiple usage. It looked
at a representative group of 87 offenders where drink was
assessed as playing a significant part in the crime. At the
start of the study in 1982, 30 individuals at the point of
admission were using other substances as well as alcohol
(predominantly cannabis). By 1984 (one year post-release), 56
had used illicit substances (in addition to alcohol) in the
previous six months. The main drugs of choice were
amphetamines and cannabis. Nineteen people were spending in
excess of £10 per week on drugs (the majority of whom were
spending around £50) and three were spending £100 a week.
Within this group, heroin and amphetamines were predominant
(Wilson, G., unpublished study).

Although limited, the evidence supports the impression of
many clinicians that multiple drug use (including alcohol) is

a significant phenomenon among their clients. Treatment agencies are also becoming increasingly aware of the problems associated with substance substitution. Of 50 people interviewed following discharge from a Regional Drug Treatment Unit, 11 reported that they had substituted alcohol for their previous drug of misuse and one had developed a severe alcohol problem (Murphy, 1985). The excessive use of alcohol is also a common problem among clients who are discharged as drug free from residential projects for problem drug takers.

Even if it can be shown that multiple substance misuse and substance substitution are not issues for the majority of clients presenting for help, there is some evidence that clients see themselves as having similar problems, whatever their substance of misuse. For example, research at the Leeds Addiction Unit found the major difference between drug and alcohol users was their age, rather than their associated problems and that the clients themselves favoured combined treatment (Raistrick, 1985).

The perception of homogeneity by clients may also be illustrated by Turning Point's experience in operating Drugline projects. A significant proportion (in some cases 50%) of new contacts are self-referrals by individuals with problems arising from the use of prescribed drugs (usually tranquillisers). In these instances, the client has self-determined the existence of a drug problem and has seen a project which purports to be for illicit users as being equally capable of serving needs despite the stereotypical image of drug addiction and drug use.

The most significant differentiating factor between the drug and alcohol user population which has not yet been mentioned is that of legality. Society has become increasingly disapproving of the effects of excessive alcohol use, e.g. the greatly increased penalties now being imposed by courts for drinking and driving. Whilst the substance may be approved, the unacceptable use of it is not. This is certainly not the case for illicit drugs at the moment except in the case of cannabis where the ready availability and apparent lack of significantly harmful side effects have resulted in a much more general defiance of the law than is found with other illicit substances. However, the growing social acceptability of cannabis use has resulted in a trend amongst law enforcement bodies to take a much more relaxed approach to its possession and this is spreading now to people found in the possession of other drugs (although not those selling them). Thus, the user of the illicit drug is being increasingly seen by the law as not requiring penal sanction. One hears with increasing frequency of police officers informally referring users to treatment or counselling centres rather than proceeding with legal action. This change in police practice is broadly comparable with the changes which have taken place in the area of alcohol, especially in the

177

care of habitual drunken offenders, over the last 20 years. It is only in the area of unacceptable behaviour associated with alcohol that the law becomes more strict in its enforcement. Thus a policemen is concerned particularly with drinking and driving, vandalism or assaults rather than drunkenness per se. Similarly, with drug use, apart from illegal trading, it is the consequent behaviour of theft, burglary and assaults which occupy most police attention. This effective change in the implementation of the law further assists us in recognising the similarities between alcohol and drug users with the result that working with them as an homogeneous group is increasingly viable.

Despite these changes, certain legal constraints do however, continue to cause significant problems and tend to emphasise artificial differences. These are the professional codes placed upon certain statutorily employed individuals. Doctors, for example, are expected to notify in the case of illicit drug users, and some social services authorities have blanket policies which relate to the maintenance of child at-risk registers which will be applied to drug users. These statutory requirements tend to mitigate against clients coming into contact with care agencies. Of themselves, however, they do not necessarily affect the potential for working with clients as a unified group (some authorities would equally feel that the child of a severe alcohol user should be placed on the register). Clearly, the boundaries of legality and illegality are no longer as relevant as the may have been in the past. Given Orford's theoretical framework, the experience of agencies who have identified a shift both in number of multiple users and their attitudes towards each other and the weakening of legal differentials, it can be argued with some justification that substance users should be reviewed as a totality. This has considerable implications for the structure and funding of services and, particularly,for the way in which these services sell themselves to the potential client or user.

THE PROBLEMS OF DEVELOPING COMBINED SERVICES

In considering the development of combined services for alcohol and other drug users one has to take into account the framework within which existing services operate. Central policies have always taken into account the relative importance of individual substances of misuse to the economic needs of the nation, e.g. that the alcohol industry employs a large number of the population both in its distribution, dispensing and marketing, has a significant effect on the economic well being of the country. There is considerable political influence attached to the alcohol industry and its ability to wield this power is evident (witness the non-publication of the Think Tank report in 1978).

Drug users, on the other hand, do not contribute a great deal to the legal economy and there are not, as far as I am aware, major illicit drug dealers who have any significant influence on government policy. In the case of legal drug manufacturers there are certainly close links with the political process. Relative political importance in terms of the strength of the relevant lobbies provides some understanding of the historical development of differential responses towards different groups of substance users. Government policy has always been one of pragmatic response rather than any attempt at long-term financial planning focusing on developing and changing needs.

The Allocation of Resources

Responsibility for national co-ordination and development of policies and services for all substance users rests with the same section of the DHSS. Despite this, they do not have the responsibility for determining resource levels or the actual implementation of services. They also have no effective means of controlling those who do. Consequently, although the DHSS might view drug and alcohol use as a unity and see it as being a major problem requiring significant resources, its ability to follow this through is restricted by financial considerations and the current climate of restraint on public spending. Thus there will be continuing pressure on financial grounds to cut back allocations, and to re-allocate money from one section of the budget to another in the absence of further resources. The policy of financial control as an end in itself does not take into account what is needed in terms of service development. This can be changed only by political will.

Athough political opinion over the last 10 years has moved towards the acceptance of a requirement to provide services for drug users of all types, the levels of resources allocated remain insufficient to meet the needs of the client population. In such a situation, planning is meaningless. It is further complicated by the lack of central control of service delivery planning. At local level decisions are more likely to be at the mercy of relatively uninformed individuals in health or social services committees holding the same stereotypical views of substance users that are held by the wider population. Since they have no statutory duty to provide specific services for these groups, it is not difficult to see how, when faced with conflicting demands for scarce finances, they will tend to vote against resources for substance users.

Health authorities have been instructed by government to raise services for drug users to a higher priority level, with inspection of their proposals also being introduced. Recent allocations to health authorities have tied money to drug services and thus there has been a limited move towards

central government control over priority determination. This
has not happened in the area of alcohol use where central
government has completely withdrawn from involvement and this
lack of direction is reflected in the low priority accorded to
services for alcohol users at the local level.

These differential policies in service development have
failed to take account of changing needs, and do not recognise
the modified characteristics of the substance using client
population. This has led to an underutilisation of many of
those services that do exist. The new drug services, both
residential and non-residential, in some cases duplicate
underutilised alcohol services and in some areas the drug
service will itself be underused. On an economic basis alone,
the current system is extremely wasteful, and it would make
financial sense to look towards a combined service.

The Relationship Between the Statutory and Voluntary Sectors
Alongside the chaos in planning and resource allocation one
must also look at the source of service delivery. Given that
service planning and funding have been increasingly
decentralised, one would expect that this would have become
the responsibility of the local statutory agency i.e. health
or social services. However, this has not been the case, for
the most significant area of growth has been in the voluntary
sector. The voluntary bodies, although largely maintained by
statutory funding, are for political reasons seen as entirely
independent and do not have any significant say in the
formulation of central policies. This gives rise to major
difficulties in attempts to change resource allocations and
priorities.

At an operational level they vary betweeen larger
national agencies and small one-off amateur groups with
minimal professional or managerial experience.

Statutory involvement has generally been in the provision
of health service run clinics and detoxification units, e.g.
DDUs and ATUs. The number of community responses by statutory
authorities is very small. Only one rehabilitation house for
drinkers in England is provided by a local authority,
(Manchester), and there are none for drug users anywhere in
the country.

The health service clinics and treatment units have
tended to separate clients who use different substances. Even
where the two groups of clients are treated in the same unit,
they tend to be separated both physically and in treatment
models. (In a few notable cases such as Newcastle and Leeds,
there have been attempts to run an integrated combined
service.)

The majority of state provision is idiosyncratic and depends
on the personal preferences of the managing specialists,
normally consultant psychiatrists. Thus, depending on one's
geographical location, there will be variations in, for

example, the willingness to prescribe opiate substitutes on a maintenance basis for drug users and emphasis or non-emphasis given to total abstinence or controlled drinking in treating alcohol problems. There are few places where the state service may be said to adopt a non-doctrinaire pragmatic approach which focuses on the needs of the individual client.

The voluntary agencies tend to be equally idiosyncratic, particularly since there is little provision (or desire) for quality control. There are also serious problems over the perceived status of services. This can be illustrated by the fact that due to poorly co-ordinated policies, non-statutory rehabilitation services for drinkers and drug users are seen as residential care homes, a category which includes the long-term mentally ill, the elderly and others requiring permanent care. As a consequence the method of working, quality of staff and their style of practice may be dictated not by professional experience and practical need but by regulations applied by a registration officer who will frequently be an inexperienced administrator who has little understanding of the issues involved in working with substance users. In some cases the registering authority has refused to permit more than one defined group of users in a house or has required inappropriately high staffing levels or environmental provision.

Additionally, because of the stigma attached to both groups of clients (particularly drug users), some planning departments will restrict planning permission to closely defined client groups. Extraneous factors of this type have considerable impact on the work of the voluntary agencies and their ability to make appropriate responses to changes in client needs.

The positive side of relying on the voluntary sector is that where there is no dramatic interference through a registration or planning process, then it may be possible for the agency to introduce alternative ways of working with clients or respond to changes in population. This has been the case in a number of instances, including my own organisation, Turning Point, where regular illicit drug users have been introduced into residential units which predominantly deal with alcohol problems. There is no evidence to suggest that either group of clients do any better or worse in either, but there is some evidence to show, as with Leeds, that the identification of commonalities confronts stereotypical views the clients hold of each other, and prevents the problem of substance substitution in other treatment.

The global issue of acceptability of substances and political will has already been examined; but in the frontline services other significant barriers exist to setting up combined services. The training of social workers in the subject of substance use is limited. It is not seen as an essential in basic qualifying courses. Furthermore, the existing service structure tends to guide those people opting for work with substance users into one or other of the specialist areas, i.e. a social worker attached to a drug clinic will become a drug specialist with little knowledge of an alcohol unit, the converse also being true. Even the voluntary sector worker will (unless fortunate enough to join an agency which spans the whole field) become a specialist in one or other substance. In a combined service, therefore, the need for additional training becomes of paramount importance as does the changing of workers´ preconceived ideas about other client groups. Training is a neglected area, especially in the voluntary sector where resources are poor. Staff resistance to working with a "different" client group has also proved to be a difficult barrier to overcome.

Management Issues
Staff training and staff perceptions of individual client groups are problematic, but the management of services poses more significant difficulties. As well as funding, questions about resource issues remain as there is little quality control of services (particularly those in the non-statutory sector), and confusion as to their aims (ranging from housing to therapy). This confusion, instability and lack of control will tend to make the management of the services conservative in their approach; for example, the desire for change is not likely to exist in the case of a residential project where restrictions to one group of client, and funding tied to that group, are the basis of financial solvency. Furthermore the limited vision of an agency which has been set up to work with a single substance mitigates against consideration of wider needs unless the service appears to be under financial threat This has been evident during the Government Drugs Initiative where a number of alcohol advisory services changed their title to addiction services to try and get "drugs" money.

When considering the need for change to relate to new client characteristics, it must be remembered that there may well remain for the foreseeable future a considerable number of people who will personally identify their problem as being either drugs or alcohol, and will present in this way. The treatment programme assessor may feel that these may be more effectively dealt with by single substance units. A continued role for such services may be required, but they should be in addition to combined services and not instead of them.

To summarise, the most significant problems to be overcome in developing combined services are those of political policies, the interpretation of the nature of substance use and the removal of substance specific ties from resource allocations. At the same time, training for staff is of major importance as is modification to the legal obligations of those staff. In the voluntary sector there is a much greater need for monitoring the quality and effectiveness of the service being undertaken, especially among the non-residential agencies. Greater regulation of these, together with a form of registration which authorised people to work on a combined basis, would be beneficial. There needs to be a greater understanding on part of the agencies, both statutory and non-statutory, of the similarities and differences between the client groups in establishing priorities.

The final and perhaps major requirement is that there is a need not only for a change in attitudes but a real commitment to improving resources to this sector and using them in the most cost-effective way. Combined services can be more financially viable compared to single substance services but they can only be so if adequate resources are available. Furthermore, in order to maximise their cost-effectiveness they will have to work in a much more methodical and market-orientated fashion than they have done hitherto.

TOWARDS A NEW APPROACH TO SERVICE DELIVERY

There is no great mystique attached to any model of combined services. Essentially what we are talking about is the development of all-purpose facilities where the variables taken into account are not just the individual substance of use, but rather or more importantly the social and personal characteristics of the presenting client. Therefore the delimiting factor on admission might be one of age. Similarly, a combined service could be an effective method of working with women, for their needs are rarely met in existing drug and alcohol rehabilitation houses because they are normally in a small minority of clients. As drug use (particularly illicit drug use) continues to become more widespread, a greater part of our population of potential service users is likely to have experience with multiple substances and thus the single substance approach must become less important. With projects targeted at specific groups using a range of substances, the opportunity exists for more effective early intervention via advisory services. Service planning has to date tended to focus on the chronic end of the market. This is particularly true of hospital-based or rehabilitation agencies where existing provision geared towards those with established problems is not likely to be appropriate for the less-established drug user or drinker. This will be recognised by both the operating agency and the client.

Ideally, the service being offered in a combined operation should be flexible and should involve both residential and non-residential components. The latter can be a means of identifying potential service users early on in their using career.

Combining Alcohol and Drug Services

The development of the "vertically" integrated multi-substance service able to link the client to the most appropriate care regime is now long overdue in the areas of substance misuse. This is the most appropriate way of reaching clients, whose use pattern has changed and is likely to continue to do so. To provide a variety of treatment options for clients who have more significant commonalities than simply using substances should be the aim of all services.

This has implications for the voluntary sector and particularly for the health service since the current hospital service is limited. The development of young persons´ units or other multiple services which do not focus on individual substances would seem to be a way forward.

Self-Esteem and the Marketing Approach

The basic problem in substance use services in the UK is that there are too few of them and they are too limited in their scope. To compound this, they do not undertake the marketing exercise which is required to penetrate the substantial population of potential clients whose needs are not currently being met. It is suggested that as well as redefining the structure of services to provide a vertically integrated multi-substance approach, the marketing of those services to the public - and for that matter to the politicians and funders - is absolutely crucial.

Many practitioners have long accepted that the drug and alcohol specifications will continue to remain the Cinderellas of health and social services since they are of limited importance to politicians, funders and the public as a whole. This lack of confidence is much to blame for the current inadequate level of service provision. To remedy this it is imperative that marketing of services should be undertaken using the well established techniques in the commercial world.

Before embarking on this course, a number of other steps are necessary. Perhaps the most confusing issue for all decision-makers who are being asked to provide services has been the longstanding, often vitriolic debate, between the proponents of various theories of addictive behaviour. The result of this has not only been to effectively wreck any opportunity for sensible advice being given to those with the power to initiate service development, but also to reduce the potential for the sympathetic consideration of requests.

Some debates have been not only damaging but futile. If other variables apart from substance are important in determining the method of working with a particular client, then a range of different treatment approaches needs to be considered to enable the individual´s requirements to be met. It may well be that there are clients who are happier to work within the disease model and find it of assistance in attaining recovery. If this is the case why should they not be able to do so? There are clients who, however, have alternative ways of understanding their problem. They too must be offered the freedom of choice. It is as wrong for the treater to impose a theory of treatment on an individual client as it is to see clients fitting into narrow groups.

A further issue which requires resolution is the regular change in emphasis on type of service. Since the mid-1960s there has been a progression from hospital to residential units, to day care, advice and latterly to the employment of experts to advise primary care workers (CATS and CADETS). Each of these services has been viewed separately and often seen as an alternative to its predecessor. This is particularly true of alcohol services but is also apparent in the drugs field. The exponents of each approach tend to project their part of service provision as being the most successful and ascribe almost messianic qualities to it as being the way forward. This is presumably because of the scarcity of funding. It is obvious that this is not true and that all varieties of service have some part to play.

The move into integrated services providing a range of options for potential clients both enables and requires the treatment field (voluntary and statutory) to undertake a far more extensive marketing campaign. The concept of marketing is alien to many health and social care practitioners and it is probably the most underdeveloped and least considered aspect of any service aimed at reaching the public. A major difficulty is that the treater frequently wishes to see his or her self as being a "professional" and thereby somehow divorced from the commercial realities of the wider world.

Many services are considerably underused. The reasons are basically fivefold:

1. There is often insufficient advertising of availability of the service.
2. Accessibility to the service may be limited either geographically or by criteria of admission.
3. The potential client may not perceive the service as being appropriate, due to the image which it projects.
4. Publicity techniques used may be amateur and therefore unlikely to appeal.
5. Ideas about such services among the public may suggest that they are likely to be ineffective.

Given that many clients will have difficulty in recognising their own need to deal with problematic substance use, many of the above provide real barriers to engagement. To dispel such misconceptions marketing of services is crucial.

Combining Alcohol and Drug Services

PROMOTING THE MULTI-SUBSTANCE CENTRE

Methods of projecting a multi-substance centre to the general public will now be considered.

Firstly, the service must have a professional image to the public and not, as many drug agencies do, relish its own amateurism. It must be authoritative and show conviction in its work. It must be able to convey the importance attached to confidentiality, and be seen as an independent and objective body where the needs of the individual client are paramount.

It must be able to provide the prospective client with a range of options and be able to adjust its services to meet changing needs and changing populations, including the needs of multi-drug users. It must be multi-purpose and non-judgemental.

It must be managed effectively. The control of services and their administration is a different discipline from that of being a practitioner. As many practising specialists would admit, be they psychiatrists, psychologists or social workers, they are not the world's best managers. The disciplines that they work with in some respect operate against established management practice.

The service must be financially viable. This may mean self-funding, or adequate grant aid in the case of voluntary bodies and realistic support in the case of statutory agencies. This can probably only be achieved by activity on the part of the managerial rather than practice staff. Service providers need advocates to speak for them - beyond those who carry out the work.

The services must be sold. The professional techniques used in selling prescribed drugs to doctors or alcohol to the general public can be applied to the selling of substance services. This does not necessarily imply that one reduces the status of the health service to a packet of frozen peas but simply that one looks at the best way of maximising the take up of service, i.e. by convincing potential customers to purchase what is on offer, or to instigate through demand the creation of new or varied services. Marketing techniques are a discipline of their own. They are not likely to be within the life experience of most practitioners or indeed of many managers. It may therefore be time to look at the development of completely new professions within the health and caring agencies similar to those in industry, but borrowing from the experience of welfare rights. A welfare rights officer encourages the take up of benefits and is in effect marketing the service to potential recipients of those benefits. Such posts do not by and large exist within the health and social services. Marketing should reduce the incidence of underused services which are a significant barrier to the development of comprehensive treatment service for substance users.

To summarise, therefore, the world has changed dramatically in the last 20 years. The old models of client and substance use are no longer valid and the services we have are increasingly irrelevant to the needs of a new population of multiple users or substance substituters. Thus many existing services are becoming underutilised. Similarly, a failure to structure services to respond to changing needs has been accompanied by misguided actions on the part of practitioners leading to models of services being seen to be all-important with no attention really being paid to their marketing either to funders or to clients. If the increasing needs of the substance using population are to be met, the whole structure of treatment services in the UK must be changed as a matter of some urgency. This can only be done by employing specialists in service delivery systems and marketing, and the elevating of the service planner to a more central role. It will also require constant review of both practice and resources to be undertaken externally. This will result in a more dynamic and cost-effective service which can not only adapt itself to individual needs but can change with prevailing external circumstances.

REFERENCES

Bruun, K. (1982) Alcohol Policies in United Kingdom. Sociologiska Institutionen, Stockholm (Concerning the Report of Central Policy Review Staff in 1979)

DHSS (1978) The Pattern and Range of Services for Problem Drinkers. Report by the Advisory Committee on Alcoholism. DHSS, London

DHSS (1981) Treatment and Rehabilitation. Report of the Advisory Council on the Misuse of Drugs. DHSS, London

DHSS (1982) National Voluntary Organisations and Alcohol Misuse. DHSS, London

Murphy, J. (1985) The Overlap-Zone. Paper presented at NDSAG Conference, Cardiff, May 1985

Orford, J. (1985) Excessive Appetites. Wiley, Chichester

Raistrick, D. (1985) Some Advantages and Disadvantages of Combined Alcohol and Drug Misuse Services. NDSAG booklet No. 10

Wilson, G. (1985) An Outcome Study of Drinking Treatments on a Population of Recidivist Offenders at HMP Pentonville. Unpublished report

PART THREE

SPECIALIST COMMUNITY ALCOHOL SERVICES

Chapter 10

THE EXETER HOME DETOXIFICATION PROJECT

Tim Stockwell

INTRODUCTION

In 1985, the Exeter Community Alcohol Team (CAT) began to
promote the idea of detoxifying problem drinkers in their home
environment, as opposed to either an out-patient or in-patient
hospital setting. Initially, the need for such a service was
demonstrated by the results of a survey of local general
practitioners' attitudes and management practices (Stockwell
et al, 1986). From this base, and from earlier clinical
experience among CAT staff, a well defined set of procedures
for the conduct of home detoxification (HD) was developed and
"sold" to both GPs and hospital services. While the DHSS
funded evaluation of this service will be reported in full
elsewhere, this chapter will outline the rationale for a HD
service, describe the characteristics of the Exeter CAT
approach and discuss the practical problems and pitfalls in
setting up such a service.

First, it is important to avoid any confusion which may
be created by using the term "detoxification". For present
purposes, it will be used only to refer to treatment designed
to control both the medical and psychological complications
which may occur temporarily after a period of heavy and
sustained alcohol use. It is well established that only a
small minority of problem drinkers are likely to experience
distressing withdrawal symptoms such as delirium tremens or
convulsions (Orford and Wawman, 1986). Furthermore, in only a
tiny percentage of cases is there a risk of fatal complication
(Sparadeo et al, 1982). However, it will be argued here that
the effective, safe and humane management of alcohol
withdrawal is an essential component of an integrated
community alcohol service.

Home Detoxification

ALCOHOL WITHDRAWAL: SIGNS AND SYMPTOMS

It is possible that the consumption of any dose of alcohol by
any person is always followed by "rebound" or withdrawal
phenomena - however mild and brief these may be. Feelings of
irritability and increased sensitivity to bright lights or
loud noises commonly associated with the "hangovers" of
occasional heavy drinkers may be but one illustration
(Hershon, 1973). A few experimental studies of both
laboratory animals (MacDonnell et al 1975) and social drinkers
(Zilm et al, 1981) indicate that the threshold for minor
withdrawal symptoms may be lower than many people realise. By
contrast, the more dramatic, even alarming, manifestations of
alcohol withdrawal in severely alcohol dependent drinkers have
been studied in more detail.
    Gross and colleagues (1971) identified three quite
distinct elements or factors comprising the alcohol withdrawal
syndrome:

1. The psychological and physiological signs of mood
   disturbance and, in particular, of anxiety. Subjective
   experiences such as panic, heightened fearfulness and
   objective signs such as sweating and tremor are
   included in this category.
2. Perceptual "distortions" and hallucinations (visual,
   auditory and tactile). Related symptoms include
   nausea, muscle pain and sleep disturbance.
3. Disturbances of consciousness such as confusion and
   disorientation.

Edwards (1982) has elegantly described the nature and
variety of withdrawal symptoms with which problem drinkers
present clinically. In his account of the alcohol dependence
syndrome he explains how the intensity of early morning
withdrawal is a useful indicator of severity of alcohol
dependence. Waking after several hours sleep is likely to be
the time when a regular, heavy drinker has lowest blood
alcohol levels during any 24 hour period. The mildly
dependent problem drinker may be aware of some anxiety and
slight tremulousness in his or her hands - especially when
performing fine movements requiring careful coordination e.g.
writing or pouring a cup of tea. A desire to drink more
alcohol may develop as the morning progresses. At the other
extreme, the severely dependent drinker often awakes in the
middle of the night drenched in sweat; the whole body may be
shaking violently and, subjectively, feelings of panic and
strong urges to drink more alcohol are experienced. In both
instances, the psychophysiological signs of the anxiety
element in withdrawal are present, though at different
intensities.

The second element of alcohol withdrawal described by Gross has its fullest expression in the notorious state known as "delirium tremens" or DTs. The leading sign of this state is the occurrence of vivid visual hallucinations, which often have a nightmarish quality to them e.g. animals or insects which attack the sufferer. While such visual hallucinations may occur during a period of heavy drinking they have been described as typically occurring 24 to 72 hours after abstinence from alcohol and gradually abating over a period of between three and five days (Edwards, 1982). Furthermore, the maintenance of very high blood-alcohol levels over many days is thought to be a prerequisite for the occurrence of DTs (Gross et al, 1975). While this aspect of withdrawal is thought to affect only the most heavy and dependent drinkers, there is interesting evidence that even the DTs may be but one extreme on a continuum. Some individuals who drink heavily experience a reduction in time spent dreaming during sleep, as shown by a reduction of "rapid-eye movements" or REM. When there has been a sustained reduction of REM sleep, whether due to sleeplessness or high alcohol intake, a compensatory increase or rebound may occur during alcohol withdrawal (Greenberg and Pearlman, 1967). One clinical study of severely dependent drinkers undergoing acute alcohol withdrawal charted the development of such REM rebound culminating in the full-blown DTs (Vojtechovsky et al, 1969). Such a view of the origins of DTs is not universally accepted, however, and definitive research has yet to be conducted in this area. Nonetheless, the DTs clearly do vary a great deal in the severity of their presentation and for that reason are often missed. Edwards (1982) quotes the following descriptions given by people who experienced them in a mild or, at least, transitory form:

I would be driving along the road and suddenly something would run across in front of the car - a dog, a cat, I couldn't be sure - and I would slam on the brakes. A real fright. And then I would realise there was nothing there.

I'd be walking down the road and, zoom, a car would come up behind me and I would jump on the pavement. Frightened out of my life. But it was all imagination.
(p. 67)

Whichever aspect of alcohol withdrawal one is considering, the likelihood of its occurrence and the severity of its presentation will be approximately related to the quantity and frequency of recent alcohol intake. An assessment of severity of alcohol dependence displayed during recent drinking can also be another useful predictor of withdrawal severity (Stockwell et al, 1983). In general, the likelihood of both psychological and medical complications increases with alcohol withdrawal states of greater severity.

COMPLICATIONS OF ALCOHOL WITHDRAWAL

An occasional medical complication of alcohol withdrawal in the severely alcohol dependent drinker is the occurrence of grand mal fits. These attacks consist of generalised epileptic convulsions, a sudden loss of consciousness and convulsive movements in both arms and legs. Withdrawal fits usually occur within 24 hours of abstaining, but may also be experienced up to four days later. Edwards (1982) describes a case where such a fit resulted in a fatal driving accident. Not only is there the risk of accident or injury, but a one in three chance of delirium tremens developing which itself carries a small but significant risk to life (Orford and Wawman, 1986).

Another occasional complication which may be encountered during alcohol withdrawal is the acute development of the Wernicke-Korsakoff Syndrome. Loss of appetite, which frequently accompanies withdrawal from alcohol, may contribute towards thiamine deficiency in producing this clinical syndrome. The following case, again from Edwards (1982) illustrates the need for early thiamine treatment in order to minimise the risk of harmful (occasionally fatal) consequences.

A woman aged 48 who had been drinking a bottle of whisky each day for 19 or more years was admitted to a psychiatric hospital for peripheral neuropathy (weakness, tingling and pain in the legs). On the evening of admission, she was found to be rather confused, to be complaining of double vision, and to be staggering. By the next evening, she was stuporose and her eye movements were uncoordinated (external ocular palsies). At this stage, and very much too late, she was started on massive doses of thiamine - the classical pictures of confusion, neuritis, staggering gait and ocular palsies would have alerted the staff to the dangerous onset of a Wernicke's syndrome. After 5 days of acute illness, the confusion cleared and the patient was found to have a grossly impaired memory for recent events, a tendency to make things up to fill her gaps in memory (confabulation), and very little ability to remember new information, as witnessed by her difficulty in finding her way around the ward. This amnesic syndrome (Korsakoff's psychosis) showed very little recovery over the ensuing months and arrangements had to be made for the patient's transfer to long-term residential care.

Such dramatic, though rare, medical complications aside, the main problems experienced by the person undergoing alcohol withdrawal are of a more psychological nature. Intense craving or urges to drink, gradually waning over the first ten days of withdrawal may occur (Funderburk and Allen, 1977). Similarly, acute anxiety and depressed mood, recovering slowly over a period of two or three weeks have been charted in numerous studies of in-patient problem drinkers (Freed, 1978). These subjective experiences are not only likely to interfere with general functioning both socially and at work, but possibly jeopardise the very success of an attempted withdrawal from alcohol. The discomfort of the experience may be too great and the individual unable to refrain from further drinking.

It would appear, therefore, that a careful combination of medical and psychological care represents the ideal conditions for an individual to undergo alcohol withdrawal safely and successfully. However, many people, probably the great majority, undergo alcohol withdrawal completely unaided. Sometimes this may be due to reluctance to seek help for a problem as socially stigmatised as a drink-related one; at other times admission to hospital or prison may precipitate acute withdrawal, maybe quite unexpectedly.

Traditionally, the common practice has been to treat alcohol withdrawal in a general or psychiatric hospital ward, an alcoholism treatment unit or a special detoxification centre (Orford and Wawman, 1986). The next section will discuss the many advantages of non-institutionalised settings for managing alcohol withdrawal and those of the drinker's home environment in particular.

THE RATIONALE FOR HOME-BASED DETOXIFICATION

In a recent major review of alcohol detoxification services, Orford and Wawman (1986) state there has been an increasing recognition that detoxification frequently occurs outside residential institutional settings. It has also been argued that such non-residential settings may even be superior in some respects.

There are several possible advantages of a non-residential setting for detoxification:

1. The individual need not be removed from job, family, or any other community support systems.
2. Continuity of care by primary care and specialist community workers can be maintained.
3. Many problem drinkers who refuse to accept hospital admission may be willing to be cared for at home.
4. Non-residential care will normally be less expensive.

In the United States, most discussion of non-residential detoxification focuses upon medical out-patient settings. These reports stress the need for careful screening of suitable cases, followed by monitoring of withdrawal symptoms coupled with daily administration of medication (Whitfield, 1982; Stinnett, 1982). Factors considered important when screening for suitable cases included there being no previous history of delirium tremens or withdrawal fits. Providing these standards are met, it has been reported that out-patient detoxification can be just as safe and effective as in-patient care, while offering greater accessibility to patients and smoother linking with aftercare (Sausser et al, 1982).

Given the success of out-patient programmes, it seems a short step to recommend detoxification at home under the responsibility of a family doctor. However, is it possible to replicate the degree of close and expert supervision available in the out-patient setting?

Orford and Wawman's review (1986) discovered only one detailed discussion of home-based detoxification. This was an account of the important role of the district nurse in liaising both with GPs and the patient's family (Rix, 1979). It concluded, however, that with good nursing care and knowledge of warning signals, home detoxification will usually be uneventful and successful. Warning signs indicating the need for hospital admission were given as the following:

1. rising pulse with falling blood pressure;
2. hypothermia;
3. seizures;
4. severe diarrhoea, especially if accompanied by excessive fluid loss from sweating and vomiting;
5. deteriorating level of consciousness even if medication is withheld.

There would seem, then, to be a sound rationale for a reliance on the home as the setting of choice for most people undergoing alcohol withdrawal. There are also a number of possible pitfalls which need to be anticipated.

POTENTIAL DIFFICULTIES WITH HOME DETOXIFICATION

Abundance of Drinking Cues in the Home Environment

During the 1960s and 1970s a number of experiments were conducted, mainly in the United States, in which in-patient problem drinkers were given free access to alcohol. Typically, it was found that many patients (or "subjects") either resisted drinking completely or did so in a fairly controlled fashion (Mello and Mendelson, 1978). In one study, alcohol dispensers were provided in every bedroom (Lawson et al, 1975) and it was described how some patients would successfully resist the use of these for several weeks and yet relapse completely when on weekend leave. It would appear that the cues and temptations for drinking alcohol were specific to their usual, home environment. By comparison, hospital would seem to be a relatively "safe" environment not only on medical grounds but in terms of protecting the abstaining drinker from the high-risk drinking situations of the outside world.

Admission to hospital can be seen as just one type of **avoidance strategy** which is sometimes advocated in the behavioural management of alcohol and drug-related problems (Stockwell, 1985). Gloria Litman studied the coping styles of individuals who either "survived" or "relapsed" following hospital treatment for an alcohol problem (Litman et al, 1984). Interestingly, reliance on avoidance strategies (e.g. avoiding drinking acquaintances, avoiding drinking situations) was associated with "survival" in the first few weeks after treatment. However, longer-term survival was associated with switching to a more active coping style.

It can be anticipated that if drinking normally takes place at home, perhaps with other family members or visiting drinking partners, and if local access to alcohol is easy, then this environment may provoke more and stronger urges to drink than a hospital environment.

The Likelihood of Family Tensions
Another area of potential difficulty concerns family relationships. Alcohol is frequently cited as contributing to marriage breakdown and child abuse (Orme and Rimmer, 1981; Orford, 1977). In general, family problems and alcohol problems tend to go hand in hand. Whether it is family difficulties which are driving the drinking, or vice versa, it is likely that family tensions will place a stress on the person who is attempting to "dry out" at home. One carefully conducted study found a strong relationship between the degree of warmth and support from family and successful outcome of treatment for an alcohol problem (Moos et al, 1981). "Giving the family a break", and sometimes even the drinker, is often given as a reason for hospital admission in its own right.

Risks of Unsupervised Detoxification
At its loosest, "home detoxification" may mean a GP prescribing medication for the relief of alcohol withdrawal to a problem drinker. That this is a very common practice was confirmed by a questionnaire survey of West Country GPs (Stockwell et al, 1986). As shown in Table 10.1, this study suggested that in around half of all detoxifications arranged by GPs, the drinker remained at home. While in the majority of cases, medication was held by a friend or relative of the drinker or a nurse, in many instances (38%) the drinkers held the medication themselves.

Home Detoxification

There is much cause for concern about the widespread practice of unsupervised home detoxification, particularly if the medication chosen is chlormethiazole (brand name Heminevrin).

Table 10.1: Arrangements Made by West Country GPs for Detoxification from Alcohol

SETTING	SUPERVISOR	ESTIMATED NUMBER PER YEAR	%
Home	Self	46	(19)
	Family/Friend	55	(23)
	Nurse	22	(9)
	All	122	51
Psychiatric Hospital	Nursing Staff	96	40
General Hospital	Nursing Staff	22	9
A L L S E T T I N G S		**240**	**100%**

Table 10.2 shows that deaths from chlormethiazole poisoning have been substantial over a ten year period from 1974 in England and Wales (OPCS, 1974-84). Chlormethiazole was the most popular drug for alcohol withdrawal among the West Country GPs (75%) and a significant minority admitted to prescribing for 10 days or more without any supervision. The likelihood of such a practice resulting in the dangerous combination of chlormethiazole with alcohol when home detoxification fails cannot be underestimated.

Both chlormethiazole and other drugs commonly used to treat alcohol withdrawal (e.g. chlordiazepoxide) are potent drugs of dependence. In addition to the risk of overdose, with or without alcohol, their unsupervised use will also place the drinker at risk of either substitute or joint dependence upon alcohol.

Of psychological interest in this context is the finding that self-administration of drugs induces dependence more readily than does their passive use on an externally determined schedule. For example, withdrawal symptoms were more severe for experimental animals which had been self-adminstering morphine than their "yoked" controls who had only passively received an infusion of morphine (Siegal, in press). It may well be, then, that it is unrealistic to expect problem drinkers to self-administer their own drugs when undergoing alcohol withdrawal. They may find it extremely hard to reduce the dose, even if this has been recommended by their GP.

Table 10.2: Deaths from Chlormethiazole Poisoning for England and Wales (1974-1984)

CAUSE OF OVERDOSE	CHLORMETHIAZOLE	CHLORMETHIAZOLE AND OTHER DRUGS
Accidental	135	24
Suicide	228	45
Undetermined	111	17
TOTAL	**474**	**86**

NB: No satisfactory data are available for 1981 and so these figures refer to a total of 10 years.

Failure to keep to a recommended reducing regime may well result in problems in either over-or undersedation. Over-sedation will increase the risk of a fall or other accident. Undersedation may lead to distressing, even dangerous, withdrawal symptoms. Furthermore, even if a medication regime is adhered to exactly as prescribed, it is most unlikely that the regime will be the correct one. Severity of withdrawal is very unpredictable, varying not only from person to person but also from one occasion to another (Gross et al, 1975). Only repeated observations of the patient can ensure that the correct dose is being taken. The various possible benefits and risks of detoxification from alcohol at home are outlined in Table 10.3.

The successful out-patient detoxification programmes described above were clearly able to both screen patients carefully and monitor the withdrawal process on a daily basis. Thus they were able to minimise the risks and gain some of the benefits depicted in Table 10.3. In the following section, an approach to the practice of home detoxification will be described which aimed to replicate the same degree of supervision, safety and effectiveness.

Table 10.3: Possible Benefits and Risks of Home Detoxification in Comparison with Traditional Medical Settings

BENEFITS	RISKS
1. Client retains family and social support	1. Domestic tensions may adversely influence the procedure
2. Greater confidentiality	2. More cues associated with drinking, may provoke more intense withdrawal and urges to drink
3. Less stigma	3. Abuse of medication if unsupervised
4. Greater acceptability to the clients	4. Poor compliance if unsupervised
5. Continuity of care by primary and/or specialist community agents	5. Less medical cover in the event of severe complications (e.g. fits, DTs
6. Possibly less expensive	

SUPERVISING DETOXIFICATION AT HOME: THE EXETER METHOD

Source of Referrals

At the outset of the Exeter HD Project in mid-1985, Exeter CAT were involved in only one HD every two or three months. By contrast, our GP survey suggested in the region of 10 HDs were being arranged per month. Encouragingly, however, 75% of GPs replying to the questionnaire indicated they would value CAT supervision of HD for a significant number of their problem drinking patients. Just over one year later, CAT nurses are now involved in up to five HDs per month.

As Exeter CAT has become better known to local people, clients have increasingly referred themselves. Now a clear majority are either referred by a friend or relative or make the first contact themselves (57% in 1985). Thus when HD occurs it is usually a case of the CAT contacting the GP rather then the other way round. In only 8 of the last 30 cases has the GP referred the drinker for a HD. The evaluation of our HD service will examine the question as to whether GPs are continuing to arrange as many unsupervised HDs without CAT involvement. Since only a small minority of our clients are likely to experience distressing withdrawal symptoms when reducing or stopping their drinking, a careful assessment is conducted before a HD is started.

Assessing Suitability for Home Detoxification

Both assessment of suitability and subsequent supervision of HD are conducted exclusively by community nurses working with the CAT. A senior community nurse receives referrals, either directly from the GP or via a CAT counsellor, and arranges an assessment interview within 24 hours whenever possible. Exeter District Health Authority is divided into five localities each of which is covered by at least one community nurse who has experience in conducting HDs. While all local GPs have been leafleted (twice) and all CAT staff have been educated as to which clients are suitable, the final decision is always left with the nurse who would be supervising the HD if it went ahead. The assessment procedure consists of answering two basic questions: is there a need for any medication to cover withdrawal symptoms and if there is, are there any strong reasons for not keeping the client in the home environment while it is administered? The considerations discussed are summarised in Table 10.4.

1. Establishing the Need

No matter how severely dependent upon alcohol a client may be, it is pointless arranging HD unless the client is expressing a clear wish to stop drinking completely for at least a few weeks. If this is not forthcoming, CAT staff never use a "hard sell" approach but wait until motivation is expressed clearly.

If the client is very keen to stop, supervised medication will only be required if it seems likely that severe withdrawal symptoms would otherwise be experienced. A picture of very recent, heavy and continuous alcohol, and maybe, drug intake right up to the day of assessment would be one indication. Even one week of very heavy drinking (e.g. one bottle of spirits per day or more - i.e. 30 "units") could be sufficient to induce distressing and prolonged withdrawal. A rule of thumb that we use is that it is unlikely medication will be necessary for women drinking less than 12 units or men less than 16 units of alcohol per day.

It is vital to take a recent history of other drug use, especially for any drugs such as tranquillisers or barbiturates which may complement alcohol's CNS depressant effects. The common combination of alcohol and tranquillisers will result in a more severe and prolonged withdrawal period.

Drinkers who experience withdrawal signs every day upon waking and who soon take more alcohol (or other depressant drugs) to reduce these are very strong candidates for detoxification. If they have had any recent whole days of total abstinence from alcohol and drugs then their experience of withdrawal on such occasions will also be useful indicators. The Severity of Alcohol Dependence Questionnaire (Stockwell et al, 1983) can be a useful assessment tool here, especially the first three sections, as these provide severity scales for both physical and psychological withdrawal symptoms experienced during a recent heavy drinking period.

Table 10.4: Guidelines for Assessing Suitability for HD

---

1. **Establishing the Need**

   a) Clear desire to stop drinking

   b) Severe withdrawal symptoms indicated by recent alcohol and drug use history

---

2. **Assessing the Risks**

   a) No history of withdrawal fits

   b) GP confirms no other serious physical and psychiatric condition

   c) Home environment quiet, not unsupportive, alcohol and drug free

---

3. **Gaining Consent**

   a) Client understands procedure and gives consent

   b) Any close friend or family give informed consent

   c) GP willing to prescribe medication.

---

2. Assessing the Risks

Even highly motivated drinkers who are very likely to experience severe withdrawal symptoms will be deemed unsuitable if they have a history of withdrawal fits. The client's GP, who takes medical responsibility during HD, will be asked to be sure on this point as well as on whether there are any other medical grounds demanding admission either to a general or psychiatric hospital e.g. early signs of delirium such as an odd voice heard or fleeting vision. If we assume the absence of serious and unmanageable physical or psychiatric conditions, then the home environment must be carefully assessed. Whenever possible, the assessment

Table 10.5: Consent Form Used Before Starting Home Detoxification

---

1. CLIENT
Please sign and date this sheet as a statement that you wish to undergo detoxification at home and will comply with the following conditions:

1. That you will not take alcohol during the agreed period of detoxification and will comply with regular breathalyser recordings by CAT staff.

2. That you will take medication as agreed by GP and CAT staff.

3. Should you start drinking you will allow the CAT nurse to keep the remaining medication.

4. That you will allow CAT staff to visit your home as arranged to supervise this period and check your medical condition.

5. That you agree to your GP doing a liver function test now and also in 2 months time.

Signed: .... Date: ....

2. RELATIVE
Please sign below if you agree to the following conditions of this home detoxification:

1. That you have read and understood the information provided about alcohol withdrawal.

2. That you are willing to take responsibility for the medication prescribed by the doctor and understand the usual charge of £2.00 will be required.

3. Should any drinking take place you will return the medication to the doctor or to the CAT nurse.

4. That you will keep the daily record of medication.

Signed: .... Date: ....

---

interview is conducted in the client's home. If the client has no home, arrangements with a friendly, local landlord or landlady may be made; otherwise hospital admission will be necessary.

The home environment, if there is one, should permit the client a degree of privacy. It should not be too crowded or noisy. If there are other residents in the house, it is vital that they will either be very supportive or unobtrusive. Having no family at all can be more conducive to a successful HD than a family in which tensions are running high. It is important to discover the alcohol and drug using habits of other residents, although we have had one client who was successful with HD despite his lodger continuing to drink beer in front of him! It is also advisable to make the removal of any alcohol and drugs from the premises a condition for instigating HD. This can be done by the client him or herself without any trouble at all providing the reasons are clearly understood (e.g. reduced availability means less temptation and less craving).

If the client is both in need of detoxification and the risks of undergoing this at home are deemed to be acceptably low, the next step is to describe the procedure of HD with him or her and any important family members. Specially prepared leaflets are given out both for clients and relatives which explain these further. The client's GP is then contacted for an urgent appointment. The GP is asked if willing to take medical responsibility for HD after, once again, explaining what back-up will be provided by the CAT nurse. The GP is also asked to take a full blood count and liver function tests and to repeat these in two months time when reviewing progress. If the GP is willing for HD to proceed, a provisional medication regime is prescribed. There are no hard and fast risks about dosage regimes, the important thing being to monitor closely the individual client's state for signs of either oversedation (e.g. drowsiness, rapid fall in blood pressure) or undersedation (manifest withdrawal symptoms). An initial dosage of 25 to 100 mg of chlordiazepoxide, (or 400 mg to 800 mg of chlormethiazole) repeated three or four times daily and reduced over 5 to 9 days is recommended by the manufacturers. At this stage the client and, if available, a close friend or relative sign a form to consent to the HD proceeding (see Table 10.5). Of particular importance is the understanding that medication is only issued providing the breathalyser check on each visit is negative. It is also necessary for the client to consent to the nurse then taking charge of the medication should further drinking of alcohol take place.

Arrangements are then made for either the nurse or a reliable friend or relative to collect the prescription and look after this throughout. The length of HD has, to date, varied between 3 and 14 days depending upon problem severity.

Typically, medication is prescribed for no more than 7 days and the nurse visits twice daily for the first 3 days and then daily until the HD is completed.

Procedure at Each Visit
On every visit the nurse makes sure a standard procedure is observed. A checklist of withdrawal symptoms is completed on the basis of observations and self-report. This is known as the Symptom Severity Checklist and was developed by Shaw and Murphy (unpublished report) from a scale first used by Gross et al (1973). Each of the items are rated on a four point severity scale (0 to 3) and a score of 12 or more is deemed to indicate a level for concern. Diastolic and systolic blood pressure is then taken, both as an indicator of withdrawal severity and to ensure blood pressure is neither very high nor very low. In either of the latter cases the GP should be consulted. In a low-key and relaxed manner, the client is then breathalysed using a small hand-held "alcolmeter" (Lion Laboratories UK).
At this point the nurse is able to decide whether any further medication should be issued and also whether the amount should be more or less than that agreed with the GP. Unless previously sanctioned, large discrepancies are discussed with the GP.
In addition to these formal procedures, advice and support are given to the client and any "carer" who is involved. Reassurances are given and future plans for treatment made. As soon as practically possible, a "key-worker" or "counsellor" is allocated to the client and his or her family and, if this cannot be the nurse, a joint visit is made with the nurse before HD is completed.
It is important to stress here that the breathalyser checks are used not only for safety reasons but also to make the procedure more effective. Providing encouragement and medication contingent upon continued abstinence provides a powerful contingency contract - a tried and tested behavioural technique (e.g. Bigelow et al, 1976). By altering the client's perceptions regarding the immediate pay-offs of drinking as opposed to maintaining abstinence, it is believed this procedure both reduces urges to drink as well as the likelihood of drinking behaviour itself.

COORDINATION AND ACCESS TO THE HD SERVICE

While a detailed evaluation of the Exeter Home Detoxification Project will be reported elsewhere, it can be reported at this stage that only 6 out of our first 39 clients failed to complete HD successfully. Furthermore, some of these 6 achieved abstinence within the following fortnight, three by virtue of hospital admission and one entirely unaided.

Home Detoxification

Despite the apparent success of the service some problems have been encountered which are worthy of mention.

Initially, nursing staff were insistent that HD could only take place if a reliable friend or relative could be found to "hold" the medication. In fact, the district health authority had a policy that prevented community nurses holding patient's medicine under all circumstances. In effect, this greatly limited the clientele that were deemed suitable for CAT supervision, while GPs continued to offer many unsupervised HDs. Fortunately, it was possible to persuade the Health Authority to change its policy so that nurses were permitted to carry medication for the whole duration of a HD. As a result, several single people living alone have been helped to withdraw without recourse to hospital admission.

Another problem we have encountered concerns the conflict between needing a rapid, responsive service and the restricted hours community nurses are contracted to work. While hospital-based staff are permitted to work overtime, their colleagues in the community are denied this opportunity. Unfortunately, our experience has been that it is hard to suddenly fit a HD involving two hours or more extra work per day between 9 am and 5 pm Mondays to Fridays. Had it not been for research funding of the project, including an allowance for overtime payments, it would have been impossible to maintain the standards we set ourselves of a quick response followed by close supervision. When a quick response is not available the client very often loses interest or takes the risk of withdrawing without any medication at all.

As has been mentioned already, Exeter District Health Authority is now divided into five different localities with separate mental health teams covering each of these. At the outset of the project, specialist CAT nurses based at the 59 Centre in Exeter offered supervision of HD throughout the district and offered cover for each other during leave. More recently, CAT nurses each had to cover one particular locality only, which left two localities uncovered for a period of time. Since many referrals for all localities still come into the 59 Centre, coordination of the initial assessment and supervision of HD has sometimes been problematic. As more staff become familiar with the procedure involved in HD it can be anticipated that these problems will ease and the service will become increasingly localised. It can be anticipated that a variety of nursing personnel could become involved in supervising HD - for example, district nurses (Rix, 1979) and practice nurses.

SUMMARY

It seems likely that there have been people experiencing alcohol withdrawal in their home environment ever since alcohol has been consumed "at home" - or anywhere else for

that matter. Many methods, procedures and places have been
used to assist this process. Hospital settings have usually
been recommended as the safest for severe cases in which there
is a risk of some medical or psychiatric complication.
However, a method for supervising Home Detoxification has been
described in this chapter which promises to avoid any loss in
terms of either safety or effectiveness. While informal
methods involving GPs, family and AA can often be successful
they may also place the drinking client at real but avoidable
risk. An evaluation of this new service is underway and will
be reported towards the end of 1987.

REFERENCES

Bigelow, G., Strickler, D., Liebson, and Griffiths, R. (1976)
Maintaining disulfiram ingestion amongout-patient
alcoholics: a security-deposit contingency contracting
procedure. Behaviour Research and Therapy, 14, 378-381

Edwards, G. (1982) The Treatment of Drinking Problems. Grant-
McIntyre, Oxford

Freed, E. (1978) Alcohol and mood: an updated review.
International Journal of Addiction, 13, 173-200

Funderburk, F. and Allen, R. (1977) Assessing the alcoholic's
disposition to drink. In Gross, M. (ed) Alcohol Intoxication and Withdrawal, Volume 313. Plenum, New York

Greenberg, R. and Pearlman, P. (1967) Delirium tremens and
dreaming. American Journal of Psychiatry, 124, 133-142

Gross, M., Rosenblatt, S., Malenowski, B., Broman, M. and
Lewis,E. (1971) A factor-analytic study of the clinical
phenomena in the acute alcohol-withdrawal syndrome.
lcohologia 2, 1-7

Gross, M., Lewis, E. and Nagareijan, M. (1973) An improved
qualitative system for assessing acute alcohol psychoses
and related states (TSA and SSA). In Gross, M. (ed)
Alcohol Intoxication and Withdrawal Experimental
Studies. Plenum Press, New York

Gross, M., Kierszenbaum, H., Lewis, E. and Lee, Y. (1975)
Desire to drink - relationship to age, blood alcohol
concentration and severity of withdrawal syndrome on
admission for detoxification. Paper presented April 1975.
National Council on Alcoholism. Milwaukee, Wisconsin

Hershon, H. (1973) Alcohol withdrawal symptoms:
phenomenology and implications. British Journal of
Addiction, 68, 295-302

Lawson, D., Wilson, G., Briddell, D. and Ives, C. (1976)
Assessment and modification of alcoholics' drinking
behaviour in controlled laboratory settings: a cautionary
note. Addictive Behaviours, 1, 299-303

Litman, G., Stapleton, J., Oppenheim, A., Peleg, M. and
Jackson, P. (1984) The relationship between coping
behaviours and their effectiveness and alcoholism relapse

and survival. British Journal of Addiction, 79, 3, 283-292

MacDonnell, M., Brown, S. and Davy, B. (1975) Hyperexcitability in the neural substrate of emotional behaviour in cats after alcohol withdrawal; evidence of a rapid development of alcohol dependence. Journal of Studies in Alcohol, 36, 1480-1492

Mello, N. and Mendelson, J. (1978) Alcohol and human behaviour. In Iversen et al (eds) Handbook of Psychopharmacology, Volume 12, Drugs of Abuse, Plenum Press, New York and London

Moos, R., Finney, J. and Chan, D. (1981) The process of recovery from alcoholism: 1. comparing alcoholic patients and matched community controls. Journal of Studies on Alcohol, 42, 383-402

Office of Population Consensus and Surveys (1974-84) Deaths from Poisoning by Solid or Liquid Substances, Table 10, Series DH4, Nos. 1-10. HMSO, London

Orford, J. (1977) Impact of alcoholism on family and home. In Edwards, G. and Grant, M. (eds) Alcoholism: new knowledge and new responses, 234-243. Croom Helm, London

Orford, J. and Wawman, T. (1986) Alcohol Detoxification Services: a review. Paper prepared for DHSS, Addictions and Homelessness Research Liaison Group

Orme, T. and Rimmer, J. (1981) Alcoholism and child abuse: a review. Journal of Studies on Alcohol, 42, 273-287

Rix, K. (1979) Alcoholism and the district nurse. Community Outlook, 275-280

Sausser, G., Fishbourne, S. and Everett, V. (1982) Out-patient detoxification of the alcoholic. Journal of Family Practice, 14, 863-867

Siegal, S. (in press) Drug anticipation and drug tolerance. In M.H. Lader (ed) The Psychopharmacology of Addiction. British Association for Psychopharmacology Monographs, London

Sparadeo, F., Zwick, W., Rvggierds, D., Meek, D., Carloni, J. and Simone, S. (1982) Evaluation of social setting detoxification programme. Journal of Studies on Alcohol, 43, 1124-1136

Stinnett, J. (1982) Out-patient detoxification of the alcoholic. International Journal of the Addictions, 17 (6), 1031-1046

Stockwell, T. (1985) Behavioural approaches and alcohol sensitising agents. In Edwards, G. and Littleton (eds) Psychopharmacological Approaches to Alcoholism Treatment. Croom Helm, London

Stockwell, T., Murphy, D. and Hodgson, R. (1983) The Severity of Alcohol Dependence Questionnaire: its use, reliability and validity. British Journal of Addiction, 78, 2, 145-155

Stockwell, T., Bolt, E. and Hooper, J. (1986)   Detoxification from alcohol at home managed by general practitioners. British Medical Journal, 292, 733-735

Vojtechovsky, M., Hart, V., Simane, Z., Brezinova, V., Krus, D. and Skala, J. (1969) Influence of centrophenoxine (lucidril) on the course of sleep deprivation in alcoholics. Activ Nerv Sup, Praha, 11, 193-201 (Cited in abstracts of Quarterly Journal of Studies on Alcohol).

Whitfield, C. (1982) Out-patient management of the alcoholic patient. Psychiatric Annals, 12, 447-458

Zilm, D., Kaplan, H. and Cappell, H. (1981) Electroencephalographic tolerance and abstinence phenomena during repeated alcohol ingestion by non-alcoholics. Science, 212, 1175-1177

Chapter 11

THE 'ACCEPT' COMMUNITY PROGRAMME FOR PROBLEM DRINKERS: A
COMPARISON WITH GENERAL HOSPITAL-BASED CARE.

Gregory Potamianos and Yiannis Papadatos

INTRODUCTION

The last two decades have witnessed a significant number of
studies concerned with all aspects of problem drinking,
particularly treatment outcome. The majority of these studies
have been carried out in specialised alcohol treatment units
and/or psychiatric hospitals with special facilities for
problem drinkers (Heather and Robertson, 1983).

A substantial number of patients attending the general
medical psychiatric sevices of a general hospital (e.g.
gastro-enterology clinics, liver units, general psychiatric
services etc.) are thought to be excessive drinkers, although
patients seeking the above services tend to present primarily
for physical or psychiatric complaints rather than problem
drinking itself. Recent findings (Jariwalla, 1979; Jarman and
Kellett, 1979) suggest that some 20% of all patients admitted
to a district general hospital suffer from an alcohol-related
problem.

Community-based treatment and/or projects concerned with
the prevention and treatment of problem drinking have been in
existence for the last 10 years. ACCEPT (Addictions Community
Centres for Education, Prevention and Treatment) is one of the
largest community-based services in the country, the
headquarters of which are based in south-west London. This
organisation offers a free service to problem drinkers who
either refer themselves directly to the Centre, or are
referred by a variety of sources in the community. As many as
100 new referrals per month are dealt with at the ACCEPT
centre in Fulham.

In spite of the increasing numbers of patients referred
to district general hospitals or seeking help directly at
community-based services, very little is known about the
structure within which such regimes operate and their
effectiveness in the treatment of problem drinking. In this
chapter we examine the structural differences that exist

between the two treatment regimes: one, a community-based day centre, the other an alcoholism clinic based in a district general hospital. We also report the main findings from a recent clinical trial (Potamianos et al, 1986) aimed to evaluate the effectiveness of the community-based centre.

TWO MODELS OF TREATMENT

We will use the word "model" to mean a particular way of construing the notion of problem drinking, upon which the treatment framework/structure is based. Models, by definition, are heuristic devices which aid conceptualisation, understanding and definition of a problem.

Table 11.1 summarises the main differences between the hospital and the community-based models of treatment. The treatment approach adopted by the former operates mainly with in a "medical/organic" paradigm which focuses, primarily, towards the medical/psychiatric management of alcohol-related problems. The latter adopts a "psychosocial" approach to treatment, based mainly on individual and group counselling, although other psychological techniques are also employed.

The two models of treatment will be examined in terms of their structure and their approach towards problem drinking. Structure of treatment will be discussed in terms of: (1) referral system; (2) process of treatment; (3) follow-up and after care. Approach towards problem drinking will be discussed in terms of: (1) therapist/patient interaction; (2) attitudes to treatment.

STRUCTURE OF TREATMENT

Referral System
All patients presenting to Northwick Park Hospital with alcohol-related problems are referred from their general practitioners to either the general medical or psychiatric services of the hospital. In contrast, the majority of problem drinkers approaching the ACCEPT services are self-referred. This difference in the mode of referral may have an influence on the person's motivation to seek treatment. Patients referred to the hospital may have to wait a few weeks before they are seen by a consultant or a member of his team. Unless the patient is strongly motivated to seek treatment, the chances of not attending the appointment are high. There is evidence (Hyslop and Kershaw, 1981) to suggest that the drop-out rate on the initial consultation is associated with the length of time a patient had to wait before he consulted his doctor. ACCEPT's clients are seen within 48 hours of making an initial appointment. The almost instant availability of the community-based services may enhance client motivation and prevent further complications arising.

211

Table 11.1: Difference Between the General Hospital and Community-Based Models of Treatment

	Hospital	Accept
1. Referral System	Mainly from general practitioners, accident and emergency and cross departmental referrals	Primarily self-referred clients
2. Appointment	Formal letter – 2-3 weeks before patient is seen	Appointments over phone or by walking in. Clients seen within 48 hours
3. First Interview	Short. Directed mainly at medical and psychiatric symptoms	Long and informal. Directed towards social and psychological issues. Matching of client to counsellor
4. Attitudes to Problem Drinking	Negative and often hostile	Warm. A number of counsellors recovered problem drinkers
5. Treatment Procedure	Out-patient appointments. Short admissions for clinical management and detoxification. Social work and referral to specialised alcoholism units	Daily attendance. Individual and group counselling, plus a variety of other groups. Home visits and support for families
6. Follow-Up	Variable. When patient does not respond usually discharged or referred elsewhere	Variable. Clients are encouraged to keep in touch. Evening groups to monitor abstinence.

Process of Treatment

With regard to the hospital services, the majority of patients are seen initially in out-patient clinics (both medical and psychiatric) unless urgent hospitalisation is required, such as for some patients presenting to the accident and emergency services of the hospital. In view of the fact that an out-patient clinic is usually quite busy, and the lack of special facilities for problem drinkers, the latter are seen along with the general medical or psychiatric patients. The intitial interview tends to be brief and concentrates mainly on the presenting symptomatology. Depending on the circumstances and the severity of the presenting problems, patients may be given medication and advised to cut down their drinking. A further appointment may be arranged, at the discretion of the doctor, within the next 2-3 months. If admission to the hospital is necessary, this is usually arranged as soon as a bed becomes available. Admission to the hospital usually lasts for a week and is aimed at detoxification and medical/psychiatric management. Involvement of other professionals such as social workers during the admission is arranged as necessary. Drug treatment is the main focus during the short stay at the hospital, particularly with patients likely to experience severe withdrawal symptoms. No other special procedures are employed and the usual ward routine is applied to problem drinkers, as with the rest of medical/psychiatric patients.

Problem drinkers presenting at the ACCEPT services are faced with a procedure and resources available to them different from those described above. Contact is usually made by telephone to invite the client to attend an interview with one of the centre's counsellors. The latter are usually recovered problem drinkers who have received appropriate training at the centre. Interviews last for about an hour and tend to focus on psychosocial dysfunction. Particular emphasis is placed on the circumstances and factors relevant to the client's current difficulties. It is interesting to note that, where possible, an attempt is made to match client and counsellor, in terms of age, educational and social background. The reason for such an approach is that the closer the match the more confident and at ease the communication is presumed to be. Upon completion of the initial interview, the client is shown around the centre and is introduced to the principles and ideology of his subsequent treatment. Following this, the client is assigned to a therapist for individual counselling, usually two to three times per week, and is asked to participate daily in the centre's activities. These are mainly group meetings, although special treatment regimes such as relaxation classes, yoga and transactional analysis are also available. Evening groups are available for clients' relatives and for a small

number of clients who are not able to attend during the day.
In addition to the above, daily supervision is offered to
those clients in receipt of medication. Length of treatment
varies according to individual progress and severity of
dependence. Referral to other agencies, usually local
hospitals, is made for clients in need of medical or
psychiatric management.

Follow-Up and After Care
With regard to hospital treatment, length and frequency of
follow-up is determined by agreement between doctors and
patients. Follow-up takes place in the out-patient clinics,
unless further hospitalisation is required. If, after several
follow-up appointments, patients are unable to abstain, they
are referred to special alcohol treatment centres. There is
no formal follow-up procedure for clients attending ACCEPT.
Upon completion of the treatment package clients return to
work but are strongly advised to keep in touch with the
centre, mainly by evening group attendance. This is often
construed as a "second phase" treatment, the aim of which is
to help the client maintain sobriety.

THERAPEUTIC APPROACH TO PROBLEM DRINKING

Therapist/Patient Interaction
The importance of therapist/patient interaction is reflected
in increasing numbers of reports in the literature. Problem
drinkers, like any other patient, respond psychologically to
the kind of relationship they develop with their
doctor/therapist. Edwards (1982) in describing the "basic
work" of treatment of alcoholism notes:

> It is, though, vital that attention should be given to
> the subtle and important range of happenings which occur
> whenever patient and therapist meet and interact, the
> what, when and how of what is felt and said and done
> between them. Otherwise, we are at risk of throwing out
> as packaging what is, in fact, the essential content of
> the parcel.

Clinical experience suggests that problem drinkers are
vulnerable, guilt-ridden and have low self-esteem. Initial
contacts with the therapist tend to be vital for the
therapeutic process that follows. The therapist with the
ability to show warmth and understanding as well, as inspire
hope, is likely to generate continuity with his patient but
also to achieve better therapeutic outcome (Hopson, 1981).
The therapeutic relationship that occurs between the patient
presenting to the hospital and his doctor, and the self-
referred client presenting to the centre and his lay therapist
are of equal importance for the treatment, irrespective of the

diversity of skills and/or qualifications of the therapist. The extent to which use of the therapeutic ralationship is made is likely to differ between the treatment models under consideration. Such a difference does not necessarily suggest that therapists from one setting are more capable of making use of such an issue than those from the other. Possible differences between the treatment regimes may be due to the attitudes held towards alcoholic patients and the way problem drinking is construed by each treatment model.

Attitudes to Treatment

Attitudes and perceptions held by staff and patients have been considered to have important implications for the response to treatment in both organic and psychological disorders (Mogar, 1969). This may be particularly important for problem drinkers since their condition may involve both physical and psychological disorders. In spite of this, research on staff and patient attitudes has been relatively neglected. With regard to general hospital treatment of "alcoholism", it seems likely that many alcholics in general hospitals are not identified because of negative medical staff attitudes. Two further studies, one by Rankin et al (1967) and the other by Wolf et al (1965) found negative attitudes towards the medical treatment of "alcoholism" amongst Australian physicians and negative attitudes towards alcoholic patients, respectively. As the authors of the later study put it, physicians prefer a medical diagnosis to one that includes psychosocial dysfunction. Thus, it rarely occurs that the physician views the alcoholic as a person with an illness that has certain physiological, psychological and social concomitants; the typical occurrence is rather the diagnosis of a particular physical or systems disorder in a person who also happens to be an "alcoholic".

Concentrating purely on the medical or the psychiatric disorders associated with problem drinking not only fails to appreciate its complexity and the importance of team work but also possibly reinforces the patient's perception that a solution to excessive drinking may be found by alleviating just the physical or psychiatric symptoms. Two recent studies (Potamianos et al, 1985 and Potamianos 1985b) carried out at Northwick Park Hospital confirm the above picture. The first study investigated hospital staff and general practitioners' perceptions of problem drinkers. It was found that both hospital staff (doctors and nurses) and general practitioners hold a negative stereotype with regard to problem drinkers, irrespective of speciality in the former group. The second study examined the attitudes held in relation to "alcoholism" treatment both by staff and patients in terms of preference shown towards a "medical" or a "psychological" approach to the problem. Not surprisingly, doctors and nurses favoured a "medical/organic" model of treatment. It is interesting to

215

note, however, that patients' preferences were significantly more medically orientated. Such attitudes are likely to have implications for the way that treatment for problem drinking is construed by staff and patients. As the authors put it, "On the basis of the present findings, it appears that patients are likely to hold the staff responsible for their treatment in a way that their contribution towards successful outcome becomes minimal". In other words, problem drinkers approaching the hospital hold the same attitudes as, say, patients referred to a surgeon for an operation. This kind of interaction would necessitate the surgeon taking almost total responsibility for a successful outcome, while the patient's contribution is minimal.

With regard to ACCEPT treatment, the attitudes and perceptions held by the centre's staff have not been investigated. In view of what has been discussed in relation to the treatment process, one can speculate that staff attitudes would be less negative given their background and the general ideology of the centre.

ASSESSING TREATMENT OUTCOME

We have discussed, so far, the way that two distinct services operate, and highlighted the main differences between them. One of the best ways to assess treatment effectiveness is by means of a randomised controlled trial. This task was undertaken by the first author (GP) and his colleagues at Northwick Park Hospital in England. We now report details of how the trial was carried out and the main findings and conclusions to be drawn from them.

THE CLINICAL TRIAL

Background
The study was carried out at Northwick Park Hospital and in association with the MRC Clinical Research Centre both of which are situated in Harrow, Middlesex. Northwick Park is a general hospital without a specialised unit for alcohol or drug problems. With the exception of a weekly alcohol clinic run by a consultant psychiatrist, the majority of referrals for alcohol problems are dealt with by the consultant physicians in general medicine or by consultant psychiatrist in the course of their normal duties.

During 1980 a Harrow District Planning Team for Alcoholism was established. As a result suitable premises for a centre were identified (the Broadway Clinic in North Harrow, approximately three miles from Northwick Park Hospital) and the Harrow District Management Team approved the establishment of the day centre for a period of three years. The day centre's activities (day to day running of the centre, designing of therapeutic regimes, funding of staff and so on) joint advisory committee including key personnel from the hospital was established.

AIM OF THE STUDY

A randomised controlled trial of day centre treatment of alcoholism was undertaken, the main aim of which was to compare the services offered by the ACCEPT day centre with the conventional in- and out-patient management provided by a district general hospital in the treatment of problem drinking.

METHODS

Subjects
One hundred and fifty-one new patients were recruited for this study. A new patient was defined as someone who had not received treatment for alcoholism either at Northwick Park or ACCEPT for at least one year before admission to the study. All patients were referred to Northwick Park from general practitioners in the hospital's catchment area. A very small number of patients who referred themselves to the hospital, were advised to contact their GP first and follow the usual referral procedures. Patients were referred to the study either via general medical or psychiatric specialities. Most patients in the former instance were referred from two general medical out-patient clinics although a small number of patients were referred from the departments of cardiology, physical medicine and accident and emergency. These latter patients were transferred to one or other of the above consultant physicians for follow-up purposes. Psychiatric referrals came from four consultant psychiatrists.

Criteria for Inclusion
Subjects included in the study fulfilled the following criteria:
1. Patients of either sex referred from either the medical and psychiatric service of Northwick Park and who, in the view of the referring consultant, suffered from an alcohol problem;
2. aged 18 to 60 inclusive;
3. alcohol consumption 80g of alcohol daily during a heavy drinking period;
4. all patients considered for the trial had to agree to accept the treatment which was recommended to them and be prepared to travel to Northwick Park or the ACCEPT day centre;
5. the referring consultant had to agree that his/her patient would be randomly allocated to either treatment;
6. patients had to agree that they had an alcohol-

6. patients had to agree that they had an alcohol-
related problem and wanted treatment for it.

Criteria for Exclusion

Patients who did not meet the above criteria were excluded
from the study. The decision to exclude patients from the
study was taken jointly by the research psychologist and the
referring consultant. In addition, we excluded patients who
had serious psychiatric or physical disorders such as organic
brain damage, psychoses or acute liver failure. Itinerants
and registered drug addicts were also excluded.

Randomisation

Each patient was assigned at random, after the initial
interview with the first author, to either hospital or ACCEPT
treatment. Randomisation was stratified so that the sexes and
source of referral (medical or psychiatric) were balanced
between the treatment groups. The necessary arrangements for
randomisation and treatment were made by the statistician and
research assistant. The psychologist was not involved in
either treatment and was unaware of patients' randomisation.
Thus, the trial was single-blind in order to reduce any bias
regarding follow-up assessment.

Procedure for Initial Assessment

As already noted, patients were referred via the general
medical and psychiatric out-patient clinics. As soon as a
patient was identified as a problem drinker by a consultant or
a member of his team, the clinical psychologist was called to
make arrangements for an assessment. When admission to the
hospital was not necessary an appointment, within a week, was
given to the patient. Patients were asked to abstain from
alcohol particularly on the day of the assessment. A brief
introduction was given to all patients with regard to the
assessment procedure. The importance of a few days abstention
was highlighted to all patients in view of the fact that most
questionnaires were self-administered, and required
concentration and acccuracy. Care was taken to ensure that
patients had consumed no alcohol on the day of the assessment.
This was done subjectively by smelling the patient's breath
and also checking with an informant. Similarly, when a
patient was admitted for medical or psychiatric management,
assessment did not take place until a week after admission.
With very few exceptions, all patients considered for
assessment had approximately a week's abstention from alcohol.
All patients were asked to come for assessment with an
informant if at all possible - usually husband, wife, close
relative or friend.

The initial assessment was carried out in two parts. In
the first part, the purpose of the study was explained to the
patient and his suitability was considered. Once the patient

agreed to participate, provided he met the criteria for inclusion, the assessment proper began. Depending on the circumstances, the informant was interviewed while the patient was completing the self-administered questionnaires or he/she was interviewed by the research assistant. The research assistant was given two months training in interview techniques with particular reference to alcohol history taken from the informant. After completion of the questionnaires, blood was taken from the patient for routine laboratory tests. Finally, patient and informant were given an appointment for their 3 month follow-up. All assessments took place in the hospital and lasted for two hours.

Procedure for Follow-up Assessment
The follow-up assessment procedure was similar to the above. Three weeks prior to each follow-up, patients and informants were sent a letter to remind them of the date and time of their interview. Patients who, for a variety of reasons, did not respond to the reminder, were sent another reminder or were contacted by telephone. Two patients who had twice failed their follow-up appointments agreed to be interviewed at home. With the exception of the above, all follow-up assessments were carried out at the hospital. Each assessment lasted for one and a half hours.

Procedure for Drinking Assessment
At the initial interview, patients were asked to indicate a recent period of time when their drinking was heavy (their own definition). An exact period of time was identified in order to establish what was considered to be typical of their recent drinking. This was done by probing and checking the patients' reports in order to obtain as accurate a picture as possible. Drinking amount and type was recorded and later converted into grams of alcohol. This was particularly important, since a significant number of patients drank beers or lagers which contained twice the alcohol of other brands.
Follow-Up Assessment: First an inquiry was made regarding the time the patient was abstinent between interviews. This was recorded in terms of days' abstinence, and at one year follow-up the days of abstinence were added up and converted into weeks of abstinence during the year of follow-up. Drinking amount was recorded in terms of units of alcohol and then converted into grams of alcohol. Once the days of abstinence were noted, patients' drinking amounts were recorded in terms of low drinking days (up to 4 pints of beer or the equivalent amounts), "moderate" drinking days (up to 8 pints of beer of the equivalent amounts) and "heavy" drinking days (16 pints of beer or more). The results were analysed in terms of grams of alcohol consumed per day.
Drinking Amounts: Patients were asked to indicate where they did most of their drinking. Responses were recorded in terms

of drinking at home, public houses, both at home and pubs or other places (e.g. work, park benches etc.).

There has been much debate concerning the truthfulness of self-reported alcohol consumption by problem drinkers participating in treatment research studies. Contrary to the lay view that "alcoholics are liars", useful levels of agreement have been reported between self-reports, and informants' reports, as well as with more objective measures such as blood alcohol level (Polich et al, 1980). Perhaps the most prudent course is to assess alcohol intake by all of these means and to check the degree of consistency between them.

Such an approach was adopted in the present study with equal importance being placed on the patients' reports of their drinking, their informants' reports and also the results of physical tests.

TREATMENT

The treatment procedures have already been described. Patients who dropped out or refused a particular item of treatment, whether from the hospital or ACCEPT, were still regarded as members of the relevant treatment group and were followed up as assiduously as possible.

OUTCOME ASSESSMENT

Treatment outcome was assessed using the following questionnaires and laboratory tests.

Patients' Interview Schedule
Data were elicited in the following areas: personal details, medical complications, drinking history, drinking pattern, drinking amount, drinking ambience, criminal involvement, use of other drugs and a physical symptoms checklist. With the exception of personal details, the same questions were asked at 3, 6 and 12 month assessments.

Informants' Interview Schedule
This is similar to the above and was designed to elicit data from the informants which could be compared to patients' reports. It was repeated at 3, 6 and 12 month intervals.

Eysenck Personality Questionnaire (EPQ, Adult Form)
The EPQ was developed and validated on British populations by Eysenck and Eysenck (1975). As its name implies, it measures personality on three dimensions: extraversion, neuroticism (or "emotionality") and psychoticism (or "tough-mindedness").

Crown-Crisp Experimental Index (CCEI)
The CCEI was developed and validated on British populations by Crown and Crisp (1979). It is designed to obtain a close approximation to the diagnostic information that would be gained from a formal clinical psychiatric examination. It is divided into six sub-scales which intend to measure, respectively, free-floating anxiety (A), phobic anxiety (P), obsessionality (traits and symptoms) (O), somatic concomitants of anxiety (S), depression (D) and hysterical personality traits (H). It also provides a total score as a measure of overall psychopathology.

The Adjustment Inventory (Adult Form)
This questionnaire was developed and validated on North American populations by Bell (1963). It provides five separate measures of personal and social adjustment, namely; home, health, social, emotional and occupational adjustment as well as a total score. It is a relatively short and reliable self-administered instrument although it has a slight disadvantage of being standardised with North American populations. In the absence of a short and self-administered British equivalent, the adjustment inventory was chosen to measure social adjustment in the present study and it was used at admission, 3, 6 and 12 month follow-up, in order to assess possible changes over the period of one year.

Treatment Expectancies Questionnaire (TEQ)
The TEQ, together with the Direction of Interest Questionnaire (DIQ) and Attitudes to Treatment Questionnaire (ATQ) constitute the Claybury Selection Battery. The battery is intended to select patients for appropriate treatment regimes. Its use is described in greater detail elsewhere (Potamianos et al, 1985). The TEQ measures patients' expectancies regarding psychological and psychiatric treatment. It is a short and self-administered questionnaire, which aims to differentiate a psychosocial attitude to treatment from an organic/medical one. The TEQ was administered at admission to investigate the extent to which it may relate to treatment outcome.

Wechsler Memory Scale
This is a clinical instrument designed to identify memory deficits primarily in cases of organic brain disease. It was developed in the USA by Wechsler (1945) and has been used widely in this country. Although seven sub-test scores are possible, each supposedly measuring a different facet of memory, only the total score indicating overall ability will be reported here. The rationale for using such a scale was to assess pre-treatment cognitive status and possible changes that might have occurred as a result of treatment, particularly after long-term abstinence. Since patients with

organic brain disease (as assessed by the referring physician/psychiatrist) were excluded from the study, the scale was not intended to detect dementia.

Severity of Alcohol Dependence Questionnaire (SADQ)
This instrument was developed and validated on British samples of problem drinkers by Stockwell et al (1979). It is based on the notion of the alcohol dependence syndrome and it measures dependence on alcohol along a continuum of physical and psychological symptoms. Scores on this questionnaire range between 0-60, with a cut off score of 30 and above indicating severe dependence. The SADQ was employed, in this study, for two main reasons: to assess patients severity of alcohol dependence at entering the trial and the subsequent changes that may occur during treatment and secondly, to determine whether severity of alcohol dependence is related to treatment outcome. The SADQ was administered at entry, 3, 6 and 12 months follow-up.

Hepatic and Haematological Indices
The following hepatic and haematological indices were used: (1) gamma glutamyl transferase (IU/l), (2) mean cell volume (fl).

Blood counts were performed within 24 hours of blood collection with a Coulter Counter Model S. Liver tests were performed by standard laboratory methods. The above indices were used to (1) determine the extent of liver damage in our sample; (2) to examine the possible changes that might occur during treatment and (3) to establish their relationship to treatment outcome. Tests were performed at entry to the trial and at 3, 6 and 12 month follow-ups.

Further Outcome Measures: Extra Help Received and Treatment Details
Problem drinkers in receipt of a prescribed course of treatment often seek addtional help for their condition (Edwards et al, 1977). In order to determine the type and frequency of any additional help that patients had received a structured interview schedule "Extra help received" was administered, the present study at 3, 6 and 12 month intervals. Additional help including AA meetings, social work, and welfare services were recorded. With regard to additional help, details of treatment, number of out-patient medical and/or psychiatric appointments were recorded, as well as the number of days as an in-patient in a medical or psychiatric ward.

Details of the ACCEPT treatment were noted in terms of days attending the centre. Moreover, the number of sessions which patients received at the day centre were also noted. The sessions recorded were under the following activities: Gestalt (transactional analysis), relaxation classes, yoga, art, workshop, individual counselling, self-assertion and group therapy.

STATISTICAL ANALYSIS

The patients´ improvement for every outcome variable was assessed from the difference between the value at recruitment and that at the one year follow-up. The difference between mean improvement in the two treatment groups was assessed by the paired t-test. Multiple regression was used when several explanatory variables were considered.

RESULTS

Recruitment was carried out between October, 1981 and June, 1983. During this period, 184 patients were referred to the trial. From those patients, 20 refused treatment although they recognised the existence of an alcohol-related problem. Ten patients did not attend the initial assessment although they agreed to participate in the study when first referred. Two patients lived outside the hospital´s catchment area which made commuting to either the hospital or ACCEPT difficult and one patient was excluded on the grounds of being a registered drug addict.

Table 11.2 shows the number of men and women who participated in the trial divided into medical and psychiatric referrals. One hundred and fifty-one (151) patients were admitted to the trial. Of those, 105 were men (70% of the sample) and 46 women (30% of the sample). When the sample was divided into medical and psychiatric referrals, it was found that half of the sample were referred from the general medical services and the rest from the psychiatric services of

Table 11.2: Number of Men and Women Admitted to the Trial

Referral Source:	Medical	Psychiatric	Total
Men	52	53	105
(%)	(50)	(50)	(100)
Women	24	22	46
(%)	(52)	(48)	(100)
Total	76	75	151
(%)	(50)	(50)	(100)

the hospital. This was fortuitous and no conscious effort was made to include equal numbers from each source.

Randomisation resulted in generally satisfactory matching of the hospital and the ACCEPT groups, except that the latter group had on average, a higher stated alcohol consumption, although a lower GGT. This has been taken into account in the analysis. Fifty-one men and 19 women were randomised to the hospital group and 54 men and 27 women to the ACCEPT group. At one year, 115 patients (79%, including 5 patients who died during the trial) were successfully accounted for at follow-up (see Table 11.3).

Table 11.3: Follow-up Rates for Patients and Informants at Admission and Follow-up

	Patients		Informants	
	n	(%)	n	(%)
Admission	151	100	77	100
3 month follow-up	113	75	59	78
6 month follow-up	106	71	41	54
12 month follow-up	115	76	39	51

Figure 11.1 shows the results of the main outcome variables for all patients who completed the trial. For most variables in both groups there was a considerable improvement at the 3 month follow-up assessment, and this was maintained throughout the follow-up year. Alcohol consumption, as reported by the patients, was considerably lower at 3 months and this pattern continued throughout the year. Reports on alcohol consumption from informants and patients on admission to the trial were in fair agreement ($r = 0.52$, $p < 0.001$).

Tables 11.4 and 11.5 show mean daily alcohol consumption in the groups at recruitment and at one year follow-up. Consumption was about halved in all groups. Multiple regression analysis showed a significant difference for source of referral ($p = 0.053$), the improvement in psyciatric referrals being greater than in medical referrals. Although the difference between the sexes was not significant, Table 11.4 shows that intake was lower (as expected) in women. The apparent trend for women to benefit more from ACCEPT than hospital treatment and the reverse for men, also failed to reach statistical significance.

Figure 11.1: A Comparison of ACCEPT and Hospital Subjects Before Treatment and at Follow-Up Points on Main Outcome Measures

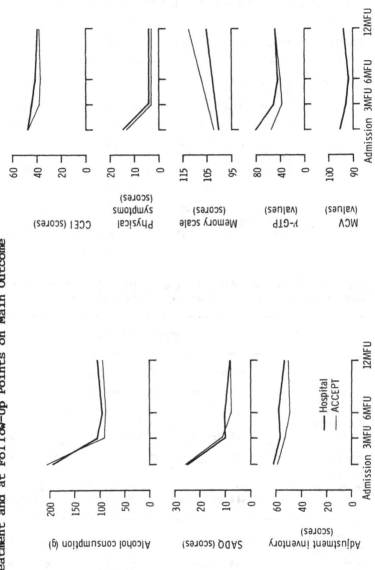

Table 11.4: Average Daily Alcohol Intake (Units) before Treatmer and at 12 Month Follow-up for the Two Treatment Groups

TREATMENT	ASSESSMENT	MEN	WOMEN	TOTAL
Hospital	Pre-treatment	25	17	23
	Follow-up	15	12	14
	% Decrease	40% (n=28)	30% (n=25)	37% (n=53)
Accept	Pre-treatment	27	25	26
	Follow-up	14	9	12
	% Decrease	50% (n=40)	63% (n=22)	55% (n=62)
Total	Pre-treatment	26	21	25
	Follow-up	14	10	13
	%Decrease	45% (n=75)	63%(n=40)	47% (n=115)

Table 11.5: Average Alcohol Intake (Units) before Treatment According to Treatment Group and Referral Source

	REFERRAL SOURCE		
	Medical	Psychiatric	Total
HOSPITAL			
Pre-treatment	22	23	22
Follow-up	17	11	14
Decrease%	24% (n=28)	52% (n=28)	37% (n=53)
ACCEPT			
Pre-treatment	25	28	26
Follow-up	12	12	12
Decrease %	51% (n=32)	58% (n=30)	55% (n=62)
TOTAL			
Pre-treatment	24	26	25
Follow-up	14	11	13
Decrease %	39% (n=60)	56% (n=55)	47% (n=115)

Table 11.6 gives the scores on psychosocial indices and blood tests in the two groups. There were no significant differences between the groups for any of the outcome

measures. 17% of patients attending ACCEPT and 10% of those attending the hospital were abstinent for the 12 month follow-up period.

The use made of health services (out-patient appointments, in-patient admissions, and GPs visits) did not differ between the two groups. The average in-patient costs over the year for the ACCEPT and hospital groups were £498 and £687, respectively. In addition, there was less use of out-patient and GP facilities by the ACCEPT group. Out-patient costs were, respectively, £72 and £70 and GP costs £39 and £37 for hospital and ACCEPT patients over the year. Unemployment rose by only 2% in both groups.

Table 11.6: Psychosocial and Biochemical Indices by Treatment Group Before Treatment and at One Year Follow-Up

Index	Hospital		Accept	
	Pre-treatment	Follow-up	Pre-treatment	Follow-up
*SADQ	23.9	7.6 (40)	23.9	8.4 (49)
*CCEI	48.0	37.6 (41)	47.3	37.7 (54)
Adjustment Inventory	64.7	52.2 (40)	58.7	50.4 (50)
Wechsler Memory Scale	101.2	104.7 (43)	104.7	111.3 (50)
Mean Cell Volume (MCV)	96.3	94.0 (46)	95.7	94.2 (51)
GGT (IU/1)	83.4	53.8 (37)	54.6	51.6 (47)

N.B. Values are given as the arithmetic mean except those for GGT which are geometric means. Number of subjects are shown in parentheses. See text for statistical analysis.
* SADQ = Severity of Alcohol Dependence Questionnaire; CCEI = Crown-Crisp Experimental Index.

It is worth noting that over 80% of all patients who were followed up were satisfied with their treatment, irrespective of the group to which they were assigned. More importantly was the fact that all but four patients felt that the follow-up assessments were as therapeutic as the treatment they received, irrespective of the group to which they had been randomly assigned.

CONCLUSIONS

We have attempted to outline the differences between two distinct forms of treatment for problem drinkers. We have also reported the main findings of a clinical trial designed to compare the two treatment settings.

No differences in outcome were found between the two patient groups, apart from stated alcohol consumption. These findings should be interpreted with caution since the probability of obtaining a significant difference at 5% in at least one out of eight outcome variables purely by chance is 34%. However, since stated alcohol consumption was the outcome variable of main interest, the difference in the two groups in favour of the ACCEPT services is noteworthy, particularly as the difference is reinforced by the informants' reports.

The findings of this trial have implications for both research and clinical practice.

Research

Research regarding general hospital and community-based treatment for problem drinkers has been neglected. In addition to the above study, recent work by Chick et al (1985) has demonstrated that problem drinkers admitted to medical wards of a general hospital and received brief counselling sessions, showed greater improvement than patients who received medical management but no counselling (see Chapter 5). These results are encouraging not only because they stimulate new hypotheses to be tested but also because they suggest that the "generalist" setting may be as effective as the "specialist" one. It is well established that problem drinkers do not constitute a homogeneous population. Recent studies (Potamianos et al, 1986; Wodack et al, 1985) suggest that problem drinkers presenting to a general hospital exhibit mild to moderate dependence as compared with samples of patients attending a specialist alcohol or liver unit. Moreover, the former seem to be a relatively stable population in terms of family background, accommodation and criminal record. Discussions with the ACCEPT staff suggest that the majority of their cients present at early stages of their dependence where intervention is more likely to be successful.

The need for further research in both general hospital and community settings is only too obvious with particular reference to the following issues:

1. **The GP and the Hospital Doctor as a Counsellor to Problem Drinkers.** The question here is whether educating and sensitising doctors to alcohol-related issues may enable them to offer practical advice which, in addition to medical management, could prove effective.

2. **Inform and Correct False Expectations.** Clinical experience suggests that when a member of the day centre visited a patient at the hosptial and explained the functions of the centre and the possible course of action, this increased the motivation of the patient and their likelihood of attending the centre.

3. **Problem Drinkers approaching the General Hospital or the Community Centre.** The notion that problem drinkers constitute a heterogeneous population is well established. The questions that may be asked are: are those problem drinkers approaching the general hospital and community setting different from other groups (e.g. those referred to liver units)? This may be asked in terms of demographic characteristics, degree of dependence, medical complications and compliance with treatment, for example.

4. **Regular Assessment as a Therapeutic Tool.** We have mentioned already that the patients in our study perceived the follow-up assessment to be as therapeutic as the actual treatment they received. The hypothesis to be tested here is whether regular assessment and instant feedback on the patient's medical, psychological, social conditions may have a therapeutic value in its own right.

We have attempted to give a flavour of the kind of questions that may be investigated with regard to general hospital and community approaches to problem drinking. We can only hope that our suggestions may stimulate some further research into these issues.

Direction of Clinical Practice

The treatment of alcohol problems, whether aimed at total abstinence or controlled drinking, has been an issue of long and polemical debate. Previously published research into treatment outcome suggests that no particular treatment regime is more effective than any other (Miller and Hester, 1980). Methodological problems, mainly uncontrolled clinical studies, contribute to such a conclusion. It has been argued that both the general hospital and the community-based settings are potential sources of treatment for problem drinkers. The structural differences that define the two facilities should provide the basis for integrating these models rather than keeping them apart and in competition. As Edwards (1982) comments:

> The prime reason why the alcoholism treatment response cannot be allowed to be narrowed into any one mould (only in-patient units, only specialist services, only AA

orientation or only anything else) is that the problems
set by excessive drinking are vastly diverse.

The services offered by a district general hospital and a
community-based centre such as ACCEPT should be seen as
complementing each other. Each facility offers a range of
services that are lacking in the other. Both facilities can
offer a vast range of services so important for the treatment
of such a complex phenomenon as problem drinking. On this
basis, one could argue that clinical practice may be enhanced
by adopting a systems approach to problem drinking. This is
not simply an argument for adopting an "eclectic" rather than
a "reductionist" approach. A systems approach may enable us
to understand the very process of interaction between the
general hospital and community-based services as well as their
potential to grow and adapt to increasing demands.

Although experience suggests that there exists
communication, in terms of cross referrals, between ACCEPT and
a variety of local services (e.g. general hospital, police,
social services) this is carried out mainly on an ad hoc basis
rather than in a well planned and systematic framework.
Furthermore, such a framework should be subjected to
experimentation to evaluate its effectiveness.

Considering our results, we propose that the community-
based service has a significant part to play in the treatment
of problem drinking in a district hospital setting.

In Greece where we now work, problem drinking has been
the most neglected field of study and clinical practice in
both general medicine and psychiatry. This is particularly
alarming in view of the observed changes in the drinking
behaviour of the population, especially in younger age groups.

As a community-based psychiatric service in conjunction
with our recently developed 24 hour crisis intervention
telephone "life line", we are in the process of establishing
the first "walk in" service for problem drinkers and drug
abusers in the country.

REFERENCES

Barrison, I. (1982) Detecting excessive drinking among
    admissions to a general hospital.Health Trends, 14, 80
Bell, H., (1963) Manual for the Adjustment Inventory.
    Consulting Psychologists Press, Palo Alto, California
Chick, J., Lloyd, D. and Crombie, E.(1985) Counselling
    problem drinkers in medical wards: a controlled study.
    British Medical Journal, 290, 965-967
Crown, S. and Crisp, A. (1979) Manual of the Crown-Crisp
    Experimental Index. Hodder and Stoughton, London
Edwards, G. (1982) The Treatment of Drinking Problems: a
    guide for the helping professions. Grant-McIntyre, London

Eysenck, H.J. and Eysenck, S.B. (1975) Manual of the Eysenck Personality Questionnaire. Hodder and Stoughton, London

Heather, N. and Robertson, I. (1983) Controlled Drinking. Methuen Press, London

Hopson, B. (1981) Counselling and helping. In Griffiths, G. (ed) Psychology and Medicine. British Psychological Society, Leicester

Hyslop, A. and Kershaw, W. (1981) Non attenders of an alcoholism referral clinic.Health Bulletin, 39, No 5,314

Jariwalla, A. (1979) Alcohol and acute- general- medicine admissions to hospital. Health Trends, 11, 95.

Jarman, C. and Kellett, J. (1979) Alcoholism in the general hospital. British Medical Journal, 2, 46

Miller, W. and Hester, R. (1980) Treating the problem drinker. In Miller, W. (ed) The Addictive Behaviours: treatment of alcoholism, drug abuse, smoking and obesity. Pergamon Press, New York

Mogar, R. (1969) Staff attitudes towards the alcoholic patient. Archives of General Psychiatry, 21, 449

Polich, J.M., Armor, D.J. and Braiker, H.B. (1980) The Course of Alcoholism Four Years after Treatment. Rand Corporation, Santa Monica

Potamianos, G. (1984) The Use and Severity of Alcohol Dependence Questionnaire (SADQ) on a sample of problem drinkers presenting at a district general hospital. Alcohol, 1, 441-445

Potamianos, G. (1985a) An evaluation by a randomised controlled trial of a community-based centre in the treatment of alcoholism. Clinical Science, 68 (Supplement 11), 74

Potamianos, G. (1985b) The perception of problem drinkers by general hospital staff, GPs and alcoholic patients. Alcohol, Volume 2, 563-566

Potamianos, G,. Gorman, D. and Peters, T. (1985) Attitudes and treatment expectancies of patients and general hospital staff in relation to alcoholism. British Journal of Medical Psychology, 58, 63-66

Potamianos, G. (1986) Randomised controlled trial of community-based centre versus conventional hospital management in treatment of alcoholism. The Lancet, 11, 797-799

Rankin, H. (1967) Studies in alcoholism: a general hospital medical clinic for the treatment of alcoholism. Medical Journal of Australia, 17, 157

Stockwell,T., Hodgson, R., Edwards, G., Taylor, C. and Rankin, H. (1979) The development of a questionnaire to measure severity of alcohol dependence. British Journal of Addiction, 74, 79-87

Wechsler, D. and Stone, C. (1945) Manual: Wechsler Memory Scale. The Psychological Corporation, New York

Wodack, A.D.,Saunders, J.B., Ewusi-Mensah, I., Davis, M. and Williams, R. (1983) Severity of alcohol dependence in patients with alcoholic liver disease. British Medical Journal, 287, 1420-1422

Wolf, L. (1965) Social factors in the diagnosis of alcoholism. Journal of Studies in Alcohol, 26, 72

Chapter 12

THE RESIDENTIAL ALCOHOL PROJECT: A DESERVING CASE FOR
REHABILITATION

Fred Yates

INTRODUCTION

Rehabilitation in a small group residence for recovering
problem drinkers now makes a significant contribution to the
range of specialist alcohol services.   The 1986 Directory of
Alcohol Services for England and Wales compiled by Alcohol
Concern lists 86 such projects within the voluntary sector
which in total provide 1,048 bed spaces.   These places add up
to twice the statutory provision of 569 beds made available
under the 25 NHS specialist units for drink and drug problems.
There has been a steady growth over the last 20 years,
particularly in the 1970s when Circular 21/73 was issued by
the Department of Health and Social Security to encourage
residential projects in the voluntary sector with capital and
time limited revenue funding.   Despite the ending of central
government support in 1980, expansion has continued at the
same rate with about 20 houses opening in the six years since
then.   Interestingly, these recent additions have come mainly
from Councils on Alcoholism and hospital services which have
identified the need for a community-based residential facility
in their own client groups.   This development contrasts with
the pattern in the 1970s when such provision was largely
initiated by non-statutory agencies outside the mainstream of
existing services.   Thus the residential project continues to
be an attractive rehabilitation option for other alcohol
services.
There has, though, been no distinctive approach to emerge
from this recent expansion and the fundamental problem of
identity raised by Otto and Orford in their study of London
alcohol houses remains: "Are these houses dry working men's
hostels" or "therapeutic communities", "halfway houses" or
"group homes"? (Not Quite Like Home, 1978, p. 80).   The main
recognisable change has been the erratic development of
therapeutic house programmes derived largely from
psychological methods used in hospitals.

233

The Residential Alcohol Project

In this chapter I want to draw out some special problems of a residential establishment for problem drinkers which work against long-term rehabilitation and argue that the introduction of clinical add-ons associated with hospital programmes is a further drift away from this primary goal. This analysis will prepare the way for what I call an "Entrepreneurial Household" model which makes the community setting of residential projects a central rehabilitative resource. I will occasionally refer to findings taken from the Alcohol Services Evaluation Scheme (ASES) which is part of an internal research and evaluation programme undertaken by the Turning Point Organisation, a large UK voluntary agency provider of drug, alcohol and mental health community services. Four analyses have been undertaken so far on data collected mainly from ten Turning Point alcohol rehabilitation projects.

SPECIAL PROBLEMS IN RUNNING THE DEMOCRATIC DRY HOUSE

The first houses signalling the new wave of small residential units for problem drinkers in this country were opened in South London in the early 1960s. Their original purpose was simple enough - to provide for the homeless problem drinker set on recovery a "humane alternative" to the institutional setting of the government reception centre or the social isolation of a cheap lodging-house. They were enterprising acts of practical charity with a rehabilitative potential which was investigated in the detailed study already mentioned of group homes for problem drinkers in London reported in 1978 by Otto and Orford.

The shift of philosophy was away from paternalistic or custodial authority towards the pursuit of a non-residential democratic ideal involving residents in all aspects of house management. Otto and Orford's study included a survey of everyday decisions taken at eight London houses and found very few instances of decisions made by staff alone. Making new rules, discharging members and the management of all domestic matters were undertaken by either residents alone or jointly with staff. Only serious matters requiring disciplinary action such as the non-payment of rent were under mainly staff control.

This enlightened ethic which passes authority over to residents is the central element of a democratic house model followed by most residential projects in the alcohol field. There are many problems in its practical management and I want to look in some detail at three major ones which face staff committed to this approach.

Supervision of the Dry House Rule

The alcohol-free setting is a condition which staff can best maintain by the selection of residents with a low risk of

234

relapse and by keeping a close watch on the house group. With most houses now employing non-residential staff who are only "on call" in the evenings and at weekends, the dry house rule is not so easily checked and more trust is placed in residents to disclose infringement to staff.

An estimate of the frequency of drink-related incidents in residential work can be taken from my own evaluation work with ASES (Fourth Report on Departure Circumstances). Data collected on 223 departures from 12 projects between September 1983 and July 1985 showed that 90 were drink- or drug-related, which is a project average of slightly more than one every three months. This figure underestimated the actual number of drink infringements because it does not include those which did not result in departure. However, the management difficulties relate not so much to the frequency of these dismissals but to longer-term repercussions in the house. Every in-house relapse inevitably upsets the stability of the house and can set off a long trail of inquests to clear up residual suspicions and re-establish group integrity. A group break-out can devastate a project for several months. A practitioner running an experimental controlled drinking programme in a residential setting gave this judgement on the effect of drink defaults: "Illicit drinking in a residential programme is extremely disruptive. Dealing with such instances and their consequences (spent rent money, "bad feelings" in the group) diverts time and resources from the positive, reconstructive aspects of any rehabilitation programme "(Gilligan et al, 1983). Otto and Orford also noted the disorderly consequences of the majority of drink instances observed in their study.

Many houses now adopt a more enlightened approach to residents' drinking which does not lead to automatic discharge. This fairer treatment of the drink casualty must be welcomed but it does further complicate management of the drink rule as staff and residents can become involved in long tribunal sessions. A decision to invoke dismissal may be strongly opposed by the offender if he or she knows that a second chance can be granted. Whatever the house policy with regard to drinking, the resolution on individual cases is rarely tidy or swift and there is no smooth resumption of a planned programme.

Relational Difficulties in the House

The concept of the therapeutic community evokes a picture of a small cohesive group supporting its members through recovery and is an ideal promoted by the house publicity manifesto, not a natural condition of group living for problem drinkers. The detailed narrative account and analysis of fluctuations in social stability over 9 months at two alcohol houses given by Otto and Orford in their study related the individual strains, family squabbles and factional rivalries which actually take

place. They came to this dismal conclusion: "Rises and falls
in stability and atmosphere appeared to be the result of a
concatenation of events which often seemed beyond the control
of staff". That social disorder will be the rule rather than
the exception in the dry house is entirely comprehensible if
one adds to the normal friction to be expected from any group
living arrangement the special conditions which apply to
residence for problem drinkers.

Firstly, the composition of the resident group is
changing continuously. Staff can do their best to retain a
core of settled residents to add ballast to the larger house
group but this stability is regularly challenged by the
admission of new residents, perhaps one every week, and the
usually disruptive departure of existing members. Our ASES
data has shown more than two-thirds of departures to be
unplanned and the average length of stay to be 15 weeks. The
constant readjustment in relations works against any long-term
group cohesion and what is most likely to emerge is a
succession of leaders and group outsiders who exert their
individual influences on a passive remainder. Otto and Orford
carried out a sociometric analysis to identify leadership and
isolate attributes in two house groups. From a combined
sample of 31 men who stayed long enough to meet their
definition of leader or group outsider (isolate) they found 17
leadership reputations and 17 isolate reputations, with a
small number of mixed or no status reputations (more than one
reputation per case was possible). There were, then, as many
exclusions (isolates) from the group as contributors (leaders)
and the general picture was one of poor group stability.

Secondly, there are the numerous domestic conflicts to be
considered which arise within a client group consisting of
individuals with very different backgrounds and living styles.
It is hard to imagine a more mixed set of lifestyles than
those brought together by the commonality of their drink
problem. In our study of client intake characteristics to
projects monitored by ASES over 18 months we found the sample
of 275 clients to be widely spread over the Registrar
General's five social class categories (Third ASES Report on
Intake Information Data, 1985). Project intakes were equally
divided between the two bottom social class groups (social
class IV and V) and the three top groupings (social classes I,
II and III). Only one of the residential projects was
dominated by a single social class group (social class V).

The liberal line taken by most staff means that domestic
matters such as organising a rota for washing up and cleaning
and the imposition of house standards are largely left to this
diverse resident group. The absence of a final authority in
household disputes can turn some of the many trivial domestic
irritations into major issues. For those set on climbing out
of the state of personal neglect which problem drinkers fall
into, there is little tolerance of a deterioration in house

standards. Typically, there emerges a house-proud majority fighting against one or two residents who persist in their sloppy, vagrant lifestyle in the house. I can report an actual instance of a longstanding resident who had the habit of taking his shoes off and stretching out on the mainliving-room sofa for an afternoon siesta. This unsociable practice naturally caused offence to other residents and staff were drawn into a long in-house dispute over residents' individual rights. Another affair concerned a resident who had recently given up cigarettes and tried to introduce anti-smoking measures in the house which were strongly resisted. Again, staff time was disproportionately taken up averting a domestic crisis. These inevitable domestic conflicts are more consequential and frequent for the alcohol house because it contains extremes of lifestyle in an intolerant setting.

A third source of social disorder special to the alcohol house comes from the personality deficits and even pathologies contained within the resident group. Some problem drinkers will have carried anxieties, personality faults and even mild psychiatric disorders untreated for many years. At any one time there may be one or two residents coming to terms with these arrested psychological troubles without alcohol for the first time and the adjustment can put the house group and staff under severe pressure. I know of one case of a resident with a clear paranoid condition who discharged his deluded feelings of inferiority on other innocent members in aggressive confrontations. His problem did not surface until he had become a longstanding member of the household and was in a position to direct his attacks on new residents who were confused and unsettled by the false charges made against them. Most often these types of disruptions express no more than psychological immaturities and are not serious enough to warrant dismissal or special psychiatric treatment. The disorders of a minority and their damaging effect on the house group may take up a disproportionate amount of staff time for long periods.

Relational problems between the sexes in consideration of the small number of females encountered in residential work may be taken to be an uncommon problem (our ASES data shows roughly one in ten admissions to be women). It will be appeciated, though, that the effect of only one or two women in a male dominated household may be explosive. I have known four major breakdowns in project households attributable to sexual rivalries. Most project staff will have seen an in-house coupling which, in its formation, confused group relations and resulted in an unplanned departure. Typically, the partnership does not endure after discharge and may still continue to complicate the social lives of the remaining group of residents long after the official departure. One could presume the same problem in a house with the male-female proportions reversed but co-residential projects with female majorities are rare households at present.

One further general point should be made here about how a swift positive staff response to house disturbances is frustrated by an inability to put together a full picture of events and feelings within the house. Staff do not usually witness the disturbance and must rely on the willingness of residents to talk openly and truthfully about the matter. At best staff will have to take time to put together a number of different versions and satisfy parties that an impartial judgement has been reached. At worst, there will be a web of deceit and secrecy to contend with. This impediment to the efficient resolution of in-house disputes was indirectly recorded by Otto and Orford in their study when they asked residential staff to list the qualities in residents they most valued. "Common sense", "realism", "spoke sensibly", "forthcoming" and "brought up subjects" were picked out by the authors as representative of the most favoured resident characteristics. I would interpret these results as an expression of staff appreciation of those qualities which allow them to work efficiently and fairly with in-house conflict.

Responsibility for Residents' Practical Affairs

Residents not only bring their alcohol dependence problems to the house but also an accumulation of practical living problems. Part of the staff work schedule must be put aside for the tedious administrative duties required to translate a person's affairs to a new address. The bulk of the work is taken up in the battle against the bureaucratic inertia of the local DHSS office. A new resident is usually admitted from outside the project area and it can take up to three weeks before the first full benefit is received covering rent and the resident's personal spending allowance. Until received temporary financial cover must be arranged. Negotiation for an emergency DHSS payment, arranging a loan from a special in-house fund and the accumulation of rent arrears are the routine adminstrative nuisances at the beginning of most stays. Residents can also arrive with unpaid bills, unresolved entitlements to DHSS benefits, previous accommodation liabilities, personal property to be stored, court cases to prepare for and even separation proceedings to take out, all of which add to the bureaucratic load of the house manager.

All this preparatory administrative work for long-term residence is undone in cases of early departure and creates the extra inconvenience of claiming unpaid rents for ex-residents, sending DHSS payments, and attempting to recover in-house loans. The measure of this additional work is evident from our ASES study of departures which showed that 38% of admissions leave within the first four weeks of their stay, the majority before arrangements with the local DHSS office have been settled. The size of the problem in cash terms can be given in the amount owed to Turning Point's ten residential projects by the DHSS as accumulated back rent payments which have not been recovered or arrears currently being pursued by project staff at the end of 1985. The sum owed was £110,016.

Although most projects can afford part-time secretarial assistance for routine office duties, social work staff are inevitably drawn into these practical matters of residents' immediate welfare. Consequently, the more creative aspects of the administrative work on a rehabilitation project, finding accommodation and securing the longer-term financial independence of residents, take a lower priority. In the last three sections I have sketched three broad areas of exceptional working conditions for the residential staff team with responsibility for running a minimal dry house project. Other routine staff commitments outside the daily life of the house, referral agency visits, external assessments, attendance at management meetings and training courses, supervision of student placements, visiting ex-residents and developing move-on accommodation facilities are left out of this account. An idea of the complexity and work load of the job for the typical number of two or three staff members can be conveyed, if, to the basic managerial responsibilities required to run a small bed and breakfast establishment, one adds the practical welfare and occupational needs of each individual boarder and the group problems arising from a very difficult client group. This awesome job description asks for group diplomacy and above all a resilience to the disruptive events which can upset the organised project work going on in the house.

It is appropriate at this point to consider Otto and Orfords's summary of general operation and philosophy of the halfway houses they studied. "Lack of clarity, contradictions and misunderstanding over goals and methods seem to be the rule rather than the exception in small hostels." My verdict is that under the job conditions presented in this section the most efficient social work management team will be stretched to reach the minimum goals of a stable physical setting for rehabilitation. An appreciation of these daily responsibilities just to keep the project in operation makes it entirely understandable that no superordinate philosophy has appeared to unite the field. Staff do their best to meet the demands of individual clients which till their working day. But a work routine which is client-led pins staff to client-perceived problems and the longer-term objectives of rehabilitation work are forgotten.

Quite simply, projects have been fully occupied keeping their heads above water and dealing with the kinds of in-house problems listed. The emergence of a common approach from these conditions would be as unlikely as the production of a theory of hotel management from a scattered group of over-worked hotel keepers. The actual business of residential work is almost all taken up in the containment of a dry community, not the long-term rehabilitation of its individual members.

I would say, then, that the very nature of the work in the daily management of practical urgencies and in-house tensions has been a significant factor in narrowing the objective of community projects. Core philosophies and common working practice can come from professional training programmes and clear guidelines from higher management; but most project staff teams not part of a large organisation are deprived of this outside resource. They work largely in isolation with the limited support of an advisory committee without executive powers. So any superior policy above the short-term needs of residents is determined very much by the capability and organisation of the staff team.

It is unfortuate that few project staff stay in the field long enough to take measure of the service problems. In a snapshot survey made in September 1986 of ten Turning Point houses only one reported the same staff team working over the previous 12 months. Three projects had made one staff replacement, five had made two replacements and one project had revived itself with an entirely new staff team. A study to investigate the feasibility of an in-house training programme by the same organisation found only one-third of project and management staff to have any formal social work qualification. We can conclude that a confident, stable, organised staff team - like their resident group - is a rarity (Report of a Survey of Turning Point Staff, January 1985).

I want finally in this section to mention two other factors which have prevented projects from taking a longer view of their rehabilitative goals. Both staff and residents have their own reasons not to venture too far beyond what goes on in the house. The far-sighted worker looking towards the survival of residents in the years after departure is held back by the short-term aspirations of his client group. A stay at a residential project offers comfortable shelter from many of the realities of ordinary living, the need to make personal domestic economies, fight off loneliness, seek employment or look for alternative leisure activities. Under these artificial conditions there is a risk of a general house complacency developing from residents who put aside the day when these problems must be addressed unsupported. Problem drinkers are particularly prone to shortening their sights and lowering personal objectives because their sense of progress is fulfilled by the simple accomplishment of getting through another day without drink. For people who have dedicated their lives to self-destruction through alcohol one should not undervalue the accumulation of sober days; but this can foster the toleration of long periods of inactivity and personal stagnation which mark no advance in areas of life outside sobriety. Residents arrive on a project usually at the end of a long drinking episode with a single commitment to stay dry and so are psychologically well prepared to be passive takers in a laissez-faire setting which does not address their longer-term living problems.

The factor working against a long-term rehabilitation programme is the absence of any reliable feedback on the progress of residents after departure. Projects do not extend their vision beyond the visible goals within the house itself - high occupancy and house stability. If the longer-term goals are not measured there is no inducement to address them and without follow-up data staff will prefer to work in the area where they have greatest control and their efforts are most clearly evident. Thus, the desirable precondition of the dry settled household for a long-term rehabilitation programme becomes an end in itself and the successful project is one which achieves a stable, optimistic atmosphere and keeps up its occupancy. It was this narrow view of work objectives which Turning Point wished to remedy and led on to the implementation of the ASES programme. Follow-up information on ex-residents is now fed back to project staff by routinely collecting 6 month outcome data.

THE THERAPEUTIC MODEL

The view presented so far would meet with strong opposition from many practitioners in the field who would claim that they now operate organised programmes which directly tackle the future resettlement problems of residents while they are at the house. The more ambitious, better resourced projects have borrowed from the applied psychological methods developed in specialist hospital settings and have introduced a range of therapeutic modules (social skills training, alternatives to drinking, alcohol education, cognitive and behavioural strategies to stay dry and the therapeutic contract system). I believe, though, that these programmes are a move in the wrong direction. Firstly, there are the numerous intrusions of ordinary community living which have been listed in the previous section to battle with.

There is also a question of the suitabilitiy of this type of programme. For client groups who are ready to accept a period of settled residence with other problem drinkers the appeal and perceived relevance of in-house group sessions with a didactic flavour must be doubted. I have in another paper taken the perspective of the user of treatment to assess different treatment methods and put forward the general proposition that different styles of service response are actively sought by users depending on the perception of their drink problem and the stage reached in their drinking career

The Residential Alcohol Project

(Yates, 1985). Our ASES data has shown that 79% of residents are likely to have had hospital treatment for their drink problem in the 12 months before admission. Thus, for the majority of residents who arrive with a recent experience of clinically-based therapies, another dose may not be welcomed or taken up with much enthusiasm. I am not devaluing outright the efficacy of structured treatment programmes which teach clients problem solving skills but strongly suspect they are better received in a clinical setting by problem drinkers who have chosen to cooperate in an analytic and educational approach to their drink problem. The needs of the resident of a dry house in relation to his or her drink problem may be different.

A NEW MODEL FOR RESIDENTIAL SERVICES – THE ENTREPRENEURIAL HOUSEHOLD

What, then, should projects be doing to exert an enduring and improving effect on long-term outcome? Clients finally choose whether to drink or not in the context of major life events mostly unconnected with the treatment episode and its short-term goals. Concretely, I mean by this that finding or losing a job, making or breaking a relationship with a special person, settling in or being thrown out of good accommodation affect drink behaviour more than a brief treatment event which is sometimes little more than a marker for real life crises.

My most important reason for opposing the trend towards "therapeutic" residential work is that it throws away the chance to develop a long-term approach to rehabilitation and to influence these significant life events which is not available to non-residential services. Hospital-based alcohol services are now more aware of the restrictions of their clinical setting and the traditional post-detoxification in-patient courses are being replaced in some areas by community programmes. More staff are taken on as community psychiatric nurses, day patient groups have increased and community alcohol teams have been set up. Given these developments it seems a perversity that the vanguard of the residential project sector sees its future in an inward-looking programme of therapeutic adaption which gives second place to environmental resources.

The initial thinking for a more direct rehabilitation strategy came from an analysis of departure information collected under ASES (Fourth ASES Report, 1985). In summary we found that married people, those living with friends or relatives, those recently in employment and those who were still in, or had only just left, their last permanent address produced the best outcomes. These results are an obvious confirmation of the assertion just made that major living assets: such as stable accommodation, settled relations and gainful occupation are vital elements in the recovery process.

242

The therapeutic model is one step removed from these life events and works indirectly through the individual to equip him or her to accomplish these ends. The radical challenge ignored by the community-based residential project is to set about reinstating these conditions directly as part of the programme, repairing the environment rather than the individual. If the residents´ living problems are likened to faults in a car then the crucial departure from the conventional therapeutic model I would like to see can be expressed in a simple analogy: the new model proposed here tries to fix the car. The shift in the function of residential projects recommended here is that they do not operate as clinical outposts but despecialise themselves and take on an entrepreneurial role in the community to alter major life events in favour of the long-term interest of residents.

We are currently following the progress of a service experiment initiated at one Turning Point residential project to test this general approach. Our ASES data had shown that there was a wide spread of professional skills amongst residents and they had on average 14 years in employment before reaching the project. Yet, four-fifths of residents had not been in work over the previous six months before admission and projects were returning their residents to the dismal prospect of life without a job and the real risk of relapse which this entailed. The Entrepreneurial Household solution to this problem of residents´ unemployment is to repair the environment and create work from within the project. This thinking led us on to the registration of a Community Co-operative to undertake small-scale work and odd jobs. The experiment is still in its early stages and a full report is planned next year when the effect of the Co-op activity on ex-residents´ chances of dry living outside the project can be tested and assessed. The following is an account of developments over the first six months.

We have acquired two private gardens loaned to us by local residents grateful to see their neglected plots made use of. The vegetables grown have been used in the house and sold to friends of the projects. Two of the residents have taken up gardening courses at the local college to learn more about cultivation. Light removal work has been taken on with the acquisition of a van which also helps in the Co-op´s trading operations with nearby auction rooms. Bargain lots are re-sold privately and people wanting to get rid of old furniture or unused articles can call on the van for their removal and placement in the following week´s auction. The driver of the van is army trained, with a Heavy Goods Vehicles licence and has agreed to teach two other residents to drive. Painting and decorating work has been carried out by the Co-op to re-furbish the Turning Point house and also to earn money from outside contracts.

The Residential Alcohol Project

The weekly work programme is organised at a meeting of Co-op members made up of staff and residents, each member having one vote in any decision making. The secretarial, treasurer's and chairperson's duties are all carried out by residents. We now have a full set of official stationery, including business cards, and a proper contractual procedure for jobs undertaken. What to do with the money earned each week is decided democratically at the meeting and, without any encouragement from staff, there has been unanimous agreement that profits should be invested in tools and materials to expand the work potential of the Co-op and not be shared out as workers' dividends. Under current DHSS rules up to £4.00 per week can be given over as cash payments to Co-op members and treated as a "disregard" which does not affect their state benefit.

It is too early to assess the Co-op's impact on the normal pattern of house activity but I can report that we have lost five residents out of 13 existing residents and new admissions since the Co-op work began and the average length of stay stands at the moment at 18 weeks. These very early indications of the Co-op's effects are promising and suggest a more stable group than in the past (the average length of stay for the Turning Point Whitley Bay project was 12.6 weeks for the 18 month period up to July, 1985). Individual drink problems or deficits are not formally addressed in the house and the absence of any overtly therapeutic activity has not increased the risk of drinking or left the residents feeling unsupported. Because the house is no longer primarily a therapeutic environment individual deficiencies arise naturally in the context of Co-op work. For example, a member who fails to carry out a job delegated or volunteered at the Co-op meeting will be subject to the ordinary disapproval of other members. Thus, idleness or unreliability is treated on its own terms and its consequences for the Co-op work programme not artificially isolated as a failed action plan or a broken condition of a therapeutic contract. The risk of turning the unextraordinary troubles of residents into a social pathology is reduced.

Reaching out for community solutions to residents' problems not only normalises them but may offer a better guarantee that the recovery process will continue after departure because the community support remains. Extending the logic of the model, it would be in order to send a resident who wants specific help with a drink problem to an outside specialist agency or clinical psychologist for counselling or recommend a local relaxation class for an anxiety problem. The resident is being taught the intelligent management of community resources in preparation for leaving. Departure should be a physical move to a more desirable living situation, the resident taking his community involvement acquired at the house with him.

I have presented this description of the first few months of
the Co-op's activities not as evidence in support of the
entrepreneurial household model but to give an example of what
is meant by it. At this stage, we have only tested its
feasibility in a residential setting for problem drinkers,
with some early indications of an increase in the stability of
the resident group.

I would like to conclude this criticism of the
therapeutic turn in alcohol residential services with wider
reference to the findings of evaluation studies of specific
treatments for problem drinkers. They have shown little
relationship between client success and type of treatment.
Many reasons, most pointing the finger at slack methodology in
the research, have been given for the poor association.
However, taking the generally negative research findings at
face value, I am forced to a desperate conclusion which is
well expressed by Ffoulkes Law of Random Results, originally
applied to parenthood: "In parenthood (and alcohol treatment)
as in business, politics and war, the correlation between the
efforts of the people in charge and the results, whether
dazzling or disastrous, is negligible".

In consideration of the account presented here there is a
simple explanation of the non-correspondence between treatment
and outcome which stares you in the face - that what is
currently done by treatment agencies, including residential
projects, is not aimed at long-term outcome and it would
indeed be surprising if there was a connection, given the
actual short-term operations of most agencies.

The choice open to residential projects wishing to move
on from the laissez-faire dry house model is to continue to
therapeutise their activities, or to attack directly the
ordinary commerce of community life which may significantly
improve the long-term rehabilitation prospects of its members.
Intellectual preparation in a protected environment has yet to
be proven as an effective treatment for the problem drinker
and rehabilitation is made doubly difficult if the client is
taken out of the living current of daily existence. It means
a return and readjustment to society which is unnecessary.
The residential alcohol project is the only facility amongst
the range of specialist alcohol services able to set in motion
this social reconstruction in the lives of problem drinkers
and develop its own model of rehabilitation.

REFERENCES

Directory of Alcohol Services for England and Wales. (1986),
    Alcohol Concern, London
DHSS. (1973) Community Services for Alcoholics. DHSS
    Circular 21/73, HMSO, London

Gilligan, T., Norris, H. and Yates, F. (1983) Management problems in a small hostel with a controlled drinking programme. British Journal of Addiction, 78, 277-290

Otto, S. and Orford, J. (1978) Not Quite Like Home. Wiley, London

Turning Point (1985) Interim Report of a Survey of Turning Point Staff Training Needs Undertaken in January 1985 by Training and Staff Development Working Group

Turning Point (1986) Financial Report 31st January 1986. Turning Point, CAP House, 9-12 Long Lane, London, ECIA 9HA

Yates, F. (1985) Does treatment work? Yes, but not always in the way we plan it. In N. Heather, P. Davies and I Robertson (eds), The Misuse of Alcohol: Crucial Issues in Dependence, Treatment and Prevention. 148-157, Croom Helm, London

Yates, F. (1984) Alcohol Services Evaluation Scheme. First Report. June

Yates, F.(1985) Alcohol Services Evaluation Scheme. Second Report. January

Yates, F. (1985) Alcohol Services Evaluation Scheme. Third Report. June

Yates, F. (1985) Alcohol Services Evaluation Scheme. Report on Residents Circumstances at the Time of Departure. December

Chapter 13

A THERAPEUTIC DAY UNIT FOR ALCOHOL ABUSERS

Alan Cartwright

INTRODUCTION

The Maudsley Alcohol Pilot Project (MAPP) was funded by the
DHSS in 1973, to help understand why primary care agencies had
failed to provide effective help for alcohol abusers. The
major findings were reported in 1975 and 1978 (Cartwright et
al, 1975, Shaw et al, 1978) and recommended the formation of
Community Alcohol Teams (see Chapters 6 and 8).

Though the MAPP was mainly concerned with helping the
primary care agents to develop a more effective response, it
was always assumed that the Community Alcohol Team would be
operating within a sophisticated network of services. At the
heart of the services recommended in the 1975 monograph was
the therapeutic day unit which, it was suggested, could
effectively replace the in-patient treatment units.

Perhaps the most important function of the day unit was
to provide a therapeutic environment for clients whose needs
would be beyond the skills or resources of the primary care
agencies. By providing a day therapeutic environment it was
argued that demands on in-patient services would be reduced.
Furthermore, by taking clients with whom primary care
agencies had little hope of success, the day unit would enable
primary care agents to focus their attentions more
productively. If attempts were to be made to develop the
responses of primary care agents, then this filtering off
process would enable these workers to be initially exposed to
working with clients who would be more rewarding.

The opportunity to explore the development of a
therapeutic day unit occurred when Terry Spratley became the
Director of Alcohol Services in Eastern Kent. The author
joined him as psychotherapist to the services. With two charge
nurses we started developing the therapeutic day unit, Mount
Zeehan, as the centre of our efforts to create a new service.
By 1980 the staff complement had increased to include six
charge nurses and a clinical nurse consultant. The staff

presently consist of a consultant psychiatrist; principal
psychotherapist who is seconded part-time to the University of
Kent; a clinical nurse consultant (who is also a
psychotherapist) and six charge nurses, five of whom have
achieved the internal status of nurse therapist. Additionally,
there are three secretaries (two of whom are part-time) and a
number of trainees. These can include nursing students, a
junior doctor on rotation and students from the local social
work courses. The staff predominantly work in the Unit which
consists of an old hospital superintendant's residence which
has always been known as Mount Zeehan. Although a large
building, its twelve available rooms are insufficient for the
therapeutic community.

Mount Zeehan serves two health districts, with a total
population of 650,000, in the south-eastern corner of England.
The unit itself is situated in the grounds of a psycho-
geriatric hospital just outside Canterbury which is roughly at
the centre of the catchment area. There are many small towns,
mainly along the coast, mostly with populations of between
20,000 and 30,000 people. Groups of towns tend to form
separate cultural identities. On the northern side there are
Canterbury and the Thanet towns including Margate and
Ramsgate. Tourism is probably the dominant economic activity
in this area. Along the southern coast there are the Cinque
Ports dominated by the docks of Dover and Folkestone.
Finally, there are the inland light industrial and farming
centres like Ashford.

The therapeutic community was planned to provide a range
of therapeutic services for clients whose alcohol abuse
effectively undermined their ability to function in the
community. Such clients usually need to come to terms with
their drinking and face a number of physical, psychological
and social problems. This chapter will describe the
therapeutic community we developed and the ways our ideas are
linked to the concepts of role security and therapeutic
commitment.

Though the basic beliefs on which the community was
founded existed prior to its opening, the form in which they
are presently described only emerged from the day-to-day
experience of developing and conducting the therapeutic
programme. This has demanded continuous assessment, by the
staff, of the way we were relating to one another and to the
patients who came to the unit.

This introspective analysis has been complemented by
regular reviews of the unit based upon data gathered from the
day-to-day process of monitoring. Such reviews sometimes led
to new policies. One major change occurred a few years after
the unit opened when the group programmes were changed
radically. More commonly, however, these reviews have enabled
us to clarify different aspects of the service and to define

ways in which it could be improved. Some of this data is included in this chapter.

The view of the unit presented in this document seems to represent the consensus of staff opinion about the way they work, though the presentation of the ethos below represents my latest understanding of these ideas.

THE ETHOS OF THE THERAPEUTIC DAY UNIT

The original MAPP work had left the concept of therapeutic commitment somewhat unbalanced, stressing that an attitude of optimism, self-worth and confidence presented to the patient by a therapist, working within a clear role structure, who could draw on others for help, was a critical therapeutic element. However, it was not made clear that such an attitude was only a pre-condition for effective intervention. For the therapeutically committed therapist to become effective, these attitudes would need to be wedded to specific therapeutic skills. Although the MAPP team had argued that professional training in principle provided workers with effective skills, we were also aware that many of the workers we encountered had received academic training which had often ignored how they should apply their knowledge. They were skilled on paper alone!

From the outset an attempt was made to conceptualise our understanding of the therapeutic environment we thought would be most helpful for the patients attending the day unit. This environment is referred to as the "therapeutic ethos" and comprises the complex of therapeutically helpful experiences, values and activities which occur in the day unit.

At the heart of the ethos is the experience of being part of a community marked by "social interest". This experience was descibed by Mosack and Dreikers (1973) as

> The feeling of belonging, the feeling of being part of a larger social whole, the feeling of being socially embedded, the willingness to contribute and participate in the communal life for the common weal.

This sense of belonging, which can be equally true of a one-to-one relationship as of a group, can emerge from the experience of sharing common values and experiences. Within the day unit the commitment to growth is seen to be the "core value" around which the experience of social interest can develop.

The concept of growth is difficult to grasp but it is based upon a belief that each person has potentials which are undeveloped and unexplored. The purpose of attending the therapeutic day community is to use this opportunity to achieve total abstinence or controlled drinking within the context of greater personal development. Such development, it

is assumed, is most likely to occur when individuals achieve
greater understanding of themselves and their relationships
with others, which in turn can lead to greater freedom of
choice.

Our growth perspective demands four types of commitment.
These are:

1. Commitment to personal awareness. If people seek to
    be aware of the way they think, feel and behave, as
    well as the way they would like to be, or feel they
    ought to be, then the possibility of making the
    choices which will lead to a more satisfactory life
    are enhanced.

2. Commitment to openness. Most people, particularly
    under stress, tend to become less able to share with
    others important thoughts and feelings which they
    anticipate might cause anxiety. The commitment to
    openness involves at least trying to present to
    others these more private aspects of oneself with an
    awareness of the reason why one avoids doing so.
    Sometimes such reasons are perfectly valid.
    Sometimes we are simply not aware of thoughts and
    feelings which are anxiety provoking. The commitment
    to openness implies the willingness to become aware
    of our defences.

3. Commitment to reality. This involves giving overt
    expression to the recognition that things are not
    always the way we would like them to be, that people
    are often unpleasant and destructive and that, with
    the best will in the world, there will still be
    disagreements and conflicts which leave one feeling
    angry and impotent. Often the commitment to reality
    involves looking at our own limitations and
    confronting and adapting to the "tragic" aspects of
    life.

4. Commitment to personal responsibility. Only by taking
    responsibility for our actions can we bring about
    change. Responsibility involves making our own
    decisions about the way we wish to lead our lives.
    It does not mean that others should not give advice.
    For instance, a staff member may advise a patient to
    adopt total abstinence but the patient has the right
    to try and control drinking instead. Similarly, at
    any point in the treatment programme, a patient has
    the unconditional, and unquestioned, right to "say
    no" to requests from other patients and staff.

This "growth orientated" framework of values are ideals to
strive toward (for both staff and patients) with people
seeking to achieve that which is optimal for themselves.
However, if growth is to be encouraged within the patient

group, the attitudes and actions of the staff are critical both as facilitating factors and as models.

Perhaps the best statement describing the attitude of the effective therapist was drawn up by Strupp et al (1969) from interviews with patients whose psychotherapy had been successful:

> The composite image of the good therapist, drawn by our respondents is thus of a keenly attentive, interested, benign and concerned listener. A friend who is warm and natural, is not averse to giving direct advice, who speaks one's own language, and rarely arouses intense anger.

Experiences such as those described above are likely to occur when the therapist acts along the major principles of supportive psychotherapy.

1. **Understanding.** As I have discussed elsewhere, (Cartwright, 1981) the presence of an understanding attitude, often referred to as empathy, is probably the most important precondition for therapeutic change. The therapist who cctempts to understand the patient from the patient's perspective instead of imposing their own views is likely to be the most successful therapist.

2. **Acceptance.** The ability to accept the patient, with their strengths and weaknesses, is critical in building up a good therapeutic relationship. Acceptance does not mean collusion with the patient's defeating or destructive behaviour, but rather the willingness to encounter the patient without imposing moral judgments.

3. **Acceptance of the unit's limitations** is also required of patients. Thus the we cannot maintain the ethos of the unit in the face of very destructive, mad or intoxicated behaviour. Patients who are unwilling, or unable, to make a commitment to the ethos of the unit will be encouraged to seek help from other quarters.

4. **Encouragement.** Encouragement refers to the therapist's willingness to realistically reinforce positive aspects of the patient's life experience and therapeutic progress. This does not mean ignoring or denying the less palatable aspects.

If the community is acting within its ethos then it becomes a safe place to be. As patients realise that the therapist, or the community, is able to understand, accept and encourage, they will become more trusting and thus able to discuss both painful and intimate aspects of their lives. Thus trust is an essential quality which must evolve before people can be expected to move into those areas of self-exploration which promote personal growth.

The focus on personal awareness, openness, reality and reasonability tends to encourage a sense of detachment from impulsive emotions and often a questioning of long established values. The stress is not on instant change, but on each person needing to go at their own pace.

Experience tells us that the ethos within the patient group is often a reflection of that within the staff group. Thus when the staff group as a whole, or individual members of staff, depart from the values expressed within the ethos this is likely to disrupt the patient group. The staff have a clear responsibility to maintain the ethos of the staff group as well as help facilitate that within the patient group.

Over recent years there have been a number of publications which give formal expression to some of the values in the therapeutic ethos. Many of the underlying views develop from the work of Alfred Adler and are well expressed in an article by Mosak and Dreikurs (1973). Other influences have been the work of Yalom (1975 and 1980) and also that of Luborsky (1978, 1984).

The therapeutic programmes described in the next section all assume that the therapeutic ethos has been maintained within the unit. Yet, as will be described below, such an assumption is not always valid. The ethos is not a static phenomenon; it is something which is alive and active and must be worked upon. Conflicts between staff, changes in staff membership or changes in the client group can all undermine the therapeutic ethos, and when the ethos fails, so does the unit as a therapeutic community. Thus the primary concern of the staff must always be to maintain the ethos.

THE THERAPEUTIC PROGRAMMES

As befits a therapeutic community most programmes are based upon a group work programme. Thus patients can take part in "support", "education" and "awareness" groups each of which have different goals and functions. Generally, one-to-one work is seen as a complement to group work. Whilst we would like to do more individual counselling and psychotherapy staff resources are limited and most therapeutic contact takes place in groups. However, when the person is first seen at the unit their initial interviews are conducted on a one-to-one basis.

Assessment

When a patient is referred to Mount Zeehan they are seen within a few days by the "keyworker" for their area. There are six keyworkers, each with responsibility for a specific part of the catchment area. The keyworker initially sees all new patients from that locality and is responsible for coming to understand their needs and advising them about the ways that they might best be helped. A number of questionnaires are completed and if relatives are present they are also interviewed. Patients who are to regularly attend the unit will receive a physical examination.

Detoxification, if required, is normally conducted while the patient attends daily. Vitamins are provided and small amounts of diazepam are prescribed for for no more than seven days. Experience has shown that the majority of patients can withdraw from alcohol, within the unit, without tranquillisers. In rare cases, where serious complications are envisaged, detoxification will take place in the local general hospital. Other drugs, like anti-depressants, are never prescribed. As will be described later many patients show symptoms which could be diagnosed as depression. However, it is our view, that such "depression" is invariably a realistic response to the person's life situation. It seems inappropriate to chemically remove the signs that something is wrong when this may serve as a stimulus for a more constructive approach to difficulties.

Of course some patients are prescribed drugs by their general practitioners, though we always write to the doctor advising otherwise. The only rule regarding alcohol and drugs in the unit is that the person should attend the unit free of any alcohol or drugs that have not been prescribed. Regular drinking or drug taking can undermine a person's ability to make a commitment to the unit programmes, in which case continued attendance would be pointless.

Following assessment a treatment plan is drawn up between the "keyworker" and the patient. This may involve the patient being referred to another community agency or occasionally being seen as an out-patient. The therapeutic day unit is likely to be recommended for the person who is unable, at the time of referral, to maintain an acceptable level of functioning within the community. For homeless patients an acute dry hostel run by the Kent Council on Addiction has also been available.

The Support Programme
The hub of the day unit is the support programme. The unit is open from nine in the morning to five at night and patients may be in the building throughout that time. However, most patients attend between 10.30 am and 3 pm during the support programme. This consists of two open groups a day led by a member of staff. Topics are not set and discussion may range from the problems an individual is having in remaining sober, to people's feelings about television or social events. It is the role of the groupleader to maintain the cohesion within the group and to ensure the discussion is relevant to the unit's goals.

The number of patients present in support groups is constantly changing. If there are other groups operating it may be as few as fifteen but there have been occasions when more then forty people have wished to take part. Thirty-five is the maximum number that can be accommodated with an average attendance of about 25.

A Therapeutic Day Unit

Although the support programme is primarily attended by current patients, some former patients are usually present. Self-referral, particularly for former patients, is very easy. Patients who have relapsed, or fear they might do so, may come to the unit, providing they are free of alcohol and drugs, and discuss their situation with their peers and if necessary their former keyworker. In practice this feature enables the unit to function as an easily accessible crisis intervention centre.

Education Groups

Although a new patient will initially take part in the support programme we try to offer the education and awareness programmes as soon as possible. The frequency of education programmes depends upon the availability of staff and the number of patients wanting to take part. Education programmes are likely to run on two or three weeks each month. They will run with a minimum of three patients and a maximum of eight the same leader conducts each session.

The education programme has two primary goals: firstly to introduce people to the experience of small group discussions in a relatively secure environment; secondly to provide patients with basic information about the effects of alcohol.

The education programme lasts five days. There are two one hour meetings each day. Each group starts with a tape recording of a talk about specific aspects of alcohol. Tapes include information on physical effects of alcohol; effects of alcohol on the family; reasons for drinking; methods of recovery, etc. Most education groups include a section on relaxation training. There are a wide range of different tapes and group leaders tend to select the tapes felt to be most relevant to that particular group of patients.

Following the tape, a discussion takes place where patients are encouraged to relate the material they have heard to their own experience. The therapist's role is to maintain the therapeutic ethos within the group and, where necessary, facilitate discussion, provide information and clarification. The therapist also tends to put limits on the group. Confrontations between patients are discouraged, as is the tendency of some patients to throw themselves headlong into the therapeutic experience. In each case, the unit ethos values a slow secure approach over a dramatic and often short-lived one.

The Alcohol Awareness Programme

The patient who completes an education group may take part in the two week alcohol awareness programme. The alcohol awareness programme is designed to facilitate a greater depth of self-exploration. This aims to help members understand their drinking and enable them to develop alternative

responses to thoughts, feelings or behaviours which are considered problematic. The complete programme involves two groups
a day, over ten days, with the same leader. Groups consist of
six to eight patients and are terminated if the number drops
below three. Any person who misses more than two groups is
automatically excluded. Throughout the two week period members
are expected to be totally abstinent.

Each group starts with a written exercise which is
designed to facilitate self-exploration. For instance, the
exercise for the second group encourages members to reflect
upon the typical situations in which they find themselves
drinking, and then to explore why they are drinking in this
particular situation.

Another early exercise asks members to consider different
aspects of their personalities by comparing themselves when
drinking, drunk and sober with the ways they would like to be
or feel they ought to be. The patient writes responses to the
exercises in a private folder provided at the begining of the
group. When the exercise has been completed, the patients are
encouraged by the group leader to share what they have written
and their responses. When each person has "fed back", a
discussion follows. There are more than twenty set exercises
available for this programme and group leaders select them in
the most appropriate order for a particular group. Those
early in the sequence tend to involve helping the patients
explore and describe their patterns of drinking. Later
exercises facilitate ways of understanding the drinking, and
the final section is concerned with ways of bringing about
changes in drinking and other behaviour.

There are several reasons why written exercises are
chosen. Firstly, the process of reflecting and writing, encourages a calm and objective view on the person's situation.
Secondly, the private writing, which is only shared if the
person chooses, enables those who find difficulty in talking
in groups to think about their situation, even if they share
very little. In less structured groups, the anxious person is
often unable to function because of fears of exposure.

The role of the group leader is to create and maintain
the therapeutic ethos and to facilitate discussion. However,
in the awareness group they are less likely to be providing
information or giving advice and more likely to be trying to
help the patients understand their particular situation and
develop ways of responding which are growth-based and
constructive.

In practice the alcohol awareness group tends to combine
aspects of supportive-expressive psychotherapy (Luborsky,
1984), with existential psychotherapy (Yalom, 1980), with a
stress on changing relevant aspects of thought, feeling and
behaviour. In this group it becomes clear that different
patients have very different needs. Some require a supportive
element to help achieve and maintain sobriety; others have to

255

come to terms with a ruined life, whilst others have difficulties in personal relationships which stem from childhood.

The role of the group leader is to facilitate the procedure which is most relevant to each individual patient. Thus one person may be developing a view of themselves based on the disease model of alcoholism and recovery through AA. Another may reject this model and be hoping to find recovery through a more introspective therapeutic process. The group leader has to find ways of enabling these different perspectives to develop according to the needs of each individual person.

Additional Programmes

Three other programmes are available, mainly for those who have completed the awareness groups. First, there is the sobriety maintenance programme, lasting one-week, consisting of ten groups, and focusing upon the development of personal assertion and social skills.

The second is a family therapy programme. A family therapy team, consisting of staff members from the unit and other agencies meets regularly. The family team will work with either couples or complete families.

The final element is the dynamic psychotherapy opportunities. Dynamic psychotherapy tends to be offered to younger clients who have long-standing personal difficulties. Some patients are seen weekly by an individual psychotherapist, and take part in a weekly group meeting. Others patients only take part in a psychotherapy group. Even though the people taken into this programme tend to have quite severe difficulties, a long-term commitment to treatment is expected.

Thus the therapeutic opportunities within the day unit are broad. Whilst attending the programmes, patients retain regular contacts with their keyworker. The programmes are designed to enable patients to take from the unit that which is of most value to them.

WHO COMES TO THE DAY UNIT?

Mount Zeehan was established in 1977, though the present complement of staff was not appointed until 1980.

As Table 13.1 shows, the total number of patients referred has increased steadily and is likely to be in excess of 700 in 1986. In 1985 medical sources dominated, accounting for 59% of referrals. The sharp increase in general hospital referrals from 1984 to 1985 reflected a new policy of working with physicians in towns other than Canterbury.

Legal sources, including probation, prison and solicitors not only increased but also seemed to change in that an

Table 13.1: Referrals to Mount Zeehan 1977-1985

Source	1977	1978	1979	1980	1981	1982	1983	1984	1985
Psych.	41	56	84	89	122	86	67	63	70
Gen.Hosp.	42	29	32	41	39	28	41	40	76
GP	29	61	125	155	117	149	156	170	196
Council	6	9	13	23	26	29	25	12	4
Legal	13	25	53	61	49	57	57	69	82
Public	6.	5	19	46	69	101	99	116	135
Others	7	4	9	11	9	15	6	12	19
TOTAL	144	189	335	426	431	465	451	482	582
Sex Ratio (M:F)	1.6	3.6	2.6	2.8	2.4	2.5	3.4	3.1	3.1

N.B. Abbreviations: PSYCH = Psychiatrist; GEN HOSP = General Hospital; COUNCIL = Council on Alcoholism; PUBLIC = Self, Relative or Friend.

increasing number of referrals were of young men on remand for alcohol-related offences creating special problems described below.

Direct referrals from social services departments have always been few in number and seem to reflect a policy of asking clients' GPs to organise referrals they feel are necessary. Mostly, these are cases where it is felt that children were at risk.

The unit has always had an open referral policy whereby any person can refer themselves or a member of their family. The only condition placed upon such referrals is that the patient's general practitioner is informed. Twenty-three per cent of patients (public referrals) in 1985 came by this route. The vast majority of these were patients already known to the unit staff.

The ratio of male to female patients has averaged 2.8:1 since the unit opened. The indications are that proportionately more females are being referred in 1986.

The age of patients has not changed over the years: the average female patient being in her early to middle forties with the average male being slightly younger. However, if the male patients with criminal records (who tend to be younger than other men) are excluded the ages of male and female patients tend to be similar.

From the perspective of the day unit, two characteristics of the patients are important in conceptualising treatment. These are the severity of alcohol dependence and the degree of personal disturbance.

The SADQ (Stockwell et al, 1979; 1983) is used as part of the normal treatment process to help keyworkers to assess alcohol dependence. SADQ scores from patients have been studied over recent years. The average patient (of either gender) scores 28 on the SADQ. This is slightly lower than scores reported from other specialist treatment agencies. However, in a study which compared severity of dependence of Mount Zeehan patients with those of the patients attending in-patient facilities in Scotland using an interview schedule, differences in dependence scores were not significant (Latchman and Kreitman 1984).

The other dimension of severity, that of personal disturbance, has also been monitored over the years.

Recently, the DSSI (R) (Foulds, 1976), which provides a fivefold hierarchical classification of patients has been used. Class 0 consists of those who show no signs of disturbance whilst Class IV refers to those who report "delusions of disintegration" which fit the psychodynamic category of severe borderline disturbance. It is assumed that patients in higher categories (more disturbed) will also report symptoms associated with lower categories. Those who do not fit this model are grouped as Class V. Less than 5% of our patients are classified as Class V by this instrument. With Class V patients excluded the D.S.S.I.(R) classified 100 consecutive referrals as follows. Approximately 30% of the patients showed either no disturbance (Class 0) or only "mood disturbances" (Class 1), primarily symptoms of depression and anxiety, which can usually be understood as "normal" responses to life crises; 27% "neurotic disturbances" (Class 2), which would include signs of mood disturbance plus marked symptoms like phobias, compulsions or ruminations; 32% showed more severe disturbances (Class 3 & 4). Thus nearly 60% of the referred patient group show symptoms of "neurotic" or more severe levels of personal disturbance. There was an association between scores on the SADQ and these categories of personal disturbance. Howerver some 35% of the least dependent patients showed neurotic or more severe personal disturbance, whilst 20% of the most dependent were classified as not disturbed or showing only mood disturbance. This issues have been discussed in more detail elsewhere (Cartwright, 1985).

From the therapeutic perspective, we feel that the ethos and programmes offered by the day unit are most appropriate for those patients who show signs of personal disturbance, whether or not they are also alcohol dependent. These are the most difficult patients to help and the ones most likely to become hospitalised.

STUDIES OF THE PATIENT POPULATION

In 1982, in tandem with a study of the effects of dependence
upon relapse being conducted from the Institute of Psychiatry
patients were asked to complete a questionnaire called the
Therapeutic Effects Questionnaire (TEQ).
    This consisted of 77 items describing a range of
experiences. Patients were asked to indicate whether or not
they thought each experience had been true for them and how
helpful it had been. The Therapeutic Effects Questionnaire,
which is based upon earlier work by Yalom (1975), has been
described elsewhere (Cartwright, 1985).
    The responses of 30 patients who were considered to have
good outcomes over a ten month period were then considered.
This sample consisted of 9 total abstainers, 10 light drinkers
who had not exceeded 10 units in any day since entering
treatment and 11 improved drinkers who had drunk more than 10

Table 13.2: "Most Helpful" Therapeutic Experiences

1. Felt there was a member of staff whom I could depend
    upon and trust.
2. Felt there was at least one member of staff who
    understood and accepted me.
3. Felt there was at least one person who understood and
    accepted me.
4. Felt there was someone whom I could depend upon and
    trust.
5. Received suggestions and advice from staff about the
    things I could do in the future.
6. Learnt a lot of facts related to my difficulties.
7. Been able to see my life from a different perspective.
8. Felt understood by another person.
9. Learnt that I am not the only person with my type of
    problem.
10. Been able to view myself and others in a new light.
11. Been able to get things off my chest.
12. Received definite suggestions about the ways to handle
    my problems.
13. Been encouraged by the knowledge that others had been
    helped.
14. Been encouraged by improvements in other people.
15. Learnt that I must take ultimate responsibility for my
    new life no matter how much guidance and support I get
    from others.
16. Revealed embarrassing things about myself and yet still
    felt accepted.
17. Belonged to a group of people who understood and
    accepted me.

units but on fewer than 28 days over the 10 month period. None of the latter group had consumed more than 10 units on any day in the month before interview.

The TEQ has two questions about each item. First patients asked if they have experienced the phenomenon described in the item and, if they have, how "helpful" they felt it had been. To discover what experiences were generally considered to have been most helpful items considered to be true by at least 85% of the sample with "good" outcomes were ranked in terms of their average score on the scale of "helpfulness". The items ranked most helpful by patients are listed, in order of importance, in Table 13.2. Items reflecting the core supportive and existential aspects of the units values are dominant in this list.

It has been argued that the unit's stress on developing and maintaining a therapeutic ethos is most appropriate to the more severely disturbed patient, whether that disturbance be due to the effects of alcohol dependence or not. Support was given to this contention by a more detailed analysis of the differences in the ways various groups of patients responded to the TEQ. For instance patients who scored more highly on Eysenck's "neuroticism" scale were significantly more likely to choose the items listed in Table 13.3. It is immediately apparent that these patients seem to value experiences which emerge from the direct contact with other patients, in a climate marked by "social interest", as being helpful. They are also stressing the importance of various learning experiences within this climate.

Table 13.3: Items Rated More Helpful by High Neuroticism Scorers

---

1. Experienced continuous close contact with others.
2. Felt more able to trust other people.
3. Belonged to a group of people who understood and accepted me.
4. Found self-respect through helping others.
5. Learnt that others had parents and backgrounds as unhappy and mixed up as mine.
6. Received suggestions and advice from other patients about things I could do in the future.
7. Improved my skills in getting along with people.
8. Been able to express positive and negative feelings toward others.

There is, of course, a very strong correlation between scores on the neuroticism scale and scores on questionnaires like the SADQ and this dimension may reflect the type of psychological environment found most useful by the severely dependent patient under considerable stress.

There is only a loose association between "neuroticism" as a psychological attitude and the severity of "psychiatric symptoms" and futher investigations were conducted to see if any aspects of the helping process were associated with patients being less "symptomatic" at follow-up.

That over 85% of the patients interviewed reported having helpful "supportive" experiences whilst attending the unit, confirmed from a consumer perspective the value of this approach. Also of particular interest must be reports from the more personally disturbed patients. Whilst they rated the core values of the unit similarly to other patients they also rated highly items associated with the "cohesion" of the group process. Whilst less disturbed patients tended to show remission of symptoms once they had been sober for a short period of time, this was not true of the more disturbed, unless they also reported "insight" into their situation.

CHANGING PATTERNS IN THE FUNCTIONING OF THE DAY UNIT

It is always very tempting to assume that a therapeutic institution is able to maintain a quality of service throughout its life. In fact, changes in the patient population, changes in policies of external agencies or changing factors within the staff group, can all bring about changes in the therapeutic ethos and the quality of the service offered. The impact of patient management policies on the ethos of the unit can be illustrated by consideration of the effects of an inadvertent policy change, during 1983 and 84. At that time, staff were reporting that the topics in the support group had changed, that an air of aggression pervaded the unit and that few women were attending.

To try and discover if these feelings represented a general change in the ethos, the treatment careers of two samples of patients were compared. The first of these, collected during 1980, was included in the studies of the unit described above. The second, was based upon a single month's referrals during the autumn of 1984. Each group of patients use of the unit was monitored for more than six months.

As shown in Table 13.4, in each year, about 80% of people referred attended for an assessment interview. This represents 80 people from the 1980 sample and 50 people from the 1984 sample. This apparently high assessment rate probably reflects the policy of referred patients being seen as soon as possible, usually within a few days. Of these, 62% were offered some treatment programme in 1980 and 58% in 1984. From then on, however, the differences become quite marked. Large proportions of patients during 1984 either did not start the therapeutic programmes, or if starting, did not complete them.

Table 13.4: Treatment Careers of two Groups of Patients

Programme Phase	1980		1984	
	%	N	%	N
Assessed	100	80	100	50
Joined Programmes	62	50	58	29
Started Education	56	45	34	17
Finished Education	49	39	16	8
Started Awareness	36	29	12	6
Finished Awareness	31	25	6	3

These changes were reflected in fewer regular attenders at the unit, particularly women. During October 1984, prior to obvious difficulties, 36 people were attending formal programmes within the unit; of these 10 were women (a ratio of 2.6:1, closely following the referral ratio).

During Febuary and March 1985 the numbers regularly attending had fallen to 27 and 26 respectively of whom only four were women, all of whom had longstanding attachments to the unit: a ratio of 5.75:1.

This was thought to be due to the change in the therapeutic ethos created by the referrals from the legal system. During the 1980 period, only 15% of those attending the unit regularly had more than three court appearances. In 1984 this had grown to 50% of all males. This change in the structure of the patient population was due to an increased willingness, on the staff's part, to provide reports for people awaiting trial. Many of these men were also offered the opportunity to enter treatment. Their attendance at the unit often seemed to be motivated by the hope that this would help them receive more lenient treatment in the courts and once their trial was over they tended to disappear. Their lack of commitment radically changed the unit ethos and other groups of patients became reluctant to attend.

By April 1986, when the policy of offering people awaiting trial periods at the unit was abandoned, the total numbers attending had risen to 35 of whom 14 were women (a ratio of 1.5:1). The ratio of male to female referrals was 2.5:1 at this time.

Regular attenders (visiting daily usually) are only a proportion of the total numbers attending. Recently, individual attendances have been around 45 men and 25 women each week. This would include those attending programmes described above, plus people coming for individual counselling, psychotherapy, family therapy and occasional support.

THE EFFECT ON HOSPITAL ADMISSIONS

One of the most substantial claims for the therapeutic day unit was that it could provide a service for patients who would otherwise either not be treated or would be treated by admission to a psychiatric hospital.

General support for this contention was provided in a study by Latchman (1984) and his co-workers who compared the characteristics of patients receiving in-patient and out-patient treatment in Scotland and in the catchment area of the therapeutic day unit. When they compared the numbers of patients receiving in-patient treatment in their study areas they found substantially more people receiving in-patient treatment in Scotland than in East Kent. However when they included all those receiving day patient care within the catchment areas they found little difference in total prevalence between their areas. They concluded that large numbers of patients who would otherwise be treated in in-patient situations were being treated as out-patients within our catchment area. Comparisons of the severity of dependence suggested there was little difference between the various groups.

If Latchman's contention was correct and the day unit was providing an alternative to in-patient treatment then one would expect that the numbers of people being admitted to psychiatric hospital with diagnosis of alcoholism would fall after the day unit was opened.

Figure 13.1. contrasts the numbers of patients admitted to our local psychiatric hospital with a diagnosis of alcohol dependence over the first four years of the unit's operation. The reduction in in-patient admissions is dramatic, from 116 in the initial year of operation to 15 after four years. By comparison, a psychiatric hospital in an adjacent area shows a slightly raised number of admissions over this period of time. It can be seen that as the number of referrals by psychiatrists to the therapeutic day unit increases, so the number of admissions falls.

Adding together admissions and psychiatric referrals provides a relatively straight line, lending extra weight to the belief that psychiatrists were referring to the day unit, whereas formerly they would have been admitting.

There is thus substantial evidence that one of the major goals of the day unit, reducing admissions to hospital, has been successful. In this context it is worth mentioning that we have a strong impression that the unit has also affected the demands on other areas of health care provision.

We have increasingly become convinced, from clinical experience and perusal of case notes, that the mortality rate for the day unit patients is much lower than the 20% (over five years) commonly found in follow-up studies of people referred to psychiatric alcohol treatment facilities.

Figure 13.1: The Relationship between Psychiatric Admissions for Alcoholism and Referrals to the Day Hospital

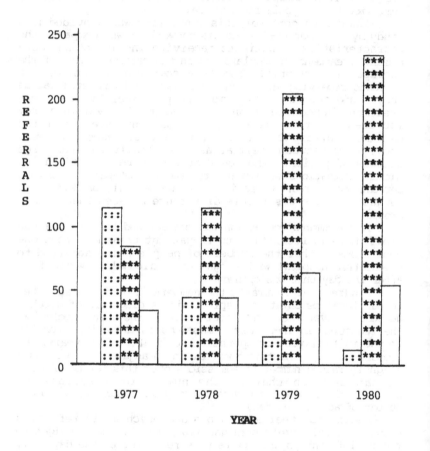

This suspicion has recently found some support from an on-going study (comparing 150 patients referred from health centres with groups of matched controls) in which no deaths had occurred.

Though this sample would not be totally representative of the population of the unit such a major difference between the actual and expected mortality rates, in line with clinical predictions, probably represents a real trend toward lower mortality rates in the unit as a whole. We believe it reflects the function of the day unit as a crisis intervention centre. Patients often report that the ability to come to the unit directly often prevents potential relapses and forshortens those which do occur. Reading through the case notes there is also a very strong suggestion that once patients have established contacts with the unit their use of acute psychiatric, medical and casualty services is also substantially reduced.

This is obviously an area that needs further investigation. Differences in mortality rates are unlikely to be due to the day unit taking less damaged clients. The two studies which have compared the unit population with those of other centres have not found the Kent population to be less damaged (Latchman et al, 1984; Yates, 1983).

SELECTION AND TRAINING OF WORKERS IN THE THERAPEUTIC DAY UNIT

The therapeutic day unit works on a keyworker system. The key-workers assess their patients needs, plan and conduct their treatment. The keyworkers are responsible for the day-to-day conduct of the groups described earlier.

It is essential that those coming to work as keyworkers should have the basic personal qualities required to contribute to and maintain the therapeutic ethos and that, furthermore, they should be acceptable to the staff group as a whole. Thus selection for staff working at the therapeutic day unit tends to be somewhat arduous, consisting of many interviews with different groups of people (including representatives of the patients) who eventually meet together to form a consensus decision about the applicant's suitability. Such appointments are rare as only three members of staff have left since the unit opened in 1977.

Because the keyworkers, who are primarily the six charge nurses, take the major treatment responsibility, it is essential that a rigorous programme of training and support be provided.

The training programme has a number of different elements. The first of these is information. All workers are expected to have a thorough knowledge of the various theories relating to the development of alcohol problems, their treatment, and the clinical management of alcohol cases. Workers should have the following skills:

1. The ability to assess patient's needs and form treatment plans.
2. The ability to provide supportive and educative counselling on a one-to-one basis.
3. The ability to conduct support, education and alcohol awareness groups.
4. The ability to assess families' needs and conduct family therapy within the family therapy team.

All of which must be conducted in a fashion consistent with the unit's ethos.

Nowadays, the first stage of this programme is attendance at the University of Kent on the Diploma in Alcohol Counselling and Consultation. This one-year part-time course provides the basic knowledge and skills which we think essential to the worker in the therapeutic day unit. This course is then supplemented by a period of supervised clinical work which normally lasts another two years.

The supervision process puts great stress on the role of counter-reactions as a source of role insecurity and low therapeutic commitment. This term refers to the ways a worker's own emotional responses to situations can create therapeutically unproductive distortions in the relationship between the keyworker and an individual patient or group.

There are two major sources of counter-reactions; those associated with role insecurity and more personal responses called counter-transference reactions.

The work of MAPP demonstrated the ways in which a worker's role insecurity could lead to attitudes of low therapeutic commitment (Shaw et al, 1978). The workers protected themselves from anxiety about their competence with a client by emotionally withdrawing from the therapeutic encounter. Such withdrawals were usually "justified" by a view of the situation which in various different ways attributed this response to the client rather than the worker.

These ideas are extended when considering counter-transference reactions. Counter-transference-based anxieties can also lead to reduced therapeutic commitment, though its source on this occasion is personal insecurity. They can also lead to distortions in the way the therapist perceives or relates to the patients. Some common sources of distortion are:

1. Distortions resulting from the keyworkers' responses to the patient's transferences. These include some patients' tendencies to idealise their keyworkers and others' tendency to use the worker as a source of admiration or

to relate to the keyworker "as if" they were somebody from the patient's past.

2. Distortions resulting from the keyworkers' tendencies to transfer similar feelings to patients.

3. Distortions resulting from emotional responses to differences in social status.

4. Distortions resulting from emotional responses to personality differences.

5. Distortions resulting from emotional responses to differences in personal values.

6. Distortions resulting from the workers' emotional responses to the emergence of threatening feelings in the relationship.

Counter-transference is mainly considered in supervision sessions which are conducted separately for individual counselling, group, family work and psychotherapy.

Individual and group work supervision often uses tape recordings of sessions and observation of the keyworker's work with groups from behind a two-way screen.

Family therapy supervision is conducted by the family therapy team using the normal methods associated with systemic family therapy.

Trainees do not undertake psychotherapy, but where nurse therapists do indicate a wish to undertake psychotherapy with patients, they have to initially undertake personal therapy and then take part in formal supervision of their cases. Generally speaking, psychotherapy work is only conducted in the unit by those undertaking a formal training in psychotherapy. The availability of supervised students from the Diploma in Dynamic Psychotherapy Skills course (at the University of Kent), which has an option for specialisation in work with drug and alcohol abusers, has enabled us to offer more patients psychotherapy.

The final element of the training process concerns the keyworker's development of "consultancy" skills. Such skills are the basis of the Community Alcohol Team approach pioneered by MAPP and considered essential for the development of such work with the primary care workers. Terry Spratley outlines this method of work in Chapter 7.

The training process at Mount Zeehan is arduous. Its stress on introspection and our belief that you should not ask patients to do what you have not done yourself is very demanding. All staff working in the unit have undertaken some period of personal psychotherapy.

People who join the staff of the psychotherapeutic day unit are actually embarking on a full professional training in counselling. When they have achieved the status of nurse therapist, they are essentially independent professional practitioners who are able to operate largely autonomously.

THE THERAPEUTIC DAY UNIT IN THE NETWORK OF ALCOHOL SERVICES

It was always envisaged that the therapeutic day unit be one part of a network of alcoholism service. Its primary function would be to provide a therapeutic environment for helping the more difficult client without the resort to traditional in-patient care. Thus one of the priorities of the day unit was to establish clear communications and links with other agencies.

This is formally done in a meeting every Friday morning, which is attended by representatives of the Kent Council on Addiction, Mount Zeehan Unit and the Consultant Physician who takes responsibility for working with patients who have physical damages. This system provides for an effective link between the different agencies. The Kent Council on Addiction provides a counselling service for the less disturbed client and an acute dry hostel with links to a number of longer-term houses. Thus the three agencies are able to use their weekly meeting to facilitate a process of referral between one another.

The therapeutic day unit described in this chapter represents a specific approach to helping those with alcohol problems. This is most strongly characterised by the tendency to view the alcohol problem as part of a complex of life and personal problems rather than as a specific focus in itself. The approach thus differs from the more fashionable medical and behavioural approaches which tend to focus directly upon the person's drinking.

To some extent this difference reflects the needs of the patient group to whom we address ourselves. It has been argued that the day unit is most appropriate to those clients who show moderate and severe levels of alcohol dependence in conjunction with marked personal disturbance, this latter characteristic being indicated by severe "neurotic", "narcissistic" or "borderline" symptoms. These patients (about 50% of all our referrals) seem to form a discrete sub-group marked by a variety of other factors. They are, for instance, quite likely to be abusing alcohol in conjunction with other drugs; amongst the younger patients these are likely to include illegal substances. Other common difficulties are gambling, eating disorders, and self-destructive patterns of behaviour. Most have difficulties in forming intimate relationships and their marriages are often stressed, children being at risk more from the parents' inability to form meaningful bonds than from direct physical harm. Those that are working often fail to achieve their full potential. Unlike other patients they rarely show a marked improvement in the psycho-social quality of their lives when they stop drinking and many relapse out of despair. Their pattern of recovery is often marked by increasingly long periods of sobriety punctuated by dramatic relapses. Sometimes these patients are involved in periods of treatment over many years before real growth and stability shows. Easy access and support from the therapeutic community is essential if this is to be achieved.

The allocation of resources to this group is justified on grounds of cost-effectiveness. If neglected they tend to be heavy users of health service resources. They demand much attention from from general practitioners, medical and psychiatric services and their alcohol problems are often complemented by a tendency to suffer from stress-related physical and mental illnesses. They are likely to make demands upon casualty and emergency services and are the patients most likely to be admitted to hospital for detoxification.

As was argued in the original MAPP work (Cartwright et al, 1975), if a service is not provided for this group, who are virtually impossible to effectively help without some form of intensive resources, then it becomes very difficult to convince community-based agents that they should start recognising and responding to other clients with drinking problems. Yet, for a unit with very few staff and many referrals the need to provide this service has made it very difficult to develop an effective community service to complement the therapeutic community.

CAT type work has primarily been focused on the probation service who have a number of recognised clients whom we find it difficult to help. Regular contact has often been established with probation officers a number of whom have developed the skills to present the educational programmes (using our tapes) in their own agencies and in the local prisons and borstals. A form of consultancy work has also begun with physicians and nurses in general hospitals in Ashford and Margate. Mostly, however, work with other agents has tended to take the form of telephone contacts and "educative" letters (Shaw et al, 1978) about specific clients, the consultancy model being applied over the telephone rather than in a face to face situation.

A satellite day unit, working in conjunction with community-based clinics, is being established in Folkestone, providing easier access for patients living in the southern part of the catchment area. This will develop in parallel with the establishment of a counselling service offered by the Kent Council on Addiction and the appointment of two community alcohol nurses who are being trained at Mount Zeehan and the University of Kent.

A major difficulty with all these developments is the shortage of resources. As staff spend more time in the community it becomes increasingly difficult for them to make the commitment required if the therapeutic day unit is to function effectively. It could be argued that the most effective way to allocate resources would be to abandon the day unit altogether and develop a preventative service based

A Therapeutic Day Unit

upon a community alcohol team model. Whilst such an argument
is possibly valid for the less disturbed person whose drinking
problem evolves slowly and imperceptibly over a long period of
time, it is perhaps less relevant to the group described above
whose drinking has often been apparent as part of a general
matrix of personal problems but who does not respond to early
interventions.

REFERENCES

Cartwright, A. (1981) Are different therapeutic perspectives
    important in the treatment of alcoholism? British Journal
    of Addiction 76, 347-361
Cartwright, A. (1985) Alcohol Dependence and Personal
    Disturbance: implications for treatment strategy. New
    Directions in the Study of Alcohol, Booklet 12. NDSAG,
    Leicester
Cartwright, A., Shaw, S. and Spratley, T. (1975) Designing a
    Comprehensive Community Response to Problems of
    Alcohol Abuse. DHSS, London
Foulds, G. (1976) The Hierarchical Nature of Personal
    Illness. Academic Press, London
Heather, N., Robertson, I. and Davies, P. (eds) (1985) The
    Misuse of Alcohol. Croom Helm, London
Latchman, R. and Kreitman, N. (1984) Regional variations in
    British alcohol morbidity rates: a myth uncovered?: 1.
    Clinical surveys. British Medical Journal, 289, 1341-1343
Luborsky, L. (1978) Individual Treatment Manual for
    Supportive-Expressive Psychotherapy: special adaptation
    for the treatment of drug dependence. Available from the
    author at the Hospital of the University of Pennsylvania
Luborsky, L. (1984) Principles of Psychoanalytic
    Psychotherapy: a manual for supportive-expressive
    psychotherapy. Basic Books, New York
Mosak, H. and Dreikurs, R. (1973) Adlerian psychotherapy.
    In Corsini (ed) Current Psychotherapies. Peacock,
    Ithaca, Illinois
Shaw S., Cartwright A., Spratley T. and Harwin, J. (1978)
    Responding to Drinking Problems. Croom Helm, London
Stockwell, T., Hodgson, R. and Edwards G. (1979) The
    development of a questionnaire to measure the severity of
    alcohol dependence. British Journal of Addictions, 74, 79-
    87
Stockwell, T., Murphy D. and Hodgson, R. (1983) The Severity
    of Alcohol Dependence Questionnaire: its use, reliability
    and validity. British Journal of Addiction, 78, 145-
    155
Strupp, H., Fox R. and Lessler, K. (1969) Patients View Their
    Psychotherapy. Johns Hopkins Press, Baltimore
Yalom, I. (1975) The Theory and Practice of Group Psycho-
    therapy. Basic Books, New York

Yalom, I. (1980) Existential Psychotherapy. Basic Books, New York

Yates, F. (1983) Survey of Referral Characteristics of ATUs. New Directions in the Study of Alcohol Group, Booklet 5. NDSAG, Leicester

PART FOUR

PREVENTION OF ALCOHOL PROBLEMS

Chapter 14

PREVENTING ALCOHOL-RELATED PROBLEMS: THE LOCAL DIMENSION

Philip Tether

INTRODUCTION

Calling on other people to "do something" is a popular activity among those concerned about an issue or set of problems. The addictions field is no exception. The rhetoric may stress that prevention is "everybody's business" (DHSS, 1986), but what is called for tends to reflect a view of "everybody" as being on the receiving end of national action: being "done to" rather than "doing". National prevention policies are, of course, essential. However, concentration on national action implies unhelpfully that any worthwhile response to some set of contemporary health and social problems is primarily a matter for central governments. This diverts attention from the wealth of local prevention resources which are so often unrecognised, and therefore, untapped. An approach to the systematic mobilisation of local prevention resources in relation to one significant contemporary "problem area" - alcohol - is described in this chapter which examines why they are important, what they are and how they can be mobilised. Based on research done in the United Kingdom for the Department of Health and Social Security (DHSS), the approach has been described in detail in a com prehensive <u>Guide</u> to local action (Tether and Robinson, 1986). The principles underpinning the <u>Guide</u> are valid for other countries and, indeed, other problems. The World Health Organisation (WHO) has expressed interest in the concept and has commissioned the production of guidelines on how to draw up a local prevention strategy which its member states could use to help combat alcohol-related problems.

    Before discussing local prevention resources and opportunities it is necessary to touch on those many recent calls to governments to "do something", for there are certain features of those allegedly inadequate current national prevention policies which are significant and have a bearing on the development of local prevention resources.

Preventing Alcohol-Related Problems

NATIONAL POLICIES

The world is full of excellent and interesting reports which,
observing that alcohol is involved in every situation where
people do harm to themselves and to others, urge governments
to "do something" (Royal College of Psychiatrists, 1979; Bruun
et al, 1975; DHSS, 1977a, 1978, 1979, 1981). The concern of
the WHO member states over the world-wide growth in alcohol-
related problems of all kinds has been expressed in a number
of World Health Assembly resolutions. The technical
discussions at the Thirty-Fifth World Health Assembly in 1982
urged member states to "develop comprehensive alcohol policies
within the context of their own national health planning"
(WHO, 1984).

Advocates of co-ordinated and "high profile" national
policies underestimate the many barriers to their development.
Too often these are identified as undefined "trade interests"
and governments´ wilful determination to maintain alcohol-
derived revenues.   Little attention is paid to what "co-
ordination" might mean or how it might be achieved, even
though alcohol is a ubiquitous substance and, in the UK as
elsewhere, virtually every government department agency has
some kind of an interest in its production and/or distribution
and/or its sale (Central Policy Review Staff, 1979). It is
assumed that problems of this kind will be readily solved if
and when governments are persuaded to act.

However, governments have only limited stocks of that
vital commodity, "commitment". They will "back" the most
contentious, difficult and "expensive" policies if the
benefits (ideological, electoral, financial etc.) clearly
outweigh the costs. Whatever the advocates of co-ordinated
national alcohol policies may think of the cost/benefit
balance, governments are less certain. Revenue and employment
considerations are obviously prominent in any government
thinking on alcohol policies but delicate issues of personal
liberty and self-responsibility must also be considered,
especially where such a widely used and socially acceptable
substance as alcohol is involved. In a democratic society,
how far can the majority be controlled in order to protect the
minority from itself? Cross-party divisions, electoral
attitudes and treaty obligations (a UK government is not
entirely free to adjust alcohol duties because of its
membership of the EEC) all combine to confuse the issue.

Moreover, those who call for determined, high profile,
committed and co-ordinated national strategies often fail to
appreciate both the range and complexity of current
"prevention relevant" policies, prescriptions, activities and
practices and the existing co-ordination processes which link
them together. As any attempt to "map" the UK´s current
prevention strategy will show, there is a bewildering array of
organisations and groups at the national level including,
among others, the Prison Officers´ Association (POA), the

Pedestrians' Association, the Royal Life Saving Society (RLSS), the Coroners' Society, the Institute of Highways and Transportation and government inter-departmental advisory committees, all involved in debating, making and implementing alcohol-relevant policy of every sort with government departments, with a constantly changing pattern of other organisations or on their own.

Out of this policy matrix emerges such significant measures as The Merchant Shipping (Means of Access) Regulation 1981, setting safety standards for gangplanks (drunken seamen fall into harbours and drown), arrangements to share data on alcohol-related drownings between the Royal Society for the Prevention of Accidents (RoSPA) and the RLSS (Tether and Harrison, 1986), and guidelines on small-scale highway improvement schemes of the kind which would save the lives of, among others, drunken drivers (Institute of Highways and Transportation, 1980).

The policy processes which lead to these and other measures are unsystematic. They are not coherently planned. But they are not "unco-ordinated". The kind of co-ordination which is continually at work is that which has been described, by Lindblom (1965) as "partisan mutual adjustment". According to Lindblom, organisations are "partisan" in that they pursue their own interests, but they are capable of "mutual adjustment" in that they adapt to the decisions made by other organisations or attempt to influence them through negotiation and bargaining. Policies which emerge from the continuous process of "partisan mutual adjustment" may not be the theoretical optimum ones but they will be ones over which agreement has been reached and which, therefore, stand a chance of being implemented.

This kind of co-ordination does not involve everyone in consultation with everyone else over every issue because, of course, alcohol-related problems fall into certain clusters; each of which is the "property" of different organisational networks. A network consists of a number of organisations having a significant amount of interaction with each other, whether this is based on mutual benefit and reciprocal exchange of resources or on conflict and hostility (Benson, 1975; Lehman, 1975). Those who participate in the network do not necessarily share the same beliefs about the nature of the "the problem", and there may not be any consensus about solutions; but there are overlapping areas of concern. On closer inspection, the bewildering array of national organisations and groups involved in alcohol-related issues appears to break down into six such networks dealing with (1) law and order, (2) health and safety, (3) advertising and the media, (4) employment, (5) education and, (6) specific alcohol agencies of various kinds. Clear boundaries cannot be drawn around any of these networks. There are sub-networks where specific issues are focused. On any given issue, network may interact with network. Nevertheless, there are typical constellations of organisations and groups concerned about a particular kind of issue and which have more contact with each other than with other constellations.

Given the nature of the policy communities outlined above, it is essential to start from where we are and work towards particular prevention goals rather than, as is often the case, to outline grand plans which merely define where the architect would like to be. If the reality is complexity, incrementalism and organisational networks, then this is where we should start. The complexity, the fluidity and, in many cases, the obscurity of the prevention policy "map" offer opportunities for innovation and experimentation and small-scale policy development.

There are a number of intervention strategies which can be used to enhance network functioning and to influence and shape policy processes, including persuasion, dissemination of information and the use of specific incentives and sanctions (Etzioni, 1968; Hanf and Scharpf, undated). If regulations about gang planks are "a good thing" then perhaps the need for regulations about bars in sports centres ought to be encouraged given the serious risks run by those who combine alcohol and water sports. If steps were taken to publicise the evidence which appears to show that many pedestrian victims of drunk drivers are themselves over the UK "legal limit" then, perhaps, the law and order network would be more interested in enforcing the obscure section of the Licensing Act 1964 which forbids the serving of drink to drunks on licensed premises and yet which resulted in only fourteen convictions in 1984 (Clayton et al, 1977).

Comparatively minor "network adjustments" could have major "prevention pay-offs". What, for instance, would be the effect if someone from the alcohol agency network was appointed to sit on the Advertising Standards Authority (ASA) committee responsible for the implementation of the self-regulatory Code of Practice which governs advertising in the non-broadcast media? Again, what would be the effect if government, as a funder of the RoSPA, insisted that all its many health and safety courses had an "alcohol and work" component?

Given the well recognised barriers to a very visible, highly co-ordinated national prevention policy, systematic network adjustment of this kind would be a relatively "inexpensive" but promising way of developing the already extensive range of national prevention policies, activities, prescriptions and practices. But these networks are significant for another reason. They are not like clouds which float free above all our heads, remote and inaccessible. Organisation networks are the foundation of a local prevention strategy. They extend down into every locality and, thus, network adjustment and enhancement can be promoted at the local level.

LOCAL NETWORKS

Most of the national groups and organisations have structures which link them with the local level and down which they discharge and implement their policies and responsibilities, some of which will be concerned with, or touch upon, alcohol-related issues. Taking safety as a case example, the Institute of Personal Managers (IPM) has 40 local branches in the UK. There are 82 occupational health and safety groups spread throughout the UK whose membership includes health and safety at work officers, personnel officers, supervisors and managers. Most are affiliated to RoSPA and, in particular, to that body's Occupational Health Safety Group's Advisory Committee (OHSGAC) where representatives from the localities sit side by side with senior safety professionals from the Health and Safety Executive (HSE), the medical profession, the unions, employers' organisations and insurance companies.

These organisations and groups are only one corner of the local "safety network". Add to it such people as coroners with their statutory right to comment about and advise on the circumstances and conditions surrounding the fatalities they deal with, local government Home Safety Committees and Road Safety Departments, the Fire Service, Accident and Emergency Departments, local branches of the newly-formed Campaign Against Drinking and Driving (CADD) - and one gets an idea of the complexity of this one network. The "local dimensions" of other networks are just as extensive.

Of course, alcohol-related issues, problems and concerns are unlikely to be prominent in most of these local networks, but they could and should be a consideration. The curricula of health and safety officers and personnel officers may not include any specific reference to "alcohol and work" problems, but it should and could. Fire brigades are unlikely to have procedures for recording the "alcohol component" in fires although evidence appears to indicate that it is extensively implicated (Woolley, 1979). Few, if any, Home Safety Committees know of the connection between alcohol and domestic accidents. Accident and Emergency Departments may or may not have an interest in, knowledge of, or keep systematic records about alcohol and accidents. In fact, the only local groups with a well recognised concern for an alcohol and safety issue are the police, magistrates and Road Safety Departments in relation to drinking and driving. But even here it is routinised and the "prevention potential" is underdeveloped.

Other local networks are equally underdeveloped. In all of them, some alcohol-related legislation is implemented, some policies are constructed, and some practices are promoted, although the activity is likely to be low-key and the concern of "specialists" - such as trainers with a personal interest in alcohol-related problems and policemen with a particular knowledge of "alcohol and crime" - who may well have more in common with similar "specialists" in other organisations than with non-specialist colleagues in their own. Such people will be at the forefront of local partisan mutual adjustment processes which may be necessary either within or between organisational networks. The police officer with an interest in "alcohol and crime" who wants to negotiate with brewery managers, pub licencees and representatives of the local public transport system over ways to reduce alcohol-related disorder, will need "reticulist", or network management skills to facilitate this inter-organisational process (Friend et al, 1984).

The purpose of a local prevention strategy is to systematically identify, catalogue and analyse the "prevention potential" of the many groups and organisations in the various local networks and to press home a simple message - prevention really is "everybody's business" and if we take local prevention opportunities seriously we do not have to wait for someone else, at the national level, to do the "something".

The opportunities for development and innovation are extensive even where national legislation and regulations appear to constrain local discretion. The literature on policy implementation emphasises that policy is frequently determined by the actions and decisions of low-ranking officials, the "street level bureaucrats", and by locally-based organisations rather than by central government (Barrett and Hill, 1981; Elmore, 1980; Hjern and Porter, 1981; Hjern and Hull, 1982).

A LOCAL PREVENTION STRATEGY

A local prevention strategy is a systematic attempt to capitalise on a wide range of local resources and can best be introduced by a brief consideration of what is meant by "local" by "prevention" and by "strategy".

What is "Local"?
In any locality the groups and organisations which go to make up the local policy networks will not be coterminous. The police force's boundaries are different from the district health authority's boundaries and both will be different from the local boundaries of the Institute of Environmental Health Officers, the Institute of Personnel Management and the local radio station. Thus, the precise definition of "local" in relation to these organisations is a matter for discovery in each locality. Local is as local does, although, on an over-all view, the most helpful definition of "local" in the UK may be the boundary agreed for the purpose of joint funding between district health authorities and local authority social service departments.

What is "Prevention"?
The concept of prevention is, similarly, not straightforward. Much prevention literature, irrespective of the particular

problem to be prevented, attempts to structure the discussion
by making distinctions between preventing the problem starting
- primary prevention -spotting the problem early and
preventing it from developing; secondary prevention; or
responding to the problem once it has developed and preventing
the further consequences of it - tertiary prevention (DHSS,
1977b; Fowler, 1983). This way of dividing up the prevention
world is very tidy in the literature. Unfortunately, the real
world is rather more complex. To begin with, few workers in
organisations which have a part to play in a local prevention
strategy are aware of the three-level prevention model. As a
result it does not inform their work, their view of their
place in relation to alcohol problems, or their relationship
with other organisations. But more important is the fact that
most organisations have the potential to respond at all three
prevention levels, and quite often they do. The distinction,
then, between primary, secondary and tertiary prevention is
unhelpful.

Another possible way of categorising the local prevention
field relates to three common conceptions of the "real" nature
of the problem. For some it is problem drinkers who are the
main focus of attention. For others the major emphasis is on
contemporary society, its drinking patterns and attitudes.
For yet others the concern is with alcohol itself (Robinson,
1980; Robinson, 1981). Each of these concerns leads to a
different prevention emphasis.

Those who see problem drinkers as the real problem
emphasise the need to prevent people who are particularly "at
risk" from developing their condition. The prevention aim is
to devise ways of getting people to recognise the early signs
of alcohol problems in themselves and in others, and to
educate them to know what action to take and where to go for
help and support (Bernadt et al, 1982; Davies and Raistrick,
1981; Edwards, 1982). Those who see the root of the alcohol
problem in the way that alcohol is used in our society focus
their attention on unhealthy drinking practices and attitudes.
The prevention aim is to increase knowledge of alcohol and its
effects and through positive health education to encourage
moderate drinking and responsible hosting (Blane, 1976;
Milgram, 1980). Those who focus on alcohol itself draw
attention to the links between levels of overall consumption
and the rates of alcohol problems of various kinds. The
preventive aim here is to regulate, through taxation,
licensing and other controls, the availability of alcohol in
the community since, runs the argument, the less alcohol there
is the fewer alcohol problems there will be (AEC, 1977;
Ledermann, 1956).

As with the three-level model of prevention, a
categorisation of preventive approaches based on these views
on the central nature of the alcohol problem - problem
drinkers, drinking habits and the alcohol itself - is fine in
the literature but unhelpful in real life. Although one

particular perspective may predominate, the activities of most organisations and groups of workers are informed by elements from each perspective. For instance, liquor licensing falls squarely within the third perspective in that it is clearly concerned with controlling the availability of alcohol. However, in addition, the licensing process itself provides opportunities for promoting education about alcohol, for shaping the drinking environment and discouraging immoderate drinking, and for fostering the development of alcohol and work policies for a particular, high-risk occupational group - the licensed trade (Tether et al, 1985; Tether and Robinson, 1986).

Thus, "prevention" in a local prevention strategy includes primary, secondary and tertiary prevention and all those activities shaped by different perceptions of "the problem". Because of the messiness of the real world, a local prevention strategy cannot be shaped around pure models and categories of prevention, however helpful they may be for clarifying thought. The only possible basis for structuring a local prevention strategy are the "networks" - within which, and between which, things are done, or can and should be done - which cut right across the neat categorisations. Thus, each chapter of the local prevention guide based on the DHSS-sponsored research focuses on a particular alcohol-related problem or issue and on the local network which is in a position to promote a constructive "prevention response": alcohol advertising, promotion and presentation in the media; alcohol and safety; alcohol and liquor licensing; alcohol and work; alcohol, education and young people; alcohol and helping professions; alcohol and statutory workers; and alcohol and the offender.

What is Strategy?
Strategy involves firstly, raising knowledge about and interest in different kinds of alcohol-related problems within appropriate networks and encouraging constructive prevention activity on every possible front.

1. Sources of Inspiration
The architect of a local prevention strategy will look in vain for a focused body of literature on how to set about such a task. On the other hand a very wide range of books, articles, reports, catalogues and even newspaper stories can provide stimulating ideas. In some cases the local relevance, the local implications, will be clear cut. The studies of city centre disorder, for example, will suggest or imply initiatives which localities could promote, ranging from changes in police supervisory practice to a review of late night public transport arrangements (Jeffs and Saunders, 1983; Hope, 1986). Studies of health education, especially those involving local campaigns of one sort or another will provide useful insights into what and and what not to say, how to say it and the kinds of results that might be expected (Wallack,

1980; Dudd et al, 1983). National reports from agencies of every kind will help to identify problem areas and indicate priorities for local action (Royal Life Saving Society, annual; CESRF, annual). Even a simple pamphlet on the duties of a coroner will, read with the right eyes, help to suggest ways in which an important and prestigious group can make a contribution to a local prevention effort (Home Office, 1981). Surveys of national policies indicate the range of things happening "on the ground" and, hence, the room for local manoeuvre (Armyr et al, 1982; Davies and Walsh, 1983). Specific discussions about prevention are obviously helpful (Grant and Ritson, 1983), while the literature on "alcohol and work" has a clear local application and relevance (Allsop and Beaumont, 1983; Health and Safety Executive, 1981; Ward, 1982; Labour Research Department, 1983; Tether and Robinson, 1985).

Given the nature of the strategic task, virtually every piece of literature about the prevention of alcohol-related problems, or about the groups and organisations which are, or could be, involved in their prevention is grist to any local mill. Perhaps the best place to start where alcohol problems are concerned is with the various local prevention intiatives pioneered by the Office of Alcohol and Other Drug Abuse Programming in St Paul, Minnesota. These are particularly interesting not only because they promote the concept of "community saturation" but for their mood, style and opportunism (OAODAP, undated).

2. Summarising the Debates

How can a local prevention strategy raise network knowledge and promote helpful prevention activities? Firstly, each network is concerned with a particular alcohol-related problem or issue. Raising knowledge and awareness involves summarising these issues in a brief and readable way, introducing key debates and, where appropriate, central facts and figures. For instance, those with a role, actual or potential, in the liquor licensing process need to know about various kinds of liquor licences, their numbers, how they are obtained and, crucially, the various debates about the place of liquor licensing in the prevention of problems. Those in the safety network should be told about the role of alcohol in accidents of all kinds and the different approaches to accident prevention which involve, on the one hand, education and publicity and, on the other, environmental modifications.

Of course, in a number of areas, the debates which must be described are unresolved. Some may even be unresolvable. However, the purpose of outlining debates is not to come down on one side or another but to present them so that "prevention options" can be considered in the light of local feeling and evidence. Thus, a local prevention strategy should not say that liquor outlets must be restricted, but point out how it might be done and the implications of doing it, for any locality which wishes to limit outlets. It should not say that alcohol advertising is a significant factor in promoting consumption, since the evidence is far from conclusive (Godfrey, 1986), but catalogue any powers a locality might be able to mobilise if it considers that action in this area is worthwhile.

3. Identifying "Good Practices"

Stimulating a re-evaluation of everyday work among a wide range of organisations and groups at the local level is an essential part of a local prevention strategy. Such a strategy must seek to overcome the belief that there is little that can be done locally to prevent alcohol problems. It must identify those good practices which will increase organisational efficiency and effectiveness in relation to alcohol problems. The examples of "good practices" that are presented in the Guide were collected from a variety of organisations in various parts of the UK. They were gathered by means of a whole series of "trawling letters" in which organisations were asked to identify any innovative practices, procedures or activities which they thought had helped them and which could help similar organisations and groups elsewhere.

The "trawling letters" identified the local health authority which, in co-operation with the local government authority, has taken steps to limit alcohol advertising on hoardings sited on public authority land; the various probation services initiatives involving offenders with drink-related problems; and the role which some environmental health departments are beginning to play in relation to "alcohol and work" issues. However, in very many areas the "good practices" were thin on the ground. The "trawling letters" more often identified the areas where "good practices" could be developed than actual examples of such practices. As a result, it was possible to identify potential "good practices" covering such diverse topics as the contents of Chief Constables' year-end reports to local liquor licensing committees and the workings of the "High Risk Offender" procedure, which is designed to identify and help drunken drivers who offend at a certain level.

4. The Importance of Records

Particular attention was paid to "good practices" involving organisational records. A recurring feature of the local groups and organisations examined was the lack of adequate record systems capable of registering the nature and extent of specific alcohol-related problems. This is significant. Problems which are not visible are not problems.

It is widely recognised that organisational preoccupations shape structures, processes and administrative systems - including records of all kinds (Garfinkel, 1967). Thus, attempts to get an organisation's members to "think alcohol" typically begins with efforts to improve knowledge about, and attitudes towards, alcohol-related problems of the kind they are most likely to encounter. The assumption is that once these are "right", supportive features of organisational life - including efficient record systems - will emerge.

Whilst the logic may be right the practical difficulties involved in affecting key attitude changes are very great. It is no easy thing to do. It might well be more appropriate to view changes in record-keeping (which can be very simple) as the starting point for encouraging the right kinds of changes in organisational practices and attitudes. The routine collection of "alcohol information" on forms, record cards and report sheets of all kinds will be one way of insinuating alcohol on to everyone's agenda and encouraging a wider organisational response.

All the "good practices" at the local level should be "do-able". That is to say, they should be possible within the constraints of existing legislation and most importantly, inexpensive in terms of organisational time and effort. Grand proposals which might have consumed large amounts of both should be eschewed. Such proposals will not catch the ear of busy people "on the run" and, of course, an incremental local prevention strategy is required precisely because local organisations do not understand, or could not possibly promote and implement, comprehensive "top-down" policies.

The identification of "good practices" in a local prevention strategy should not be seen as a blueprint which lays down what must or must not be done. Rather, "good practices" should provide a starting point to help many different kinds of people to think how they might begin to amend their organisation's practices and priorities. When the people are asked to identify ways in which their organisation might develop its "prevention potential" they can usually come up with a series of ideas.

5. Inter-organisational Contact

Many of the "good practices" can be put into operation in single organisations. Others, however, will require co-operation across organisational boundaries and these are particularly important. Activities involving more than one organisation are calculated to bring a network together in a common understanding of, and response to, a particular alcohol-related problem. A local prevention strategy should facilitate inter-organisational contact and communication by briefly describing network participants so that readers have an idea of organisational size, structure, activities and, most importantly, who to approach if some kind of joint activity is contemplated. It is, for instance, less than helpful to urge Home Safety Committees to co-operate with Social Service Departments over the provision of some training for home helps and others on the role of alcohol in domestic accidents, and not to indicate what it is which both these very different kinds of organisations do, their legal powers and how to obtain "access".

Encouraging co-operation between local organisations is so important that it may be necessary to build a network from scratch. In one alcohol-related area, that of liquor licensing, the issue was important and the existing network was small. The Guide, therefore, suggests the creation of a licensing forum, a consultative and co-ordinating mechanism which could involve a number of relevant local groups and organisations in an issue from which they had hitherto been excluded.

In any local community there are a number of agencies which have an interest in licensing decisions and are affected by the consequences of them. Social services departments, the probation and after-care service, agencies concerned with the care, rehabilitation and counselling of those with alcohol problems, various sections of the alcohol trade itself, the police, local road safety departments, Home Safety Committees, have local information and expertise on various drinking issues which could usefully be shared. Given all the organisations which have a legitimate interest in and concern with licensing decisions and their impact, a "licensing forum" would be an ideal place for these organisations to meet to discuss specific issues such as implementation and support for an overall local licensing strategy. Similar co-ordinating and consultative devices would probably be helpful in other networks.

6. A Prevention Group?

A local prevention strategy for alcohol-related problems should permeate various local networks in an essentially low-key, undramatic and incremental way. However, it is probably unwise to rely on spontaneous interest or network's pressures to bring together previously unrelated organisations into a local prevention strategy. For however straightforward the description of the issues, however simple the "good practices" described and however clear the advice on contacting and working with others, some local groups and organisations will remain untouched by the dissemination process. One reason is the sheer range of local groups and organisations with a "prevention potential". Another is organisational inertia. Even small-scale innovations may be too much for isolated individuals to carry through within their own group.

The development of a local prevention strategy and its spread would be encouraged if each locality had a group which was clearly seen to be responsible for disseminating knowledge about the prevention of alcohol problems, which lobbied local organisations to develop their prevention potential and which was the repository of ideas about good practice and a clearing house for materials and knowledge of prevention developments. This focus of local prevention activity could be a local Council on Alcoholism, a Joint Planning Team, an associated liaison committee, or an alcohol group set up specifically for the purpose. Thus, the development and promotion of a local prevention strategy would operate on two complementary and mutually reinforcing levels, one within the networks, one above and between.

CONCLUSION

The approach embodied in the proposed local prevention strategy can be criticised. It is untidy. It is "unscientific" in the sense that many of the suggested "good practices" are supported by common sense rather than measured evaluation although, of course, the monitoring and measurement of innovation is important and is addressed in the Guide. It might also be doubted whether a local prevention strategy can actually make much impact on the forces leading us to consume more and more alcohol and to experience more and more problems of all kinds. The answer is simple. There is only one way to find out and that is by taking seriously the possibility that helpful prevention activities can be developed at the local level.

Hopefully, the systematic mobilisation of neglected local resources and opportunities will have an impact on many kinds of alcohol-related problems. But however valuable this is, it is not the sole point and purpose of a local prevention strategy. We began by discussing co-ordinated national prevention strategies and how the first steps to such a strategy might be taken by developing the already quite extensive range of national prevention activities and possibilities. Local prevention strategies would help such development since they are, in part, a political strategy designed to insinuate the alcohol prevention issue on to some agendas for the first time and, where it is already an issue, to increase its importance and "visibility".

Local networks have a national dimension and any success in organisational "consciousness raising" could be expected, at least, in some cases and over some issues, to have national repercussions. Groups and organisations involved in a local prevention strategy are likely to raise alcohol-related issues and concerns with their national bodies, representatives or associations. If they take the idea of good practices seriously they can help to create policy at the periphery where developments can serve as models for national policy-makers. For good practice at the local level is often, as any policy analyst knows, tomorrow's central policy (Rhodes, 1979).

REFERENCES

Alcohol Education Centre (AEC) (1977) The Ledermann Curve. AEC, London

Allsop, S. and Beaumont, P. (1983) Dismissal for alcohol offences, Employee Relations, 5.2 and 5.5

Armyr, G., Elmer, A. and Herz, U. (1982) Alcohol in the World of the '80s. Sober Forlaggs AB, Stockholm

Barrett, S. and Hill, M. (1981) Report to the SSRC Central-Local Government Relations Panel on the "Core or Theoretical Component of the Research on Implementation". Unpublished

Benson, N. (1975) The interorganisational network as a political economy. Administrative Science Quarterly (20) 229-249

Bernadt, M., Mundorf, J., Taylor, C., Smith, B. and Murray, R. (1982) Comparison of questionnaire and laboratory tests in the detection of excessive drinking and alcoholism. The Lancet, 6th February

Blane, H. (1976) Health Education as a Preventative Strategy. paper prepared for the Tripartite Meeting on Prevention, Sept/Oct

Bruun, K., Edwards, G., Lumio, M., Makela, K., Osterberg, L., Pan, L., Popham, R., Room, R., Schmidt, W., Skog, O. and Sulkunen, P. (1975) Alcohol Control Policies in Public Health Perspective (a collaborative project of the Finnish Foundation for Alcohol Studies, the WHO Regional Office for Europe and the Addiction Research Foundation of Ontario), Vol. 25. Finnish Foundation for Alcohol Studies, Helsinki

Central Policy Review Staff (CPRS). (1979) Alcohol Policies. unpublished

Christian Economic and Social Research Foundation (CESRF) Chief Constables' Reports. England, Wales and Scotland. CESRF, London

Clayton, A., Booth, A. and McCarthy, P. (1977) A Controlled Study of the Role of Alcohol in Fatal Adult Pedestrian Accidents, Supplementary Report 332. Transport and Road Research Laboratory, Crowthorne, Berks

Davies, I. and Raistrick, D. (1981) Dealing with Drink: helping problem drinkers - a handbook. BBC Publications, London

Davies, P. and Walsh, D. (1983) Alcohol Problems and Alcohol Control in Europe. Croom Helm, London and Canberra

DHSS (1977a) Prevention and Health. HMSO, London

DHSS (1977b) Advisory Committee on Alcoholism, Prevention. HMSO, London

DHSS (1978) Advisory Committee on Alcoholism, The Pattern and Range of Services for Problem Drinkers. HMSO, London

DHSS (1979) Advisory Committee on Alcoholism, Education and Training. HMSO, London

DHSS (1981) Drinking Sensibly. HMSO, London

DHSS (1986) Prevention and Health: everybody's business - a reassessment of public and personal health. HMSO, London

Dudd, P., Gray, D. and McCron, R. (1983) The Tyne Tees Alcohol Education Campaign: an evaluation. Health Education Council, London

Edwards, G. (1982) The Treatment of Drinking Problems: a guide for helping professionals. Grant MacIntyre, London

Elmore, R. (1980) Backward mapping: implementation research and policy decisions. Political Science Quarterly (94) 4 601-616

Etzioni, A. (1968) The Active Society. Macmillan, London
Fowler, G. (1983) Prevention - what does it mean? In BMJ, Practising Prevention. Devonshire Press, Torquay

Friend, J., Power, J. and Yewlett, C. (1984) Public Planning: the intercorporate dimension. Tavistock, London

Garfinkel, H. (1967) Studies in Ethnomethodology. Prentice-Hall, Englewood Cliffs, New Jersey

Godfrey, C. (1986) Government policy, advertising and tobacco consumption in the UK. British Journal of Addiction, 81, 339-346

Grant, M. and Ritson, B. (1983) Alcohol: the prevention debate. Croom Helm, London

Hanf, K. and Scharpf, J. (eds) Interorganisational Policy Making: limits to coordination and central control. Sage, London

Health and Safety Executive (1981) The Problem Drinker at Work. HMSO, London

Hjern, B. and Porter, D. (1981) Implementation structures: unit of administrative analysis. Organisation Studies, 2, 3, 211-227

Hjern, B. and Hull, C. (1982) Implementation research as empirical constitutionalism, European Journal of Political Research, 10, 105-115

Home Office (1981) The Work of the Coroner: some questions answered. HMSO, London

Hope, T. (1986) Drinking and disorder in the city centre: a policy analysis. In Implementing Crime Prevention Measures. Home Office Research Study

Institute of Highways and Transportation (1980) Highway, Safety - Accident Reduction and Prevention in Highway Engineering. IOHT, London

Jeffs, B. and Saunders, W. (1983) Minimising alcohol related offences by enforcement of the existing licensing legislation. British Journal of Addiction, 78, 1, 67-77

Labour Research Department (1983) Alcohol Policies at Work: a bargaining report. Trades Union Congress, London

Lederman, S. (1956) Alcohol, Alcoholism, Alcoholisation, Cahier No 29. Universitaire, Paris

Lehman, A. (1975) Coordinating Health Care: explorations in interorganisational relations. Sage, London

Lindblom, P. (1965) The Intelligence of Democracy. Free Press, New York

Milgram, G. (ed) (1980) Alcohol Education Materials: an annotated bibliography. Rutgers Centre of Alcohol Studies, New Brunswick

Moser, J. Prevention of Alcohol-Related Problems, an international review of preventive measures, policies and programmes. Division of Mental Health, Office of Alcohol and Other Drug Abuse Programming, St Paul, Minnesota, OAODAP, Occasional Papers

Rhodes, R. (1979) Research into central-local relations: a framework for analysis. In Social Science Research Council, Central-Local Government Relationships. SSRC, London

Robinson, D. (1980) Prevention: a co-ordinated approach. The Alliance News. Sept./Oct

Robinson, D. (1981) Prevention. In E. Pattison et al (eds) American Encyclopedia of Alcoholism, Chapter 33, Gardner Press, New York

Royal College of Psychiatrists (1979) Alcohol and Alcoholism. Tavistock, London

Royal Life Saving Society, Drowning in the British Isles. RLSS (annual), Studley

Tether, P. and Harrison, L. (1986) Alcohol-related fires and drownings, Data Note 3. British Journal of Addiction. 81, 3, 438

Tether, P. and Robinson, D. (1985) Alcohol and work: policies are not enough. Alcohol and Alcoholism, 20, 3

Tether, P., Robinson, D. and Wicks, M. (1985) Liquor licensing: role in a prevention strategy. Alcohol and Alcoholism, 20, 4

Tether, P. and Robinson, D. (1986) Preventing Alcohol Problems: A Guide to Local Action. Tavistock, London

Wallack, L. (1980) Assessing effects of mass media campaigns: an alternative perspective. Alcohol, Health and Research World, 5, 1 17-27

Ward, G. (1982) Identifying and helping problem drinkers at work. Journal of the Society of Occupational Medicine, 32 171-179 World Health Assembly, 28.81, 32.30, 36.12 (1979, 1979, 1983)

WHO (1984) Alcohol Policies, No 18. WHO Regional Publications European Series, Copenhagen

Woolley, D. (1979) Synthetic materials and alcohol are culprits in fire death study. Fire. September

INDEX

abstinence 9, 35-6, 40, 51
  see also ACCEPT;
residential project
ACCEPT service
  and Drinkwatchers 41, 45, 47
  vs. hospital care 210-30
    clinical trial 216-28
    implications 228-30
    models of treatment 211-12
    process 213-14
    referral 211
    therapeutic approach 214-16
accidents 66, 70, 106-8, 227-9, 283
addictive behaviour 174-5
Adelstein, A. 105
Adler, A. 252
alcohol
  controlled drinking 9, 36-7
    see also DRAMS; Drinkwatchers
  dependence syndrome 192
  drinking continuum 7-9, 64-5
  and health problems 61-2, 65-6, 105-9

  prevalence 7-8, 26
  risks from 65-6, 71-2, 75-6
  'safe' drinking 41, 84
alcohol-related problems 7-11
  and children 23-4
  detection of 40, 67-71, 106-7, 109-10
  and the elderly 24-5
  and families 17, 20-2
  prevention (q.v.) 275-87
  social and political issues 25-7
Alcohol Services Evaluation
  Scheme (ASES) 234-43
Alcoholics Anonymous 9, 14-15
Allen, R. 195
Allsop, S. 283
Anderson, P. v, 2, 61-79, 87
Apte, R. 6
Arbery, B. v, 2, 143, 172-87
Armyr, G. 283

Babor, T. 37, 83
Backhouse, M. 108
Bailey, M. 17
Baker, C. 67
Baldwin, S. v, 2, 158-70